SAMUEL EYNON & SONS

The 'HERO'

TRIMSARAN
SOUTH WALES

An illustrated history to commemorate

the company's centenary.

by Vernon Morgan

Samuel Eynon & Sons
The 'HERO'

Published by Vernon Morgan.

June 2016

Printed in Wales by – Proprint, Carmarthen.

ISBN 978-0-9574045-3-3

Other titles published by the same author:

James of Ammanford (A history of J. James & Sons Ltd. Ammanford).

SWT 100 (The South Wales Transport Co. Ltd. 100th Anniversary).

Images of Old Llanelli & District (Historical views of Llanelli & District).

Cover picture: Pictured here outside Eynon's depot at Heol Waun-y-clun, Trimsaran is the very last 'New' vehicle purchased by the company – a Leyland 'Tiger' TRCTL11/3R with very attractive LAG 'Galaxy' coachwork - a rare combination as only six Leyland 'Tigers' received LAG 'Galaxy' coachwork. Registered **A802XEP,** it was captured here upon delivery on 29th June 1984, with David Eynon, youngest grandson of the company founder behind the wheel. Note the garage trade plate 018 BX on display in the windscreen. *(Vernon Morgan).*

Rear cover: **JXN 320** was one of two Park Royal bodied Leyland 'Titan' 7RT's acquired from London Transport in October 1958. They were the forerunners of numerous RTL and RT class London Transport vehicles to join the Eynon's fleet. Eynon's were extremely fond of their RTL's, which could regularly be seen working their main service, Llanelli to Carmarthen via Trimsaran. **JXN 320** (RTL 8) is seen here at Carmarthen crossing 'Towy Bridge' (River Towy) on its return journey to Llanelli in the summer sunshine of 1959.

Title page: A superb photograph of the company founder, Samuel Eynon. (*Courtesy of David Eynon*).

CONTENTS

AUTHOR'S ACKNOWLEDGEMENTS

The task of compiling this book has been both a challenge and a pleasure and I'm indebted to numerous people for their sincere help and assistance in compiling it.

First of all I would like to thank my wife Kath and my daughter Katie for their co-operation and contribution in the production of this book, proof reading my notes, correcting small grammatical errors and assisting with the layout. Katie also designed the cover of this publication.

Special thanks are due to several members of the Eynon family, David Eynon, Jean Thomas, the late Thomas John Eynon and Ieuan Lodwick for their assistance throughout the years with valuable information and the loan of several family photographs. Without their help and valuable input this book would not have progressed so well. Furthermore, David Eynon undertook the mammoth task of proof-reading the completed draft before production of the finished article.

Thanks are due also to my late brother Trevor, who worked at the establishment and regularly informed me of any vehicle movements at Eynon's. Trevor would also position vehicles for photographing whenever I would arrive at the depot - before my vocation at Trimsaran. My photograph collection would not have been so extensive without his assistance.

I would also like to thank Meirion R Morgan-Jones and Alwyn Evans of the Carmarthenshire County Council Passenger Transport Unit; Alan Mills librarian of the Omnibus Society; and David B Lloyd, Llanelli for the loan of his historical documents; David Gravell of Pinged Hill Garage, Kidwelly; the Leyland Motors Ltd (archive); Alan B Cross; the late Bertie Phillips and to my PSV Circle friends John Jones, Steve Powell, Andrew Porter, Paul Fox, Richard Evans and Robert Edworthy for supplying photographs and notes, and not forgetting the late Chris Taylor, transport historian of Cardiff who loaned me lots of valuable notes regarding the early services operated.

Most other photographs are views taken by myself or views from my large collection which are the copyright of persons unknown as they are not back stamped. No discourtesy to the photographer is intended through lack of acknowledgement, in view of which I trust they will accept my sincere thanks.

Much valuable information has also come from material in the care of Carmarthenshire County Council Cultural Services Department; Carmarthen Reference Library and Llanelli Reference Library.

Finally, I would like to thank Adrian and the staff at Proprint - Carmarthen for their professional assistance in producing the final product.

FOREWORD

Samuel Eynon & Sons of Trimsaran were once Carmarthenshire's largest independent 'bus operator, running 35 vehicles on several stage carriage services (nowadays known as local services) which included three different routes from Llanelli to Carmarthen, express carriage services, contract services, private hire and tours which extended to all parts of Great Britain and Europe.

It can truly be said that Samuel Eynon was the 'Pioneer' of road passenger transport in the village of Trimsaran, South-West Wales. Furthermore, he was called **'The Hero'** for inaugurating the community's first bus service, a logo he applied to his first charabanc.

The humble beginnings of this family business began in 1917 and spanned a period of over seventy years before passing to another sizeable family owned West Wales operator.

Eynon's had built up a tremendous reputation throughout its existence having reliably served the south-east Carmarthenshire area, especially during times of extreme weather conditions which frequently hit the area.

The management and staff at Eynon's treated their customers like family or friends in this very close knit mining community, and were known to have stopped at regular passengers houses if they weren't present at the bus stop for their usual journey to work.

The company can fondly be remembered for their very low fares, seldom having fare increases, even during their bad times in the 1970's and 1980's, when car ownership was ever increasing and passenger numbers decreasing.

However, de-regulation by the Tory Government was the final straw for the already financially unstable company. Immediately after de-regulation in August 1986, the South Wales Transport Company vigorously challenged them on their lucrative Trimsaran and Carway routes with brand new Mercedes Benz L608D mini buses branded 'Sosban Link', charging lower fares and running just five minutes in front of Eynon's. This unfortunately brought the company to its knees.

Sadly, the well-renowned and much loved company, with a name that had become a household word in the east Carmarthenshire (east Dyfed) mining communities, was sold to another Carmarthenshire (Dyfed) independent operator, Davies Bros (Pencader) Ltd, in June 1988, ending a fine story of enterprise and achievement.

This publication, which has been produced to celebrate the Centenary of the business; 'Samuel Eynon & Sons', Bryn Villa Garage, Trimsaran, is a tribute to the Eynon family and their devoted staff, and a succinct history of the business which has previously never been told.

The spelling of place names referred to in this story are taken from authenticated records of that period in time, as several welsh place names were changed to the true welsh spelling from around 1966 onwards.

INTRODUCTION

For the reader who may not be familiar with the area, we start the story with a brief history of Trimsaran, a sizeable village situated at the lower (southern) end of the Gwendraeth Valley in south-east Carmarthenshire. The village is located on the B4308 road, five miles north-west of Llanelli and three miles east of the Roman town, Kidwelly.

Until the coming of the industrial revolution, the village inhabitants had earned their living from farming and coal mining in a very small way. Coal had been mined in the area as early as 1581. Some villagers however, made a three mile trek to nearby Kidwelly each day to work at the tin works which had opened there in 1737.

The industrial revolution brought with it huge demands for coal which in turn saw the opening of several new collieries in the community. Star Colliery, Trimsaran opened in 1854 and soon passed to the Trimsaran Colliery group, known as 'The Trimsaran Anthracite Coal & Iron Co', which had been registered in January 1863. The colliery group also owned the Trimsaran iron works and Trimsaran brickworks, becoming a major employer in the community, attracting a workforce from further afield.

In 1872, the newly formed Trimsaran Coal, Iron & Steel Co. Ltd, (formerly Trimsaran Anthracite Coal & Iron Co. Ltd) had their industrial complex connected to the Burry Port & Gwendraeth Valley Railway, enabling straightforward shipment of their products to Burry Port docks and elsewhere on the nationwide rail network. This brought about a huge influx of people to work at Trimsaran, which included the Eynon family from the nearby village of Pembrey.

As Trimsaran prospered from the coal industry, it greatly expanded from a small two street village on the west side of Pembrey Mountain into a sizeable community with a population of over 3,000.

HOW SAMUEL EYNON'S BUSINESS STARTED

Samuel Eynon, the 'Pioneer' of public transport in the village of Trimsaran, south-west Wales was born at the neighbouring village of Pembrey in 1880. The family however moved from Pembrey to Trimsaran when his father Arthur Eynon took up employment as a coal miner at the Trimsaran Colliery. At the age of 14, Samuel Eynon, one of eight children began his working career as a labourer, and later moved on to work at the Trimsaran Colliery alongside other members of the family, where he held the responsible position of an engine winder-man.

In the meantime, no less than three local villagers, William Jones of Bryncaerau; Rhys Davies of Park Stores, Bryncaurau, and L Bowen of Dan-y-banc, each purchased small five seater cars in 1916 and licensed them with the Llanelly Borough Council as Hackney Carriages No's 30, 26 and 27 respectively, to operate a taxi service from the village.

Despite all the 'transport' activity in the community, Samuel Eynon of 'Bryn Villa', Waun-y-clun, Trimsaran, went ahead and purchased a second-hand American 'Studebaker' motor car in 1917, and began an un-licensed service between Trimsaran and Llanelly, causing some friction with the licensed taxi operators *and* the Llanelly Borough Council licensing committee.

Below: This is the Studebaker motor car that Samuel Eynon used in 1917 to carry local people into Llanelly.

He retained his job at the colliery, along with other members of his large family who assisted with the driving of the car. The colliery manager Evan Jones arranged their shifts so that there was always one family member available to drive, but it wasn't until June 1919 that the Llanelly Borough Council issued the first Hackney Carriage licence (No. 62) to Samuel Eynon, some two years after his humble beginnings in 1917. Competition on the tortuous route began in January 1918, when a Hackney licence was granted to James Hughes of 'Mile End' Bryncaerau, Trimsaran. James Hughes later bought L Bowen's five seater 'model T' Ford registered BX 717 in November 1918, and in June 1919 he bought a Ford 'model T' ten seater 'brake' registered BX 937 from Tudor Williams (Pioneer Bus Service) Laugharne, Carmarthenshire. Another competitor on the Trimsaran to Llanelly road was Gwilym John Davies of 4 Green Cottages, Carway who took out a licence to operate Carway to Llanelly on 3rd May, 1920.

Mention must also be made of David John Eynon-Southcott of Baglam Farm, Llandyry, near Trimsaran. Operating a GMC 14 seater charabanc by October 1920, he had no connection with the Eynon family and didn't compete against Eynon's service on the Trimsaran to Llanelly road.

Nevertheless, 'Sam' Eynon's taxi service was so successful, that a 38 horse power Fiat 18BL 25 seat charabanc was purchased brand new in December 1920 at the cost of £1,660, an enormous price in those far gone days. Registered BX1669 and fitted with solid tyres, it was the first omnibus operated by the company. The rear end panel of the charabanc was sign-written **Samuel Eynon & Sons 'The HERO' Trimsaran**, as shown below. Samuel Eynon was known locally as 'The Hero' for inaugurating the first omnibus service in the village.

Above: Three different views of the 38hp Fiat 18BL charabanc which Samuel Eynon used to inaugurate the Trimsaran to Llanelly service in 1920/1. Howell Eynon, eldest son of the founder is seen here with the Fiat at Llanelly Town Hall in 1921.

Three months after purchasing the Fiat, the Llanelly Borough Council licensing committee met to discuss the issue of licensing an increasing amount of Hackney Carriages, which by then also included omnibuses, and ultimately decided that charabancs would in future not be licensed as they were regarded as unsuitable for stage carriage service due to their construction, i.e. having individual doors to each row of seats. A month later, a date of 24th June was given by the licensing committee as the withdrawal of charabanc licences, in order for the five operators concerned to have reasonable notice to replace charabancs that were used on stage carriage. This date was further extended to 29th September 1921 and in December 1921 they said that charabancs should no longer be licensed for stage carriage service. Nevertheless, Samuel Eynon was granted further permission to use his charabanc until 23rd January 1922 with an understanding that a new 'proper' omnibus on order was imminent.

Having to purchase this second bus so soon after the charabanc almost crippled 'Sam' Eynon financially. The new bus registered BX 2404 was a Leyland G7 with Leyland 32 seat 'Edinburgh' style body identical to the 'G7' of J James & Sons, Ammanford. It arrived in February 1922, and was the forerunner of a long line of Leylands to serve the company throughout its 71 year existence. The cost of this 'real' bus was only £100 more than the Fiat charabanc - £1,760.

Above: This photograph of Samuel Eynon's new Leyland G7, BX 2404 was taken at Llanelly Town Hall, terminus of his pioneering service from Trimsaran to Llanelly. Samuel Eynon is the gentleman standing in front of the bus, with the Town Hall visible in the background. The company's fleet-name 'Trimsaran & District' was introduced with the arrival of this Leyland in February 1922.

After purchasing the new Leyland to comply with the local by-laws, the Fiat charabanc was retained for private hire, running trips to local places of interest and Sunday-school outings. It also ventured into Carmarthen un-licensed on market days during 1922-4, making Sam Eynon

Above: This view of Samuel Eynon's *first* garage alongside his house 'Bryn Villa' was appropriately named 'Bryn Villa Garage'. It was later rebuilt into two larger garages on the same plot of land, and still stand today in 2016. This image dates from 1927, and shows a rear end view of Leyland G7, **BX 2404** before conversion to pneumatic tyres, and a rear view of newer Leyland C7, **BX 5872** which had already been fitted with pneumatic tyres. Note the vintage 'Pratts' petrol pump on the right hand side of the garage forecourt. *(Courtesy of David Eynon)*

the first omnibus operator on the Kidwelly to Carmarthen road. This was the beginning of the Llanelly-Trimsaran-Kidwelly-Carmarthen service which ran un-licensed into Carmarthen until June 1924. The Carmarthen terminus for Eynon's service in those far gone days was the town's main street, Lammas Street, until the opening of a new bus station at Blue Street on 3rd August, 1975.

Delivery of the new Leyland 'G7', BX 2404 mentioned above brought with it the company's fleet-name 'Trimsaran & District' which was applied to each side of the bus by the manufacturer Leyland Motors, ironically in the same style as that of J James & Sons, 'Ammanford & District Bus Service'. The fleet-name Trimsaran & District was carried on all of Eynon's vehicles for many years before being discarded in the early post-war period.

Meanwhile, bearing in mind that some local authorities were slow implementing the new Hackney Carriage regulations, Llanelly Borough Council executed their obligations impeccably. In addition to their obligations of licensing, by February 1921 they had also allocated standing places (bus stops) for all stage carriage services arriving and departing from the Borough. Eynon's were allocated Town Hall Square, where most of the town's bus services terminated and departed from.

On the 13th December 1921, the Llanelly B C licensing committee refused an application from Reginald C Lloyd, licensee of the Star Hotel, Trimsaran, to licence a car on the Trimsaran-Llanelly route, but a month later agreed to grant him a licence if a 'proper' bus was acquired. Despite this, Lloyd was caught several times thereafter for various offences against the Hackney Carriage laws, and in February 1923 had to appear in front of the licensing committee together with joint operators of the route, Samuel Eynon and James Hughes, regarding non observance of their time-tables. However, in May 1923 Lloyd was only granted a short term licence until 30th June, due to further irregularities on the service. Renewal of Lloyd's licence had been opposed by the other operators, ending his share of the service. The only 'bus' Lloyd had ever operated, was a second-hand 'Hansa-Lloyd' of German manufacture that had been acquired from the Midlands/Black Country area in August 1922. It was afterwards parked up out of use at the nearby village of Pinged, where it was later mysteriously set on fire and burnt out completely. The insurers apparently refused to pay out as it was proven to be arson!

Bearing in mind that the business of R C Lloyd was now extinct, the road to Llanelly was still not clear for the enterprising Eynon family concern. The Trimsaran to Llanelly route was still shared between Samuel Eynon, James Hughes and John Davies of Carway, who literally *fought* it out together. John Davies with his market days only, Thursday and Saturday service; Carway-Trimsaran - Llanelly regularly complained to the licensing committee about Eynon's irregular time keeping, and in February 1924 reported them for 'Pirating' with an un-licensed bus. The so-called un-authorised bus turned out to be a brand new Leyland A9 with Leyland 'Chester-style' rear entrance 20 seat body delivered in December 1923, and ***was*** licensed. It was registered as BX 4035.

Above: Samuel Eynon stands proudly on the step of his new Leyland 'A9' **BX 4035** mentioned above, fitted with a Leyland 'Chester style' 20 seat body. It's captured here outside the 'Bird-in-hand' public house, Trimsaran, with two of his sons James (left) and Daniel (centre). This bus was known as 'Bws Fach' (the small bus). *(Courtesy of David Eynon).*

Despite all the bus activity, Eynon's were still operating cars, and still running an un-licensed taxi service. Carmarthen Borough Council however, eventually implemented their Hackney Carriage laws in June 1924, and began issuing licences to all operators running into the Borough. Eynon's licence for the Llanelly-Trimsaran-Carmarthen service was issued at this time, but the Kidwelly Borough Council were one of many local authorities that ignored their responsibilities allowing bus services a free passage through their small town until 1929.

Employees at this stage were still all family members and in January 1925, Samuel Eynon's sons Howell aged 21 and James (Jim) 17, had their first drivers licences issued, along with son-in-law, Walter Lodwick. Walter had married Sam Eynon's eldest daughter Annie who conducted on the buses alongside her sister Eleanor-Jane and brother Daniel. Eleanor's husband John Thomas also drove the buses but Daniel Eynon never drove as he suffered from epilepsy. Tickets used in these early days were the 'Bell Punch' with geographic stages as shown on page 204.

Meanwhile, another new Leyland arrived in July 1925. Registered BX5872 it was a 36hp normal control Leyland C7, again fitted with a Leyland 'Edinburgh' style rear entrance body which seated 26. Its solid tyre wheels were quickly exchanged for pneumatics which were available as conversion sets from Leyland Motors. Changing to pneumatics brought with it an improved ride and better road holding, with an added incentive (introduced in 1928) of a reduction in licence fee (road fund tax) by 20% for vehicles fitted with the softer tyre which was an added bonus for the enterprising company. Furthermore, the speed limit of 12 mph was increased to 20 mph on 1st October 1928 for vehicles fitted with pneumatics.

Above: Bus No 3, **BX 5872** was a Leyland C7 with 'Edinburgh' style rear entrance 26 seat body. It's seen here at the 'AA Box' Llandefeilog hill, on its return journey from Carmarthen, where driver Jim Eynon (right) has a break and a cigarette. His brother Daniel Eynon the conductor stands on the left with the AA Patrol man, centre. *(Courtesy of David Eynon).*

The first new bus fitted with pneumatic tyres arrived in July 1926, and was a little different from the earlier Leylands. It was an 'Allweather Coach' built by John Buckingham Ltd; Birmingham on a Leyland 30hp normal control Leyland C9 chassis. Painted in a dark blue livery it had 26 forward facing seats and a folding canvas roof. Registered BX 6996, and given fleet number 2 this also featured **'THE HERO'** lettering on the rear end panel, similar to that carried by its predecessor, the Fiat charabanc. It was later repainted red/black before finally being changed to maroon.

Trimsaran to Carmarthen Road Motor Service.

The attention of our readers is drawn to the fact that extra services have been added for the time being to the above, viz:—Wednesdays: Leave Trimsaran 9.30 a.m., Kidwelly 10 a.m., Llandefeilog 10.15 a.m., Idole 10.30 a.m.; leaving Carmarthen at 1 pm. Saturday service as on Wednesday, leaving Carmarthen at 1 p.m.

TRIMSARAN, KIDWELLY AND CARMARTHEN ROAD SERVICE.

ADDITIONAL SERVICES.

From the FIRST WEEK IN NOVEMBER the above Service will DAILY run as under:—

Leaving	Trimsaran	5.30 p.m.
	Kidwelly	5.50 p.m.
	Llandefeilog	6.10 p.m.
Arriving	Carmarthen	6.30 p.m.

LEAVING CARMARTHEN at 7.30 p.m.

The 10 a.m. Service will run on Mart Days, which fall occasionally on Thursdays and Fridays.

S. EYNON & SONS.

Sam Eynon didn't spend much money advertising his service to Carmarthen; the notice above (left) informing passengers of additional services on the Llanelly-Trimsaran-Kidwelly-Carmarthen service was extracted from the Carmarthen Journal newspaper dated 28th May 1926, and the one above right from the same source was dated 29th October 1926.

On the **right** is a front view of **BX 6996** the 30hp Leyland C9 'Allweather Coach' with its folding canvas roof in the open position. The same coach is pictured **below** with its roof in the closed position. After its early disposal in 1934 it was converted into a lorry, and ran as such until 1936. This picture was taken at Trimsaran Colliery with the engine house in the backdrop, and also shows the partial rear end of Eynon's Leyland 'Lion' PLSC1, BX 8048 which arrived new in 1927. A rear view of the C9 coach BX 6996 can be seen on the next page.
(Courtesy of David Eynon).

Above: This view of Leyland C9, **BX 6996** and Leyland PLSC1, **BX 8048** was taken inside Bryn Villa Garage with the staff, all family members, posing for the camera. **'The Hero'** lettering on the rear panel of the Leyland C9 'Allweather Coach' **BX 6996** is clearly visible, and the Hackney Carriage plate confirms its seating capacity as 26.
(Courtesy of David Eynon).

Exactly a year after the Buckingham bodied Leyland C9 arrived, another new Leyland was purchased in July 1927. This was a Leyland 'Lion' PLSC1 fitted with the 'L type' 4 cylinder petrol engine and a Leyland B31R body, again similar to the 'Lion' delivered to J James & Sons, Ammanford. This was registered BX 8048 and given fleet number 4, and consequently it allowed the company to have one additional Hackney Carriage licence, which then amounted to four licences compared to James Hughes' two and John Davies of Carway with just one.

At around the same time their first competitors appeared on the Kidwelly to Carmarthen road. The operators; J M Bacus & Co, of Burry Port (James Morrell Bacus) and The South Wales Transport Co, were granted licences on 19th September 1927, to operate an extension to their already established Llanelly - Burry Port - Kidwelly service, extending it to terminate at Carmarthen (Lammas Street), thus competing with Eynon's service between Kidwelly and Carmarthen.

Nevertheless, Eynon's survived the lean times of the depression years in the late 1920's, which had been the downfall of numerous small operators nationwide. Their business flourished as they battled on against their competitors during the bad times. On the other hand, Eynon's were warned by the Llanelly Borough Council licensing committee, known as the 'Watch Committee' in January 1928 that their licence would be revoked if they continued running irregularly.

Left: Bus No. 4, **BX8048** the Leyland 'Lion' PLSC1 with Leyland B31R bodywork is captured here on the Carmarthen road on a very wintry day in 1936. It would take a lot more snow than this to stop the Eynon's wheels from turning.
(Courtesy of David Eynon).

The model designation PLSC1 deciphered was:
P = Pneumatic Tyres.
L = Low loading chassis.
SC = Side cab driving position.

A total of 3,000 Leyland PLSC 'Lions' were built.

Above: Eynon's purchased this 1925 Ford 'model T' motor car from R Thomas, Newchurch, Carmarthen, in 1927.

As time passed, competitor James Hughes followed Eynon's into Carmarthen in 1929 with a very poor service that only operated for a short while. Eynon's were by now well established on the Carmarthen road and offered a far better time-table by owning four licensed vehicles.
Meanwhile, Eynon's applied to the Carmarthen Borough Council licensing committee for a licence to operate a service from Carmarthen (Lammas Street) to the nearby village of Croesyceiliog. This was granted in 1929, to run Saturdays only alongside Evan Morris' (Llansaint) similar service.
Consequently, in May 1930 another new bus was purchased. This was another new Leyland model known as the 'Tiger' TS1, with a 6 cylinder, 6.8 litre petrol engine and Leyland B31R body. It was given fleet No 5, and registered TH 804. After its arrival in May 1930, the Llanelly Borough Council licensing committee granted the company their fifth Hackney Carriage licence in February 1931, just a short while before the new 'Road Traffic Act 1930' was implemented.

Above: A splendid view of bus number 5, **TH 804** the Leyland 'Tiger' mentioned on the previous page. It was taken at the Leyland Motors factory on 2nd June 1930 shortly before delivery to Eynon's, and prior to its registration. It must be noted that all of Eynon's buses were built to rear entrance layout to comply with the by-laws of Llanelly Borough Council's licensing committee. Front entrance vehicles were regarded as potential fire hazards on petrol engine buses.

Right: Another view of bus number 5, **TH 804** taken sometime after delivery shows it with the registration plate.
Its powerful 6.8 litre overhead camshaft petrol engine developed 90bhp at 2,000 rpm. This particular engine was also fitted to the Leyland 'Titan' double decker chassis of the same period.
The early Leyland Tiger TS1's had that rugged looking appeal, with the characteristic square cut Leyland timber framed bodywork. Its seating however was extremely comfortable with pneumatic seat cushions.
This 'Tiger' saw almost 22 years' service with Eynon's.
(Courtesy of David Eynon)

INTRODUCTION OF THE 1930 ROAD TRAFFIC ACT

After thirteen years challenging and literally fighting with rival competitors, it came as a blessing to most operators when the new Minister of Transport, Mr Herbert Morrison announced the introduction of the 1930 Road Traffic Act. This Act of Parliament passed in August 1930 gave the Ministry of Transport's Traffic Commissioners full control of public service vehicles (PSV's), passenger services and their licensing in Great Britain.

These Traffic Commissioners, with the power vested in them, brought about improved operating conditions, an adherence to time-tables and stability of fares. All stage carriage and express service routes had to be licensed, and the granting of such licences, which had previously been under the jurisdiction of the local authorities, were then only obtainable through the Ministry of Transport's Traffic Commissioners. Licences to drive and conduct a public service vehicle also became the Traffic Commissioners responsibility. Under this new licensing system all public service vehicle operators (PSV operators) were issued with operator reference numbers, by which they were identified. Consequently, the number issued to Messrs Samuel Eynon & Sons, was TGR 311, with each Road Service Licence (RSL) applied for thereafter being given licence application numbers beginning with the operators reference number: TGR 311.

After implementing the new Traffic Act fully in April 1931, every bus operator had to re-apply to the new authority for renewal of each Road Service Licence held, and re-apply annually thereafter. Likewise, any changes to services, times, fares or new routes all had to be applied for and the licences would only be granted when approved by the Traffic Commissioners. However, the first licences Samuel Eynon & Sons applied for under the new Traffic Act in April 1931 was to renew the licences previously held by them, which were:-

TGR 311/1: Llanelly (Town Hall) to Carmarthen (Lammas Street).
via: Furnace, Cwmbach, Pen-y-mynydd, Trimsaran, Kidwelly, Glanmorlais, Llandefeilog, Rama, Idole, Cwmffrwd and Tycoch.
Service of stage carriage to operate daily Sunday to Saturday throughout the year.

TGR 311/2: Excursions & Tours starting from Llanelly (Town Hall).
[1] Tour to Aberystwyth via Llandilo or Carmarthen and Lampeter.
[2] Tour to Hereford via Brecon.
[3] Tour to Cheltenham via Cardiff.
[4] Other Excursions & Tours from Llanelly Town Hall.

As mentioned earlier, licences were only issued to the operators after a public hearing, and this particular hearing was the Traffic Commissioners first sitting at Llanelly in July 1931. Eynon's however were granted the above licences with no special conditions attached on 13th July 1931, and a week later they applied for a special short term RSL. This licence was:-

TGR 311/3: Trimsaran to Llanelly (Stradey).
via: Pen-y-mynydd, Cwmbach, Furnace, Pembrey Road and Sandy Road.

The licence was granted in order to run a special service of stage carriage from 22-24th July 1931 inclusive, on the occasion of the Royal Welsh Agricultural Show held at Stradey, which was visited by the Prince of Wales. Eynon's competitors were also granted a special short term licence to operate a service to the event.

Bearing in mind that the new Traffic Act had been operational for seven months, the company had left it rather late in applying for continuance of one other RSL. On 18th November 1931 they applied for continuance of their Carmarthen to Croesyceiliog stage carriage service:-

TGR 311/4: Carmarthen (Lammas Street) to Croesyceiliog.
via: Pibwr Lodge and Croesyceiliog Fach.
Service of stage carriage to operate on Saturdays only.

Ironically, the other competitor on this service, Evan Morris of Llansaint, near Kidwelly, had applied four months earlier for renewal of the same Saturday service, which was granted to him in December 1931. Eynon's licence renewal however was granted on 16th February 1932, with the following special condition attached:

The service is to operate on Saturdays only, as previously authorised.

Evan Morris ran his share of the Croesyceiliog service until June 1932 when he modified it to start from his home village of Llansaint, operating via Bryncoch Bach, Uplands Arms, Croesyceiliog and Pibwr Lodge to Carmarthen, Saturdays only. However, Evan Morris had abandoned all of his services by October 1937, and surrendered his remaining licences by July 1938, leaving Eynon's to continue running the Croesyceiliog service on their own un-opposed.

Meanwhile, competitor James Hughes failed to renew his stage carriage service licence for the Llanelly-Trimsaran-Kidwelly-Carmarthen service after introduction of the 1930 Road Traffic Act. He renewed his licence to operate between Llanelly (Town Hall) and Trimsaran only, (TGR 344/1) and the licence for Excursions & Tours starting from Llanelly Town Hall (TGR 344/2), as he only possessed two vehicle licences. The other competitor, John Davies & Son of Carway, with just one licensed vehicle, renewed the licence for his Thursday and Saturday only stage carriage service Carway to Llanelly via Trimsaran on 13th July 1931 with licence application number TGR 674/1.

On the other hand, Eynon's still shared the Kidwelly to Carmarthen section of their Llanelly-Kidwelly-Carmarthen service with J M Bacus & Co, of Burry Port, and South Wales Transport. However, Bacus' business was absorbed by South Wales Transport in May 1935, with the SWT continuing Bacus' daily service Llanelly to Carmarthen via Burry Port and Kidwelly.

At around the same time another PSV operator appeared in the village of Trimsaran. The operator Thomas Rees & Sons, 'Pretoria' Waun-y-clun, Trimsaran applied in June 1931 for a RSL to continue operating a workmen's stage carriage service between Trimsaran (Waun-y-clun) and Carway Colliery, claimed to have been operated by him during the previous year. Even though there wasn't any record of the service with the Llanelly B C licensing committee, the licence was granted to them on application number TGR 1193/1, and remained operational until 1936.

In December 1931, another operator appeared on the Kidwelly road, but this didn't affect Eynon's very much. It was a Thursday only market day service from Abergwili and Carmarthen to the Llanelly market, with only three picking up points on the route. Operated by Daniel Jones & Sons, of Abergwili, Carmarthen, the 'express service' carried mainly market traders and their wares, baskets of fruit, vegetables and flowers. However, the service was discontinued in March 1937.

Above: **TH 2970** was the first vehicle purchased after introduction of the 1930 Road Traffic Act. This 32 seat Leyland bodied 'Tiger' TS4 arrived in December 1932, and was again fitted with a petrol engine but of slightly larger capacity, 7.6 litre. This also gave 'Yeoman' service, almost 23 years before its sale to a showman for further use. Showing signs of its age here in September 1952, it was photographed by the late *Roy Marshall* on waste ground near Llanelly Town Hall. This is now the site of Llanelly Police Station, at Old Castle Road.

In 1932, a subtle change was made to the licensing of all services into Llanelly town centre. Special conditions were attached to the Road Service Licences of *all* operators running into the town. These conditions read:-

Granted without prejudice, and subject in all respects to the provisions of the Llanelly & District Transport Act 1930.

This condition was added to Eynon's licence TGR 311/1: Llanelly to Carmarthen upon renewal in July 1932. It disallowed the picking up of passengers between Harries Avenue, Llanelly and Llanelly Town Hall on inward journeys, and between Llanelly Town Hall and Harries Avenue on outward journeys except passengers for a destination beyond Harries Avenue. This was to protect services operated by the Llanelly & District Traction Company's tramway system, a condition that continued until deregulation in 1986! The Llanelly & District Traction Co, had this clause included into their Act of Parliament (a mandatory requirement to operate a public tramway system).

During the lean times of the economic depression which followed the 1926 General Strike, Eynon's were still looking for extra work to expand their business. Consequently three more RSL's were applied for in 1933. Firstly, on 8th March 1933 they applied for:-

TGR 311/5: Excursions & Tours starting from Trimsaran (The Square), at inclusive return fares only.
Tour to St.Ishmael's via Kidwelly. Return on same route. Price 10d.
The tour is to be run during June to September inclusive.
Max number of vehicles to be used on this tour on any one day is two.

The licence was granted on 5th July 1933, but was amended nine months later to include a list of 39 scheduled tours, with fares in line with all the other Llanelly area operators. The approved fares were set by the Traffic Commissioners to avoid fare cutting.

The next licence application on 26th April 1933 was to provide a 'new' service of stage carriage:-

TGR 311/6: Mynydd-y-garreg to Llanelly (Town Hall).
via: Kidwelly, Trimsaran, Pen-y-mynydd, Cwmbach and Furnace.
Fares: Mynydd-y-garreg to Llanelly: 1/2d single; 1/10d return.
To operate 4 journeys per day Monday to Saturday.

This application was refused on 16th June 1933, but was granted 31 months later under a composite time table combining TGR 311/1 and TGR 311/9 (see below).

The last licence application for 1933 came on 7th June. This was:-

TGR 311/7: Excursions & Tours starting from Pontyates (The Square).
A list of 39 scheduled tours was presented.

With opposition from competitor James Hughes, the licence was *finally* granted on 10th October 1933. Ironically, Hughes had applied for the same licence, which was granted at the same sitting.

The rivalry between Eynon's and Hughes inevitably continued and as a direct result of this, an inquiry was held at Llanelly Town Hall on 3rd January 1934, where it was claimed both operators had breached the conditions attached to their licences; to provide a service of stage carriage between Llanelly and Trimsaran. They were allegedly not running in accordance to published time tables. Consequently, the Traffic Commissioners decided at the public sitting to suspend the following RSL's for the period 8th to 14th January 1934 inclusive:-

TGR 311/1: Granted to Samuel Eynon & Sons, for Llanelly to Carmarthen.
via: Furnace, Cwmbach, Trimsaran, Kidwelly and Llandefeilog.

TGR 344/1: Granted to James Hughes & Sons, for Llanelly to Trimsaran.
via: Furnace and Cwmbach.

Alternatively, the Traffic Commissioner granted the following special licences to The South Wales Transport Co Ltd, to operate the suspended services without inconveniencing the travelling public:-

TGR 421/Sp/10: Llanelly to Carmarthen.
via: Furnace, Cwmbach, Trimsaran and Kidwelly, during the period 8th to 14th January 1934 inclusive.

TGR 421/Sp/11: Llanelly to Trimsaran.
via: Furnace and Cwmbach, during the period 8th to 14th January 1934 inclusive.

Surprisingly, amidst all this activity in the early 1930's, the Eynon's fleet didn't increase in size. Three Leyland saloons were acquired, one new and two second-hand to modernise the fleet by replacing earlier Leylands. First to arrive was TH 2970 a new Leyland 'Tiger' TS4 with 7.6 litre petrol engine and Leyland B32R bodywork in December 1932, followed by OF 5483 a Leyland 'Titan' TD1 (double decker chassis) with Leyland B32R body in April 1933. This had started life in 1929 as a lorry/box van with the Dunlop Rubber Co, as pictured below. The other vehicle, TJ 599, previously a Leyland Motors demonstrator was a 1933 Leyland 'Tiger' TS4 with a Leyland 32 seat coach body acquired in May 1934. Its bodywork was extensively rebuilt to B32F layout by Jeffreys Commercial Motors of Swansea after WW II. Jeffreys Commercial Motors Ltd were also the local Leyland dealer.

Below is an official Leyland photo of **OF5483** a Leyland 'Titan' TD1 of 1929 which had started life as a lorry/box van (as seen on right) with Dunlop Rubber Co, in Birmingham. The model designation TD1 was not Turbo Diesel Injection, it was a 'T' type Leyland; the 'D' was for its double decker chassis and the 1 = Mark 1. When sold by Dunlop in 1933, it was re-bodied by Leyland Motors Ltd, with this splendid looking 'new' Leyland rear entrance bus body which seated 32. It was then re-sold to Samuel Eynon & Sons in April 1933, where it carried fleet number 6, and operated until July 1950.

Above: Fleet number 8 was carried by this Leyland 'Tiger' TS4 registered **TJ 599**. This vehicle was new in 1933 as a demonstrator for Leyland Motors, carrying a Leyland C32R body, and was sold to Eynon's in May 1934. The body was rebuilt to front entrance layout and fitted with bus seats by Jeffreys Commercial Motors, Swansea, immediately after W W II ended. It is seen here in 1950 at Carmarthen (Lammas Street) - terminus of their Llanelly to Carmarthen service. **TJ 599** was withdrawn in January 1955 and sold to the open-cast mine contractor 'Sir John Jackson Ltd' as a mobile office at their Carway site. *(Alan Cross collection).*

Left: James (J
Eynon on the far
is pictured here
an outing at Co
Beach, Porthcaw
the early 1930's.
The outing
operated by these
and limousines,
it's not certain wh
car Jim was driv
on this hist
occasion. It is m
likely to be the on
the far left.

(David Eynon).

In the meantime, the ambitious Eynon family were still anxious to expand their business and eventually approached James Hughes in June 1935 with an offer to take over his business. The Ministry of Transport on the other hand encouraged larger bus companies all over the country to absorb the smaller operators. As a direct result of this, Samuel Eynon made an agreement with James Hughes, of Mile End Garage, Bryncaerau, Trimsaran to purchase his business and two vehicles pending the Ministry of Transport's approval of a licence transfer. Consequently, on 12th June 1935, Eynon's applied for a RSL to continue the service of stage carriage previously held by James Hughes & Sons (TGR 344/1) Trimsaran to Llanelly.

The application read as follows:-

TGR 311/9: Llanelly to Trimsaran
via: Furnace, Cwmbach and Pen-y-mynydd.

It is desired to operate the above service TGR 311/9 and TGR 311/1 under one RSL in accordance with the time-table supplied.

Before the licence was finally granted, a modification was made to the application on 24th July 1935, to incorporate a 'new' service to the village of Mynydd-y-garreg, a service which had previously been applied for and refused on application number TGR 311/6 in June 1933.

On 8th January 1936, the licence TGR 311/1 was renewed and incorporated the application TGR 311/9 above to absorb James Hughes & Sons' service, and also incorporated the new service to Mynydd-y-garreg. Combining the application TGR 311/9 with TGR 311/1 allowed a composite time-table on the Llanelly-Trimsaran road, which in turn allowed licence application TGR 311/9 to be cancelled in January 1936.

The new service to Mynydd-y-garreg was operated by diverting the established Llanelly-Carmarthen service TGR 311/1 from its normal B4308 route at Kidwelly (Abbey Street) into Priory Street and Heol-y-Meinciau, along one and a half miles of unclassified road to Mynydd-y-garreg Cross and back to Abbey Street, re-joining its normal route.

The two vehicles mentioned earlier as acquired from Hughes were BX 8368 a 1927 Dennis F and TH 838 a 1930 Dennis EV. They were not operated and quickly sold on to new owners as Eynon's had incorporated Hughes' time-table into theirs making Hughes' buses surplus to requirement.

James Hughes' son Tom transferred to Eynon's with his father's business, and consequently became the first Eynon's employee without a family connection. Hughes' garage which was next door to Sardis Chapel at Bryncaeuru, Trimsaran was not acquired.

Bearing in mind that the Ammanford operator J James & Sons Ltd, also ran a service through the Gwendraeth Valley to Burry Port (via Trimsaran), Eynon's were one of the few operators that didn't support James' six week strike in August 1935. The Eynon's employees, all family members were not Trade Union members. Twenty-one operators in Carmarthenshire and Glamorganshire joined the stoppage, shutting down the entire public transport system in Ammanford, Neath, Swansea, Llanelly and Gower. *A detailed history of J James & Sons Ltd, is still available from the publisher*: www.vernonmorgan.com

Meanwhile, another new RSL was applied for on 27th July 1935, to provide the following service of stage carriage:-

TGR 311/10: Trimsaran to Llanelly (Als Square).
via: Pen-y-mynydd, Cwmbach, Furnace, Atheneum Square, Church Street, Water Street, Upper Park Street, College Square and Als Square Llanelly).
Return via: Als Square, Upper William Street, William Street, Upper Park Street, Water Street, Church Street, Atheneum Square, Furnace, Cwmbach and Pen-y-mynydd.

This application was heard at a special sitting on 25th October 1935 and granted on 13th November 1935 with the special conditions stated below:-

To be run every day in the year except Saturdays, Sundays and school holidays. The service is for children only, attending the Intermediate School (Boys Grammar School) at Alban Road, Llanelly.

In 1936 there was another interesting development. It was the acquisition of another competitor, John Davies & Son, of 4 Green Cottages, Carway. On the 10th June 1936, Samuel Eynon applied for a RSL to take over the stage carriage service previously operated by John Davies & Son (TGR 674/1). In retrospect the application was:-

TGR 311/11: Carway to Llanelly (Town Hall).
via: Trimsaran (Junction of Llandyry Rd), Pen-y-mynydd and Cwmbach.
To run on Thursdays and Saturdays only throughout the year.

It must be noted that the junction of Llandyry Road was the only turning place at the lower end of Trimsaran village in those far gone days.

The licence was granted on 22nd July 1936 with two special conditions:-

[1] *The service is to run on Thursdays and Saturdays only.*
[2]*This licence is granted without prejudice, and subject in all respects to the provisions of The Llanelly & District Transport Act 1930.* (Same as TGR 311/1)

Eynon's acquired John Davies' Road Service Licence only. No vehicles or premises were acquired in the take-over owing to the fact that Davies' one and only bus was far too old. It was a 1923 Vulcan registered BX 3182.

Acquiring John Davies' licence finally gave Eynon's the monopoly of the Llanelly to Trimsaran route, yet Carway to Trimsaran was as mentioned earlier also operated by J James & Sons Ltd, of Ammanford on their Gwendraeth Valley service from Ammanford and Cross Hands to Burry Port. (*A detailed history of this service and its early operators can be found in my other publication:* James of Ammanford).

Despite all this activity, the business only moderately expanded during its first twenty years. The fleet had stayed dormant at just four buses until 1930 when a fifth bus arrived. In June 1937, a sixth bus was added to the fleet due to the extra workload mentioned earlier. Again, the company were influenced by the impressive Leyland fleet of J James & Sons, of Ammanford, acquiring another Leyland identical to James'. This was bus number 9, TH 8834 a Leyland 'Tiger' TS8, which was the company's first diesel engine vehicle, and fitted with their first metal framed body, built by Leyland Motors to B32R layout. It saw 22 years of service with the enterprising company.

Above: Leyland Motors introduced the Leyland 'Tiger' TS8 model in 1937, and Eynons acquired their 'Tiger' TS8 pictured here, with Leyland B32R bodywork, in June 1937. Carrying fleet number 9, it was registered **TH 8834** and fitted with the 8.6 litre Leyland diesel engine. This was the company's first diesel engine vehicle and saw continuous service until April 1959, when it was replaced by a 1948 'Tiger' PS1 acquired from Stratford Blue. *(Leyland Motors Archive)*

The only other changes before the outbreak of WW II in 1939 were revisions of time-tables on TGR 311/1 in January 1938 and a modification to the Excursions and Tours licence TGR 311/5, allowing passengers to be picked up (and set down on return journeys) at Kidwelly.

In addition to this, a special licence was granted to operate a service of stage carriage for one day only on Easter Monday, 18th April 1938:-

TGR 311/Sp/1: Trimsaran to Burry Port.
via: Pinged and Pembrey.

The licence was issued in order to operate a service on an unregistered route to a sports day event held at Burry Port Park.

This rear end view of Leyland 'Tiger' **TH 8834** was taken in 1954, inside the 'new' garage built in 1947 to accommodate double decker buses. By this time, the Tiger had been renumbered from 9 to 12. The double decker on the right is **WN 9474** an all Leyland TD4 which had been new to Swan Motors of Swansea in 1936. I'm indebted to Mr. David Eynon for the use of this family photograph.

THE DARK DAYS OF WAR

Just days after World War 2 began on 3rd September 1939, the company introduced an emergency time-table on their services. This decision was carried out in order to conserve fuel when fuel rationing commenced on 16th September. Their services were reduced to a very basic frequency – merely maintaining services to accommodate workers.

Ten months later in July 1940, War Department Officials toured all bus and coach operators in the United Kingdom requisitioning buses and coaches for military use, usually taking the operators best buses and coaches. In Eynon's case nothing was commandeered which was very unusual.

As war progressed, the company received additional work from the nearby Royal Air Force base at Pembrey, transporting USAF and RAF personnel to a camp near the village of Llansaint where they were billeted in 'Bell Tents'. An additional RSL had to be applied for to operate this service, but the licences were then only authorised by the Ministry of Defence (Ministry of War Transport), as were all other operational licences issued during the hostilities. Licences to operate excursions and tours were suspended in order to conserve fuel and rubber, as were the licences for Express Carriage services some three years later.

The only RSL issued to the company under the new Ministry of Defence regulations came soon after war broke out in 1939. It was:-

TGR 311/12: Pembrey Royal Air Force Base to Llansaint (Manor Farm camp).
via: Kidwelly.

Service of contract carriage to operate daily throughout the year.

Transport to convey war workers and military personnel was an absolute necessity at this point in time but the supply of new and second hand buses was very limited. All wartime purchases of buses, new and second hand had to be sanctioned by the Ministry of War Transport, and granted in special circumstances only. Eynon's however only received two vehicles through the MOWT, and both were second-hand Leylands. First to arrive in April 1944 was GJ 2397 a 1930 Leyland 'Titan' TD1 fitted with an unidentified second-hand Leyland 32 seat saloon body. It had been new to Premier Omnibus Co, London in June 1930, and passed to the LPTB as f/n L30, later TD189, for their Green Line service, but came to Trimsaran via Lewis & Jacob of Maesteg, Glamorganshire. It was closely followed in July 1944, by CBX 435, a re-registered 1930 Leyland 'Tiger' TS3 which had previously been registered UP 5095 and new to Stockton Corporation, Stockton on Tees, Teesside.

In 1944, Samuel Eynon's wife Mary, and his eldest daughter Annie Lodwick sadly passed away. At that point, the Lodwick family were also living at Samuel Eynon's large seven roomed house known as 'Bryn Villa'.

Pictured **above** is the first ex London Transport vehicle acquired by Eynon's in 1944. It was a 1930 Leyland 'Titan' TD1, registered **GJ 2397,** which had been fitted with a second-hand early 1930's Leyland B32R body sometime during WW2, as seen above.

The picture **below** shows the same vehicle **GJ 2397** carrying its original Duple C26R body when operating out of London Transport's Northfleet Garage in 1934.

THE POST WAR YEARS

After the wartime hostilities were over in 1945, the 'Trimsaran & District' fleet-name and logo were discontinued in favour of an 'E' monogram. The 'E' monogram however was rather short lived and replaced by the Eynon's fleet name as displayed below. Additionally, the company sold their ageing Leyland 'Lion' bus number 4, BX 8048 in 1945 which had survived eighteen years of arduous service, considerably well for a vehicle built with a timber frame body. Timber framed bodies normally had an average life span of around ten years.

Above: Leyland 'Titan' **GJ 2397** opposite is seen here at Kidwelly in 1946, working the connecting service from Kidwelly to Llansaint village some 500ft above Kidwelly. The driver, Willie Morris was also a member of the Eynon family.

Road Service Licences which had been under the strict control of the Ministry of War Transport throughout World War 2 and the immediate post war period, finally reverted back to the Traffic Commissioners control in September 1946, returning services to normal pre-war working, and permitting the return of Express Carriage services and Excursions & Tours licences. As a direct result of this, several modifications were made to the company's schedules and services which included alteration of time-tables, and inter-availability of return and season tickets between Eynon's on their Llanelly-Trimsaran Kidwelly to Carmarthen service, and The South Wales Transport Co, on their Llanelly-Burry Port - Kidwelly to Carmarthen service in December 1948. Furthermore, Eynon's were granted an extension to their Kidwelly-Mynydd-y-garreg service, (TGR 311/1) in May 1948, which allowed them to serve the neighbouring village of Four Roads, (one mile north-east of Mynydd-y-garreg), and permission had been given to operate double decker buses on their lucrative Llanelly-Trimsaran-Kidwelly to Carmarthen route in 1947, which of course included the villages of Mynydd-y-garreg, Four Roads and Llansaint, as the connecting services to these villages operated on the same RSL (TGR 311/1).

It may seem a little confusing but when the service to Llansaint was inaugurated under defence permit in 1939, it had application TGR 311/12 (service of contract carriage) but had been modified whilst still operating under the MOWT permit in1945/6, to application TGR 311/1 in order to carry the general public on a new stage carriage service after the RAF contract had finished.

The immediate post war period however suffered an acute shortage of new buses as most of them were built for the export market. Renewing their association with Leyland Motors, the company purchased their first new vehicle in ten years. This was bus number 12, DTH 103 a Leyland 'Tiger' PS1 which arrived in September 1947 fitted with a Duple B35F body. This was quite a change to the traditional Leyland body, due to the fact that the hard pressed body-shop at Leyland Motors were only building double decker bodies in the immediate post war period.

Above: The first 'new' vehicle purchased after W W II ended was this Duple B35F bodied Leyland 'Tiger' PS1 in 1947, which was painted in 'coach' livery, a reversal of the bus livery, cream with maroon relief. After a repaint in 1954 it received the bus livery of maroon with cream relief. It's seen here at the original Llanelly bus station in Town Hall Square, about to depart for Kidwelly.

Having been a widower for two years, Samuel Eynon remarried in 1946 and moved out of the family home 'Bryn Villa' Trimsaran, to live at Llangunnor, Carmarthen, leaving his family to operate the business, with his grandson David Ieuan Lodwick taking control as General Manager. Ieuan had joined the family business immediately after his de-mob from the RAF in 1946. The former family home 'Bryn Villa' was retained by the business and used as an office and staff canteen.

On 1st July 1947, Samuel Eynon wrote to the Minister of Transport expressing his concerns regarding the new Transport Bill – 'Nationalisation' affecting his business. In reply, the minister didn't commit himself as to whether or when the British Transport Commission would propose a transfer of the whole or any part of any particular undertaking and stated that the basis of compensation on transfer of undertaking to be quite fair. Obviously, it was a huge relief to the enterprising family when the BTC passed them by in their Nationalisation programme.

After receiving permission to operate double decker buses in 1947, a new garage had to be built to maintain and house them. A neighbouring plot of land some 30 yards away from Bryn Villa Garage was acquired where a new garage was constructed in 1947 by the structural engineers J. & P. Zammit of Llanelly. The steel framed asbestos covered garage could house 6 double decker buses of 27ft 6ins length (two lines of three buses) and became the company's main workshop.

The first double decker however arrived in May 1948, and was placed in service two months later after receiving extensive cosmetic work to its 'Leyland style' Northern Counties bodywork by Jeffreys Commercial Motors, Swansea, the local Leyland dealer. This was bus number 10, EK 8878 a 1932 Leyland 'Titan' TD2 retrofitted with a diesel engine. It had originally operated for Wigan Corporation (83), but came to Eynon's via Red & White Services, Chepstow (846).

Above: Eynon's first double decker bus, a 1932 Leyland 'Titan' TD2 with Leyland style Northern Counties L24/24R bodywork, registered **EK 8878**. Note the experimental type lettering for the fleet-name 'S E & S' in 1948.

Right: A front view of the same Leyland 'Titan' above **EK 8878** shows the rebuilding work carried out to its 'piano front' by Jeffreys Commercial Motors, Swansea in 1948, giving it a slightly modernised look. Jeffreys carried out an enormous amount of rebuilding work in the immediate post war period and simultaneously built several 'new' bus, coach and lorry bodies. They were also the Leyland, Albion, Scammell and Bedford dealers for west Wales.
Bus No.10, **EK 8878** is seen here at Lammas St, Carmarthen, fitted with a newer headlamp on its near side – probably giving more candle power!

In 1949, the Anglo-American Optical Co. Ltd, opened a new factory at Greenfield, Mynydd-y-garreg near Kidwelly. Eynon's quickly formed an association with the company and modified their time-table on the Kidwelly to Four Roads service (TGR 311/1) in July 1949, for the convenience of workers employed at the factory. This establishment later changed its title to British-American Optical Co. Ltd.

311/1—**Samuel Eynon and Sons,** of Bryn Villa Garage, Trimsaran. Stage carriages between Llanelly (Town Hall) and Carmarthen (Llammas Street). Revision of time table: (1) To delete the 8.0 a.m. journey Kidwelly to Four Roads on weekdays. (2) To introduce the following journeys for the convenience of workers employed at the Anglo-American Optical Co., Ltd., Greenfield Factory, Kidwelly :—

		*	†			*	†
		a.m.	a.m.			p.m.	p.m.
Trimsaran ..	.. dep.	7 40	7 40	Four Roads ..	.. dep.	—	—
Kidwelly ..	.. ,,	7 50	7 50	Greenfield Factory	.. ,,	5 35	4 35
Greenfield Factory	.. arr.	7 55	7 55	Kidwelly ..	.. arr.	5 40	4 40
Four Roads ..	.. ,,	8 5	8 5	Trimsaran ..	.. ,,	5 55	4 55

*—Mondays to Thursdays. †—Fridays.

It's interesting to note that the South Wales Transport Co, also ran services to the Anglo-American Optical factory. They were Service 15, Llanelly via Pwll, Burry Port, Pembrey and Kidwelly, and service 66, Upper Tumble via Cwm-mawr, Pontyberem, Pontyates, Meinciau and Four Roads.

Bus No.11, **JY 5026** the former Plymouth Leyland TD4c had the combination of an 'Oil Engine' and 'Gearless' (Torque Converter) transmission. The 'low-bridge' metal framed body seated 48.

As the company's workload increased, two more second-hand double-deckers were purchased in 1949. First to arrive was the former Plymouth Corporation Transport (108) JY 5026 (pictured left), a 1935 Leyland 'Titan' TD4c with Weymann L24/24R body, acquired from Tudor Williams Bros (Pioneer) of Laugharne followed two months later by TF 7310 a 1931 Leyland 'Titan' TD2, which had been extensively rebuilt by Jeffreys Commercial Motors, Swansea on behalf of Eynon's. It's Leyland L24/24R body was rebuilt to seat 50, losing its piano style front. TF 7310 had originally been a demonstrator vehicle for Leyland Motors. Fitted with 'Gearless' transmission, it operated with Birmingham Corporation Transport as their No.94, before passing to J James & Sons Ltd, Ammanford, converted to manual transmission in 1935, and to Williams Brothers, Laugharne in 1945.

Captured here outside the Ritz Ballroom, Town Hall Square, Llanelly in September 1952 is **TF 7310** the Leyland 'Titan' TD2 built in 1931 as a TD2c demonstration vehicle, and mentioned opposite. Its petrol engine had been retrofitted with an 'oil' engine when owned by J James & Sons Ltd, Ammanford. Eynon's had its Leyland 'piano fronted' body rebuilt as seen, by Jeffreys Commercial Motors, of Swansea in 1949. *(Roy Marshall collection)*.

At this point in time the villages of Trimsaran and Carway, and the nearby town of Kidwelly were rapidly expanding, which inevitably caused passenger numbers to increase. It can be said that the stage carriage side of Eynon's business flourished during this period, allowing the purchase of two 'new' double-deckers in 1950/1. Bus No.14, FTH831 a Leyland 'Titan' PD2/1 with Leyland L27/26R bodywork was first to arrive in August 1950, followed by No.15, GBX987 an eight feet wide Leyland 'Titan' PD2/3 with Leyland L27/26RD body, which had the luxury of manually operated platform doors. This was the first 8 feet wide vehicle to arrive at Trimsaran, and was unfortunately the last 'new' decker purchased by the company. However, the fleet only moderately expanded – consisting of just eleven vehicles in 1951: 5 double-deckers, 5 single-deckers and 1 coach. The double-deckers had ousted single-deckers on the stage carriage service, and could regularly be seen on a Saturday night arriving at Llanelly terribly overcrowded, with the conductor standing on the platform hanging on to the handrails to stop passengers from falling out, and the platform scraping the road when the bus cornered to the right from Vaughan Street into Broadway.

Having avoided nationalisation and offers of take-over by BET owned South Wales Transport in the early 1950's, the trend was now changing to underfloor engine vehicles, and the first such vehicle was bought in April 1952. Looking really modern at the time, it was the first 'new' coach purchased for many years. Registered GTH737 (No.16) it was a Leyland C41C bodied Leyland 'Royal Tiger' PSU1/15, fitted with the horizontal Leyland 600 power unit, synchromesh gearbox and vacuum brakes, and was another 'first', the first vehicle in the fleet with a centre doorway.

Above: This Leyland L27/26R bodied Leyland 'Titan' PD2/1, **FTH 831** was the first 'new' decker purchased by Eynons in August 1950. The view taken at Llanelly Town Hall (bus terminus) in the early 1950's depicts the 'E' for Eynon's monogram on the lower off-side panel. This monogram introduced in 1945 was discontinued in 1953, being replaced with the Eynon's fleet-name, as seen in the view on the opposite page.

Left: A splendid near side view of **FTH 831** shows the unusual location of the fleet number (14) on the near side alongside the bonnet.
The photograph was taken in 1956/7 at Llanelly (Town Hall), terminus of their Llanelly to Carmarthen service, with the vehicle about to depart on its 18 mile journey to Carmarthen.

Above: Bus number 15, **GBX 987** a Leyland PD2/3 'Titan' with Leyland L27/26RD body arrived new in July 1951. This was Eynon's second and last 'new' double decker which was fitted with manually operated platform doors–quite a rarity in those days. It was also the company's first 8ft wide vehicle – and had a little difficulty negotiating the 8ft 9inch wide Roman bridge known as 'Spudders Bridge' located on the main B4308 road between Trimsaran and Kidwelly. Spudders Bridge crossing the Gwendraeth Fawr river can still be seen today as an ancient monument alongside the new B4308 road.

Below: This near side rear view of bus number 15, **GBX 987** displays the layout of the manually operated doors and the enclosed rear platform, together with the emergency door in the rear end and the upper deck emergency window. This colour photo shows the company's original livery of Maroon and Primrose, and was taken at Llanelly Town Hall Square bus station in 1952.

Above: The first 'new' coach for 26 years was this unusual 'sad looking' Leyland 'Royal Tiger' PSU1/15, **GTH 737** with Leyland C41C (centre doorway) coachwork delivered in April 1952. It was also the company's first vehicle with an underslung engine, the horizontal 9.8 litre Leyland 600 unit, coupled to a 4 speed synchromesh gearbox. The brakes were vacuum, but the handbrake - must have been unreliable looking at the brick placed under the front wheel here at Eynon's yard in 1964. Interesting to note, the emergency door was alongside the driver, and probably used as a cab door also! This particular chassis/body combination didn't sell in large numbers, 145 went to BET owned Ribble Motor Services, with other BET companies taking a very small number. Eynon's were just one of a few independent operators to purchase one of these 'Leyland' coach bodied PSU1/15 Royal Tigers. Incidentally, this was to be the very last vehicle 'Sam' Eynon purchased as he passed away a year later.

As mentioned earlier, Eynon's were very much a family concern. With the exception of Tom Hughes who transferred to Eynon's in 1935 with his father's business, every employee was a member of the Eynon family, but inevitably this changed in 1952 as the business was expanding. Several 'outsiders' joined the staff at this point, fitters, drivers and conductors. These employees were very loyal personnel and some stayed with the company through thick and thin to the bitter end in 1988, namely Noel Babbage and Mel Davies.

Tom Hughes' son on the other hand didn't follow in his father's footsteps to work at Eynon's – he became a 'coach painter' with the erstwhile local coachbuilder Thomas & Thomas Coachworks at Fair Lane Works, Carmarthen. Thomas & Thomas built around 100 bus and coach bodies for several South Wales companies from 1926 to 1950. They also built lorry bodies and carried out commercial bodywork repairs and vehicle repaints until the early 1960's.

On 5th September 1953, Samuel Eynon sadly passed away at the age of 73 years, leaving his three sons and one grandson, Ieuan Lodwick to control the company. The partnership continued to trade as Samuel Eynon & Sons, but never formed a limited company. Following his death, the title on the operator's licence (TGR 311) was changed to 'The Executors of the late Samuel Eynon' in November 1953, and continued as such until October 1959. In his will published on 5th February 1955, his effects valued at £19,201-5-0 passed to his three sons Howell, Daniel and James Eynon. The former home of Samuel Eynon, 'Bryn Villa' at Trimsaran was part of the business and retained by the family partnership for continued use as an office and canteen.

As the private hire and excursions side of the business began to increase in the early 1950's, a modification to the Excursions & Tours licence (GO 3619) TGR 311/2 was asked for and granted in May 1953, to have additional picking up points at Pwll, Sandy, Park Howard, Felinfoel, Llwynhendy and Bynea.

At around the same time, school contract work increased due to the 'population explosion' of the immediate post-war period. This meant extra school buses to transport the increased number of children, resulting in the arrival of a new dual-purpose saloon: (No.18) LBX 811, a Leyland 'Tiger Cub' PSUC1/12T with attractive Willowbrook DP41F body in May 1955; a second-hand Leyland 'Tiger' TS7, registered BV 4454 with ECW C32F body in July 1954; (No.17) EVT382 Leyland 'Tiger' TS7 with Willowbrook B37F body in November 1954; (Nos.20/21) BSM170/1 Leyland 'Tiger' TS7's with 1943 ECW B35R bodies in 1955, closely followed by three all Leyland double-deckers; (No.19) BTH175 an un-frozen 'Titan' TD7 from James Ammanford in September 1955 and (No's. 22/23) CS 7034/8046 'Titan' TD5's from Western S M T, in November 1955. CS 8046 had a comparatively short stay at Trimsaran as it received extensive roof damage in 1957 when it collided with an arched bridge at Pembrey Road, Kidwelly. Working a schools contract at the time, driver James (Jim) Eynon, son of the founder had been more familiar with low-bridge type deckers – the mainstay of the fleet at this particular time. High-bridge double-deckers *could* negotiate the bridge provided they straddled the centre of the road (centre of the arch).

Above: Wash time here at the Trimsaran yard by the good old fashioned method – by hand. This Leyland 'Tiger' TS7, **BV 4454** with Eastern Coach Works C35F body was purchased from Daniel Jones & Sons, Abergwili Road Garage, Carmarthen, in July 1954.

Above: Captured here on layover at Llanelly Town Hall Square in the mid-1950's is bus No.17; **EVT382**, a rather tired looking 1937 Leyland 'Tiger' TS7, with Willowbrook B37F body. This was sold in 1958.

Above: This Willowbrook dual purpose bodied Leyland 'Tiger Cub' PSUC1/2T, **LBX 811** was new to Eynon's in May 1955. It could regularly be seen working stage carriage between Llanelly and Carmarthen, but also worked private hire when required, as seen here at Newcastle-Emlyn. The 'Tiger Cub' was very economical with its 5.7 litre Leyland 0.350 engine returning a fuel consumption of 13.6 mpg.

Right: This 1935 Leyland 'Tiger' TS7 **BSM 170** was one of a pair (BSM 170/1) purchased from Western SMT (862/3) in 1955. They both carried Eastern Coach Works B35R bodies built in 1943, and were acquired for the escalating amount of school contract work at the time. They were given fleet numbers 20 and 21 respectively but were withdrawn within two years. **BSM 170** found a new home with a new operator, Ronald G Peters, T/A: Towyn Coach Services at Pembrey, Carmarthenshire, where it worked for a further two years.

Above: Loading up at Lammas Street, Carmarthen for its return journey to Llanelly in 1957 is bus No.24 (previously No.19) **BTH 175** a 1941 'unfrozen' Leyland 'Titan' TD7 with Leyland L27/26R body. It was built during the early part of WW II before the wartime austerity specifications were imposed, to the order of Walter Alexander & Sons, Falkirk, and then stored (*or* 'frozen') together with around 200 others. The stock of 'frozen' buses under strict control of the Ministry of War Transport were eventually 'unfrozen' in 1941/2. **BTH 175** was one of a pair supplied to James, Ammanford in October 1941, this particular one passing to Eynon's in September 1955. Interesting to note that the unique Alexander style destination box was still fitted. *(Roy Marshall collection).*

Above: In November 1955, Eynon's bought two Leyland 'Titan' TD5's from Western SMT. Numerically the first one was this Leyland 'high-bridge' bodied example **CS 7034** which was given fleet No.21. It's captured here at Town Hall Square, Llanelly, working their Llanelly-Trimsaran–Kidwelly-Carmarthen service.

Above: Bus No.23, pictured here at the company's Carmarthen terminus (Lammas Street), was the second Leyland 'Titan' TD5 acquired from Western SMT (147) in November 1955. Registered **CS 8046**, this also had a Leyland 'High-bridge' body with seating layout H30/26R. It had a very sad end in 1957 when it collided with an arched bridge at Kidwelly and was subsequently scrapped.

December 1956 saw the beginning of fuel rationing in Britain, implemented by the government and brought about by a severe shortage of crude oil due to troubles in the Middle-East and the Suez Canal. The company's services were revised in order to conserve fuel – the first time since World War II ended. Coupled to the fuel shortage was a massive increase in fuel prices. With a surcharge of 20% imposed, the cost inevitably had to be passed on to the travelling public but four months later the surcharge was removed and the fares reverted back to normal.

In July 1957, a rather unusual looking coach was acquired with a bulbous front panel fitted to its fully fronted Plaxton coachwork. The style of moulding around the front grille had a somewhat 'unhappy' look about it. It was a 1950 Leyland 'Tiger' PS1 registered LKH 351, which came from Bluebird of Hull. The chassis which was intended for a 27ft. 6inch body had been extended to take its Plaxton 28ft 6inch body – the new permissible length in 1950.

Above: Fleet No. 24 was also given to **LKH 351**, this 1950 Plaxton fully fronted 35 seat coach with a Leyland 'Tiger' PS1 lengthened chassis. Its chassis had been lengthened to accommodate the 28ft 6ins body – the new permissible length in 1950. This rather unusual looking coach was sold to John Howell, Burry Port in March 1961.

For the 1958 coaching season, another 'new' coach arrived, a Duple 'Donnington' C41F bodied Leyland 'Tiger Cub' PSUC1/2. Registered RBX 394 in May 1958, it was the pride of the fleet and a few months later in October 1958, they purchased their first pair of London Transport double- decker buses, JXN 320/358, Leyland 7RT's with Park Royal H30/26R bodies dating from 1948. They were previously fleet numbers RTL 8/35 respectively, and had been refurbished by London Transport a short while before sale. Eynon's were so delighted with their RTL's they acquired many more in later years. In addition to these RTL's they purchased a 1947 Leyland 'Titan' PD1A with Leyland H30/26R body registered FOR 639 from Hants & Sussex, which had been new to their subsidiary company, Liss & District Omnibus Co, (LO51) in May 1947.

Above: Leyland 'Tiger Cub' PSUC1/2 with Duple 'Donnington' C41F body, **RBX 394** was the pride of the fleet in 1958, and was the envy of local competitors that were running petrol engine Bedford SB's. It's seen here at Newcastle Emlyn in 1958, with its regular driver, Willie Morris a member of the Eynon family.

Left: The upper deck of this 'High-bridge' bodied Leyland 'Titan' PD1A, **FOR 639** is looking somewhat battered in its final years, after regularly colliding with low tree branches at the privately owned Stradey Woods, on the B4308 between Llanelly and Trimsaran. Eynon's staff were often seen reaching out of upper deck windows of their buses, cutting off protruding tree branches. The Leyland PD1's with a chrome radiator surround had a very smart appearance. This particular one dating from 1947 was acquired in October 1958 from Hants & Sussex Emsworth, Hampshire, and gave four years of service to the company. It was replaced in October 1962 by a former Western Welsh 'low-bridge' bodied Leyland 'Titan' PD2/3.

Above: The backdrop for this view of former London Transport RTL8, **JXN 320** a 1948 Leyland 'Titan' 7RT with Park Royal H30/26R body is Heol Waun-y-clun, Trimsaran: outside Eynon's double decker bus garage. **JXN 320** was one of a pair acquired in September 1958, forming an alliance with London Transport. The house with an entrance porch visible in the right hand background is 'Bryn Villa', Samuel Eynon's former residence, by then used as the company's office and canteen.

Above: The other London Transport Leyland 7RT acquired in Sept. 1958 was RTL35, **JXN 358** with Park Royal H30/26R body. At first the maroon and cream livery was applied as seen in this view dated July 1959, but was later repainted with cream window surrounds. Note the odd headlamp on the near side, probably to give more candle-power, and the Eynon's time-table fastened to the shop wall at the company's Carmarthen terminus; Lammas Street.

From 1953 to 1959 the Eynon's business had operated on licences in the name of 'The Executors of the late Samuel Eynon'. However, on 28th October 1959 all seven of the company's RSL's and the operator licence were applied for and granted in the names of 'Howell Eynon; Daniel Eynon and James Maurice Eynon (T/A: Samuel Eynon & Sons)' from the same address and under the same licence application number TGR 311. The new registered licence holders of the business were the late Samuel Eynon's three sons.

Throughout the years, the company relied tremendously on part time labour. One part time driver, Gwynne Price, a self-employed hardware rounds-man bought a 12 seat mini-bus and a 29 seater coach, and applied for a Road Service Licence in February 1960 to operate an Express Carriage service from Carway (Bron-gwendraeth) to Mynydd-y-garreg (British American Optical Factory), via Pontnewydd (Glyn Abbey) on unclassified road - which was a different route to Eynon's. The proposed service to run on working days at the factory had application number TGR 4834/1. Objections to the application were made by Eynon's; J James & Sons Ltd, Ammanford and The South Wales Transport Co, on grounds of encroachment. Support for the service was given at the hearing by Carmarthen R D C, but the licence was refused. Gwynne Price continued working part time for the company for many years afterwards until his own coach business established itself, nowadays operated by his two sons Ceri and Arwyn Price, ironically from the former Eynon's garage at Trimsaran.

The intake of vehicles for the 1959/60 period were all second-hand. The list included GUE 250 a 1948 Leyland 'Tiger' PS1 with Northern Coach Builders B34F body from BET subsidiary, Stratford Blue in April 1959; TAB 577 a two year old Leyland 'Tiger Cub' with Duple 'Britannia' C41C body in May 1959; KAW 677 a 1954 Leyland 'Royal Tiger' PSU1/17 with Leyland B44F body from Whittle, Highley, Salop, in January 1960; DBX 260 a 1947 Leyland 'Tiger' PS1 fitted with a second-hand (1946) Burlingham B34F body which came from another BET subsidiary company, J James & Sons Ltd, Ammanford (200) in January 1960, followed by LTG 269 a 1952 Leyland 'Royal Tiger' PSU1/15 with a Leyland C41C body from BET subsidiary Rhondda Transport (329) in March 1960.

Bearing in mind that the fleet at this stage was increasing in size, the stage carriage services had already passed their peak. Passenger numbers were beginning to fall, and this was evident on some off peak journeys, especially the Kidwelly to Llansaint service, as the company had withdrawn some Saturday journeys on this route three years earlier in September 1957. Additionally, increased costs were leading to higher fares, and rural services nationally were in danger of being curtailed or withdrawn because of rising costs. As a direct result of this, in February 1958 the Western Welsh Omnibus Co; South Wales Transport; James of Ammanford; United Welsh Services and several smaller operators appealed to Carmarthenshire C C to support a campaign for the abolition of the excessive tax on fuel oil, which was tax exempt when used on the railways. The local authority agreed to support the campaign provided that any reduction in the fuel tax duty would be reflected in cheaper fares.

Similar appeals had been made by operators throughout the country until finally the fuel duty rebate scheme was established under section 92 of the 'Finance Act 1965' nowadays known as 'Bus Service Operator Grant'. More details of this financial assistance will be mentioned later.

Above: The very last vehicle to carry a fleet number with Eynon's, in this case 28, was this 1948 Leyland PS1 'Tiger' **GUE 250** with Northern Coach Builders B34F body. Purchased in April 1959 from Stratford Blue Motors, Stratford upon Avon, it was crew operated and gave 'Yeoman Service' until September 1964.

Above: Captured here on the forecourt of Eynon's garage is **TAB 577** a 1957 Leyland 'Tiger Cub' PSUC1/2T with attractive Duple 'Britannia' C41C coachwork. It was fitted with the Leyland 0.350 engine, constant mesh gearbox and two speed axle. The driver was the company's garage foreman at this particular time, Thomas John Davies. *(Robert Mack collection).*

Above: New to Whittle, Highley, in 1954 and acquired by Eynon's in January 1960 was this Leyland B44F bodied Leyland 'Royal Tiger' PSU1/17 registered **KAW 677**. After giving lots of trouble it was sold to the dealer, Arlington Motors and resold to Morlais Services, Merthyr Tydfil in October 1962.

Above: A second Leyland 'Royal Tiger' PSU1/15 with Leyland C41C coachwork was purchased by Eynon's in March 1960. This was a second-hand example and came from a BET subsidiary; Rhondda Transport (329), Porth, Glamorganshire. Registered **LTG 269** in April 1952, it operated with Eynon for four years before passing to a contractor, Maberly Parker, Tongwynlais, May 1964.

The 23rd April 1960 was an extremely harrowing day for all members of the Eynon family, and all Eynon's staff. Samuel Eynon's second son Daniel, who suffered from epilepsy, fell behind a bus that was reversing out from the garage, and died from his injuries. Driver of the reversing bus, was Daniel's elder brother Howell who was exonerated of any blame.

On 27th April 1960, the company applied for a new RSL to accommodate employees of a car components factory at Felinfoel near Llanelly. The application was as follows:-

TGR 311/13: Trimsaran (Bird-in-Hand) to Felinfoel (Morris Motors Ltd, Nuffield Works),
via: Pen-y-mynydd, Cwmbach, Furnace and Llanelly (West End).
To operate Express Carriage (Workers) Mon–Sats, throughout the year.

An objection to the application came from The South Wales Transport Co, and after a public hearing the licence was granted on 8th June 1960, with the following Special Condition:-

No passengers to be picked up or set down between Furnace Square and Felinfoel, Nuffield Works.

Only one vehicle was purchased in 1961 and this was another first. It was the first Leyland 'Leopard' and the first coach with Burlingham coachwork. This L2 type 'Leopard', fitted with the Burlingham 'Seagull 70' C41F body was registered XTH 300 and licensed in May 1961. It was a pretty rare model, as these bodies were only in production for a few months in early 1961. The coachbuilder H V Burlingham of Blackpool was taken over by the London based coachbuilder Duple Motor Bodies, Hendon in 1960, who discontinued the Burlingham design in favour of new Duple products in mid - 1961.

Above: The rare Burlingham 'Seagull 70' bodied Leyland 'Leopard' L2, **XTH 300** mentioned above is captured here at Blackpool whilst on tour in 1961.

An amendment to the Construction and Use Regulations in 1961 brought Britain into line with most of Europe. All buses and coaches, single and double decker could then have a maximum length of 36ft (11 metres) and a maximum width of 8ft 2½ inches (2.5 metres). Eynon's however didn't take advantage of the new regulation when they exchanged their Leyland 'Tiger Cub' coach, RBX 394 in 1962. The replacement coach 818 ATH was the second Leyland 'Leopard' L2, but this one carried the newly developed Plaxton 'Panorama' C41F body to the old maximum length of 30ft. A very attractive design which grew in popularity.

More second-hand vehicles arrived at Trimsaran in 1962 including LYF 150 (RTL 1209) another Leyland 'Titan' 7RT from London Transport; JTH 791 a Leyland 'Tiger Cub' with Duple Midland body from Davies Bros, Pencader; EUH 959/964 Leyland 'Titan' PD2/3's from Western Welsh (959/964) in October 1962 followed by sister buses EUH 953/966 (953/966) in March 1963.

Above: Eynon's purchased this 1954 Duple Midland bodied Leyland 'Tiger Cub' **JTH 791** from Davies Bros (Pencader) Ltd, in March 1962, where it had carried fleet number 46. *(Vernon Morgan).*

The Eynon's livery had always been maroon with primrose relief and black wings, with coaches carrying a reversed livery of primrose with maroon relief and black wings until the purchase of the Western Welsh Leyland Titan's mentioned above. From that point, the maroon was changed to red and the primrose to cream for all subsequent purchases and repaints over the preceding years, with the balance of colours changing to around 50%. The process of re-painting into the new standard livery took 5 years. However, not every vehicle received fleet livery. Numerous second-hand and three new vehicles, OBX 1J; WTH 255M and GNY 431N operated in the liveries they carried when purchased, and a few double-deckers received all-over advertising liveries.

Above: This attractive looking Plaxton 'Panorama' 41 seat coach on a Leyland 'Leopard' L2 chassis arrived at Trimsaran in June 1962. Registered **818 ATH,** it was the first coach to display the new 'Gothic' style lettering of Eynon's fleet-name. It was sold to West Wales Motors Ltd, Tycroes, Carmarthenshire, in 1965 where it operated until mid-1984.

Above: Former London Transport RTL 1209, **LYF150** a 1951 Leyland 'Titan' 7RT with Park Royal H30/26R body joined the Eynon's fleet in August 1962, giving 6 years of excellent service. It's seen here at the original Llanelly bus station (Town Hall Square) about to depart for the ancient town of Kidwelly.

Above: The company's 'new' livery of red and cream superseded the old maroon and primrose livery in 1962 with the arrival of four identical ex Western Welsh Leyland 'Titan' PD2/3's with Leyland L27/26R bodies in 1962/3. One of the batch **EUH 964,** seen here at Carmarthen terminus, shared the same stable as EUH 959/966/953 at Trimsaran. Dragon Stores were apparently one of the earliest off-licenses in Llanelly.

Mention should be made here of the dedicated staff employed at Eynon's, and how well they coped on the Kidwelly to Carmarthen road during the Arctic conditions that hit south Wales on 9th February 1963. The A484 trunk road from Kidwelly to Carmarthen was closed for several days – blocked by 10ft high snow drifts that were only partially cleared to allow single file traffic with passing places along the 10 mile road. These dreadful conditions didn't improve for several weeks, the freezing temperatures continued without a thaw, with further snow falls until the end of March – but the buses kept on running.

In June 1963, everyone was surprised to see the arrival of 405 CTH a 'new' Bedford SB5 with Duple 'Bella Vega' coachwork. It was the first of many 'lightweight' Bedford's - a breakthrough from the traditional Leyland which had been the mainstay since 1922! This Bedford was the first vehicle to pioneer continental travel for the company, when it toured Germany with the famous 'Scarlets' (Llanelly RFC) in 1963. Eynon's coaches later visited every country in Western Europe.

The company however were extremely satisfied with the reliability of their Leyland RTL's from London Transport and went ahead to buy a further five of that marque in September 1963, ousting two of the Western Welsh 'Titans' acquired a few months earlier. I can recall the spectacular sight of seeing all five travelling west in convoy along the newly opened Cowbridge by-pass, on a Sunday afternoon, 15th September 1963, still wearing their LT liveries, three in central area Red, and two in country area Green; all displaying Carmarthenshire garage 'Trade Plates'.

Above: Breaking from the traditional Leyland marque for the first time since 1922, this Bedford SB5 with Duple 'Bella Vega' C41F body, **405 CTH** was purchased new in June 1963. It was also the first Eynon's vehicle to embark upon Continental Touring with a tour to Germany in 1963 conveying the famous Llanelly RFC, known as the 'Scarlets'.

Above: Eynon's adored their former London Transport RTL's. This 1951 Park Royal bodied Leyland 'Titan' 7RT, **LYF 35** (RTL1111) was one of five purchased in 1963, all giving eight years of service.

Above: Former London Transport RTL1114, **LYF 38** was another Park Royal H30/26R bodied Leyland 'Titan' acquired in Sept. 1963, and is captured here crossing the Gwendraeth Fawr river by means of a Bailey Bridge, erected by the open cast mine contractor 'Sir John Jackson Ltd' to divert their heavy lorries off the old Roman 'Spudders Bridge'. It was located alongside 'Spudders Bridge' on the B4308 between Trimsaran and Kidwelly.

Above: Another former London Transport RTL acquired in 1963 was **LYF 40**, (RTL 1116) captured here at Oscar Chess Garages, Pensarn, Carmarthenshire on lay-over between school workings. This bus also had a Park Royal H30/26R body, and gave eight years of service before being replaced by a former Plymouth, Leyland PD2 'Titan'.

Above: Seen here at the Llanelly Town Hall bus terminus sometime in 1964, awaiting departure for Kidwelly via Trimsaran is **LYR 959** (RTL1311) another one of the five Leyland 'Titan' 7RT's with Park Royal bodies acquired from London Transport in September 1963. Both **LYR 959/LYR 808** arrived at Trimsaran in full London Country - green livery, but were soon repainted into the Eynon's livery. *(R. H. G. Simpson collection).*

Above: Only one vehicle was purchased in 1964 and was the second Bedford in the fleet. The Bedford **695 ETH**, was a VAL14, with Plaxton 'Val' C52F coachwork, new in May 1964, and was another 'first' – the first 36ft long vehicle and the first tri-axle vehicle in the fleet. Apparently the Bedford VAL's had notorious braking systems!

Surprisingly, Eynon's didn't object to the South Wales Transport's application for a RSL in April 1964, to operate a stage carriage service from Trimsaran (Bryncaerau Shop) to Cynheidre Colliery shaft No. 1 & 2. It was a service that operated three shifts per day for National Coal Board employees only, working at Cynheidre Colliery.

With the company beginning to expand, the one coach business of Oliver Rowlands, Carway, was absorbed in July 1964. No vehicles or premises were involved in the transaction but Rowlands' petrol engine Commer 'Avenger I' registered FBX 489 was borrowed during the summer months of 1964, and maintained by Eynon's staff throughout the season. The Commer was returned to Rowlands at the end of the season, September 1964, and laid up at his garage 'Brynamlwg' in Carway until it was sold in 1969.

Running costs at this point in time were ever increasing and the company reluctantly applied to the Traffic Commissioners in December 1964 for an increase in fares, to bring them into line with the fares granted to the South Wales Transport Co earlier that year. This application was objected to by two local coach operators; H G Sage, Burry Port and Jenkins Tours, Llanelly, operators that didn't work any stage carriage themselves. Nevertheless the fare increase for the Llanelly-Carmarthen service was finally granted in April 1965, and to regularise fares, their other services followed in June 1967.

However, when the RSL's were due for renewal in January 1965, they were again modified due to the deaths of two shareholders, brothers Daniel and Howell Eynon. It was only a change of entity to James Maurice Eynon & David Ieuan Lodwick (T/A: Samuel Eynon & Sons) senior partners of the business. As mentioned earlier, Ieuan Lodwick was a grandson of the founder Samuel Eynon and was also the General Manager of the business.

Due to the change of entity above, the Traffic Commissioners issued temporary special licences until authorisation had been granted. The special licences issued on 27th January 1965 and expiring on 27th February 1965 were:-

TGR 311/Sp/2: Llanelly (Town Hall) to Carmarthen (Lammas Street).

TGR 311/Sp/3: Carmarthen (Lammas Street) to Croesyceiliog.

TGR 311/Sp/4: Carway to Llanelly (Town Hall).

TGR 311/Sp/5: Trimsaran (Bird-in-Hand Square) to Felinfoel (Morris Motors Works).

Meanwhile, after forty years of competition on the Kidwelly to Carmarthen road, Eynon's ultimately became the *only* operator between the towns in June 1965. This came about after a re-organisation of services by the South Wales Transport Co, when their un-remunerative service 15 (TGR 421/31: Llanelly - Carmarthen via Burry Port and Kidwelly) was curtailed at Castle Garage, Kidwelly. Additionally, on the 30th November 1986, the service was curtailed even further - at the village of Pembrey, abandoning the town of Kidwelly altogether!

In 1964, the company took advantage of the new permitted 36feet maximum length for buses and coaches which had been introduced three years earlier. The first 36ft long vehicle to arrive was 695 ETH a Bedford VAL14 with Plaxton 'Val' coachwork, followed a year later by another Bedford VAL14, BTH 987C with Duple 'Vega Major' coachwork. The VAL14's had Leyland 0.400 engines mounted at the front, and were accompanied by a pair of Leyland 0.375 engine Bedford SB13's, CBX 9C/CBX 238C, all purchased through the dealership of Arlington Motors Ltd. The two year old Bedford SB5, 405 CTH was part exchanged for one of these Bedford SB13's in May 1965, exchanging it for a Leyland engine vehicle – the company's preference!

Other purchases during 1965 were a pair of second-hand Leyland 'Tiger Cubs' with Weymann B44F bodies from Western Welsh O C, (1025/7) HUH 25/7 and two more Leyland RTL's from London Transport (RTL708/876) KXW 58 and LLU 866. These RTL's replaced the last two former Western Welsh Leyland 'Titan' PD2/3's which were part exchanged at Passenger Vehicle Sales (Dealer) in Essex.

Another very important issue must be mentioned at this stage – the spelling of **Llanelly** was changed to the correct welsh spelling – **Llanelli** on 1st January 1966, and will therefore be spelt as such from this point even though, Eynon's destination blinds continued to display Llanelly.

Above: In 1965 the company purchased no less than three new coaches, all Bedford's. First to arrive in May 1965 was this Leyland 0.400 engine Bedford VAL14, **BTH 987C**, with Duple 'Vega Major' C52F coachwork, and had left the fleet in less than two years. It's pictured here at Coney Beach Coach Park, Porthcawl, even though the destination blind states Blackpool. Coney Beach wasn't the Welsh equivalent to Blackpool but was a very popular destination for Sunday School and Social Club outings in those far gone days with its Amusement Park and beach, plus the seasonal Firework Displays.

Above: Quite a rare combination was this Bedford SB13, **CBX 9C**, with Harrington Crusader IV, 41 seat coach-work, but the Eynon partnership had a penchant for coaches that were different to their competitors vehicles.

Above: This Weymann 'Hermes' bodied Leyland 'Tiger Cub' PSUC1/1, **HUH 25** was new to Western Welsh (1025) in 1953. It was purchased by Eynon's in October 1965, and after receiving two serious accidents was regarded to be an unlucky bus, so was passed on to Arlington Motors the dealers after just nine months. It then passed to Silcox of Pembroke Dock where it worked until 1976.

Above: **KXW 58**, formerly London Transport RTL708, a 1950 Leyland 7RT 'Titan' is captured here outside T P Hughes department store known as 'London House' at Lammas Street, Carmarthen. London House was Eynon's terminus for more than 50 years until the opening of a bus station at Blue Street. Note the 1961 Austin FGK40 2 ton delivery lorry YBX832 owned by T P Hughes (TPH), London House.

Right: The very last RTL acquired by Eynon's happened to be RTL876, in 1965. Registered **LLU 866** it's seen here at Star Square, Trimsaran in 1966, and was affectionately known as 'LULU' a name derived from its registration number. It was repaired after being involved in a fatal accident near Kidwelly in February 1966 but left the fleet soon afterwards. *(V. Morgan).*

As mentioned earlier, bus operators throughout the country had campaigned to the Tory Government for several years to have the excessive tax on fuel abolished to assist failing services. Consequently, under section 92 of the 'Finance Act 1965' the 'Fuel Duty Rebate' was established to assist operators of local bus services only. The F D R of 10d a gallon was only 50% of the fuel tax, but this was increased to 100% from January 1st 1969, a tremendous help to rural bus service operators such as Eynon's. This vital financial assistance was given to the bus industry by a Labour Government that had taken control a year earlier in 1964.

22nd March 1966 was another very sad day for everyone involved with the company, when news of a tragic accident arrived at the depot. General Manager of the business, Ieuan Lodwick (grandson of the founder) and the garage foreman John G Morgans were on their way to inspect a second-hand vehicle at Gloucester, in anticipation of purchasing it when they were involved in a serious three vehicle accident at Penhow near Newport. John Morgans died of his injuries, and Ieuan received serious injuries to which he recovered, continuing his role as General Manager of the Eynon's partnership.

Going back to 1962, a second car components factory had opened at Felinfoel, Llanelli. The factory, a pressings plant owned by Fisher & Ludlow Ltd, made body panels for BMC cars, later BLMC. On 5th October 1966, Eynon's applied for a RSL to operate an Express Service to this new factory, to accommodate the workforce on a three shift per day work pattern Monday to Friday, only when the Fisher & Ludlow Factory was working. The application read as follows:-

TGR 311/14: Trimsaran (Bird in Hand Square) to Felinfoel (Fisher & Ludlow Factory), via Pen-y-mynydd, Cwmbach, Furnace, Llanelli (West End), A476 to Felinfoel, and Llethri Road (Fisher & Ludlow).

Proposed fare from Trimsaran to Fisher & Ludlow Factory was 1/7d single, 2/10d return.

After an objection by The South Wales Transport Co, the licence was granted on 14th December 1966 with a special condition:

No passengers to be picked up or set down between Furnace Square and Felinfoel (Fisher & Ludlow Factory).

In addition to this, when the company applied for a modification of the time-table on their main route Llanelli to Carmarthen (TGR 311/1) in October 1966, another objection was made by the tour operator – Jenkins Tours, Llanelli, which resulted in another public hearing at Shire Hall, Carmarthen on 2nd February 1967 where the modification was granted.

It was assumed that there was a great deal of resentment by Jenkins Tours regarding Eynon's expansion into the coaching market with a fleet of six new coaches, three delivered in 1965 (mentioned above) and three more Bedford's in 1966:- ETH 210D/320D, Plaxton bodied VAM14's and ETH 260D a Duple bodied VAL14. Coupled to that was the fact that Eynon's had encroached upon Jenkins Tours' weekend breaks to the Blackpool Illuminations.

Above: Captured here at Tenby Coach Park working an end of term school outing in July 1966, is Plaxton Panorama C45F bodied Bedford VAM14, **ETH 210D** carrying an incorrect registration number plate ETH 120D. It carried this number plate for eight months before being detected and replaced. *(Courtesy of David Wright).*

Above: Another photograph of the Bedford VAM14, **ETH 210D**, seen here a year later in July 1967 carrying its correct registration number plate. It left the fleet after just twenty months.

Above: A superb view of **ETH 320D**, the second Bedford VAM14 purchased by the company in June 1966, is captured here in August that year. This also had a Plaxton 'Panorama' C45F body, identical to ETH 210D on page 60 but had an even shorter stay at Trimsaran – just seven months!

Above: **FTH 989E** a Bedford VAL14 with Duple 'Viceroy' C52F coachwork arrived in May 1967 ready for the summer season and was sold seventeen months later in October 1968. Eynon's can't have been happy with the Bedford's as they exchanged them quickly for more heavyweights – Leylands, and even tried AEC's.

(Courtesy of David Eynon).

Left: **GBX 542E** was another Plaxton 'Panorama' bodied Bedford VAM14 which the company purchased new in May 1967. It was the third and last Bedford VAM in the fleet, and was sold to Arlington Motors the dealer in October 1968, who quickly sold it on to Edwards Bros, Beddau, near Pontypridd in October 1968. That company is nowadays a very large concern known as Edwards Coaches, of Llantwit Fardre, Pontypridd.

From this point in the mid 1960's, the company's loyalty to Leyland Motors deteriorated. The change to Bedford in 1963 was only the beginning. As mentioned earlier, four 'new' Bedford coaches were purchased in 1964/5 and five more between 1966/7, and as the years passed other marques of chassis were tried. In 1967/8 three second-hand AEC 'Reliances' arrived followed by three *new* AEC 'Reliances' in May 1968. These were JTH 92F with a Duple 'Commander' C45F body and JTH 424/5F with Plaxton 'Panorama' I bodies, seating 51 and 43 respectively. The Eynon's management may have been influenced by the salesperson at Arlington Motors Cardiff, as most of their vehicles purchased at this time were supplied by Arlington Motors.

Left: The first AEC acquired by Eynon's was this 1960 'Reliance' 2MU3RA, with Duple 'Britannia' C40F body. Registered **YXD 14** it arrived in August 1967 from K. W. Motors, of Daventry, and in 1970 was part exchanged for a 1967 Bedford VAL14.

(David Eynon).

Above: The second AEC 'Reliance' 2MU3RA acquired in August 1967 was this rare Burlingham 'Seagull 70' bodied example. Registered **933 DVA** in 1962, it's captured here at Eynon's yard in early 1968.
(David Eynon).

February 1968 saw the arrival of two former Western Welsh Leyland 'Tiger Cub' PSUC1/1's. **JBO127 above**, with Weymann 'Hermes' B44F body was new to W W O C as 1127 in 1954, and is seen here at Llanelli Bus Station about to depart for Carmarthen. Eynon's converted it to PSUC1/1T specification by fitting a 2-speed axle.

Above: Former Western Welsh O C, Leyland 'Tiger Cub' 1107, **JBO107** was looking rather tired and battered when photographed here at Church Street, Llanelli in 1969. It was replaced by an ex London Transport RT in January 1970.

Above: This view of Eynon's *second* garage was taken in October 1967. Visible on the depot yard are: **CBX 238C, GBX 542E, TAB 577, YXD 14** and two RTL's. The only access to their premises in those far gone days was by means of the narrow river bridge in the foreground, which formed part of Heol Waun-y-clun. Most of this parking area was lost to a road improvement scheme in 1977, resulting in an alternative parking area being acquired after the purchase of land to the rear of the garage in 1975. Also visible is part of Bryn Villa Garage top left of picture. *(Courtesy of Aled Roberts).*

As mentioned earlier, under a Labour Government in January 1968, the Minister of Transport Mr. Richard Marsh announced details of the 1968 Road Traffic Act, which gave stage carriage bus operators financial grants of 25% towards the purchase of new service buses, provided that they complied with certain obligatory requirements of the Ministry of Transport, including for example an extreme front entrance doorway under driver supervision. The intention of the grant scheme was to encourage operators to modernise their fleets and make buses more competitive in terms of comfort with private cars. The scheme applied only to buses used primarily on stage carriage services initially, but by 1970, when the grant was increased to 50% it was agreed that coaches could also qualify for grant if used to a sufficient extent on such bus services, provided that the coach bodies were built with minor essential modifications such as 'jack knife' entrance doors and other features which complied with the bus grant specification. The conditions attached to the 'New Bus Grant' were that operators would have to refund the grant if they sold the vehicle or ceased to use it for stage service within 5 years of its delivery.

The scheme which came into being on 1st September 1968 and ended in March 1984 was a blessing to most operators, but simultaneously put several operators deep into debt by purchasing vehicles they could ill-afford, a situation that caused the downfall of many operators nationwide. In addition to the bus grant, provision was made to increase the fuel duty rebate introduced in 1965 to 100%, from 10d to 1/7d a gallon, paid to operators of rural bus services from 1st January 1969, and also the introduction of 'Rural Bus Grants' – subsidising un-remunerative rural bus services.

Despite having all this financial assistance, the company applied for a fare increase on 16th October 1968. The increase was granted on 11th December 1968, and is published on page 66 opposite.

Furthermore, Eynon's were amongst the first handful of West Wales operators to order grant aided buses, placing an order for two Leyland 'Leopard' PSU3/3RT's with Willowbrook dual purpose 49 seat bodies. These were ready for delivery in full Eynon's livery from Arlington Motors, the dealer in May 1969 as LBX 547/548G, with a photograph of LBX 547G appearing in 'Commercial Motor'. LBX 548G was delivered and entered service in July 1979 but LBX 547G was described as being 'un-acceptable in a non-standard livery'. It eventually passed to West Wales Motors at Tycroes, Carmarthenshire in October 1969, after a re-paint into their livery and re-registered MBX 86H. The re-registration was due to the change of year suffix in August that year, voiding the 'G' suffix.

Right: This type of appointment card would have been posted to the operator of a particular vehicle informing them of a forthcoming vehicle inspection. In this case, the examination of a former London Transport RTL; LYR808 by Mr. G. H. Price the vehicle examiner. The vehicle examiners in those far gone days multi-functioned, they were also driving test examiners. Mr G. H. Price conducted my PSV driving test in July 1965, and a short while later administered my practical mechanical examination, authorising me to carry out class IV MOT tests on cars.

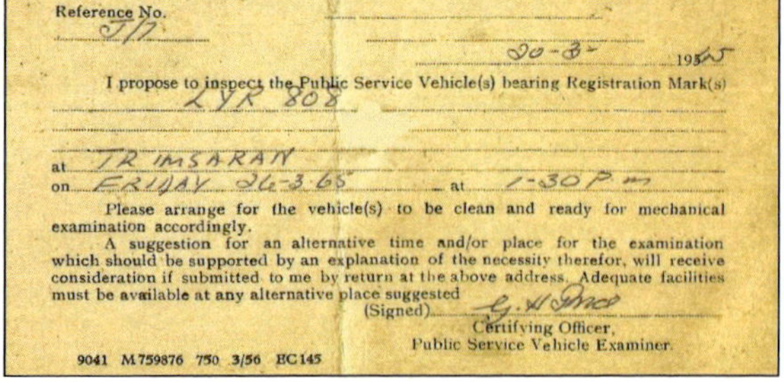

P.S.V. 43G

THE LICENSING AUTHORITY FOR PUBLIC SERVICE VEHICLES
SOUTH WALES TRAFFIC AREA

Reference No. J/7

20-3- 1965

I propose to inspect the Public Service Vehicle(s) bearing Registration Mark(s) LYR 808

at TRIMSARAN

on FRIDAY 26-3-65 at 1-30 P.M.

Please arrange for the vehicle(s) to be clean and ready for mechanical examination accordingly.

A suggestion for an alternative time and/or place for the examination which should be supported by an explanation of the necessity therefor, will receive consideration if submitted to me by return at the above address. Adequate facilities must be available at any alternative place suggested

(Signed) G. H. Price
Certifying Officer,
Public Service Vehicle Examiner.

9041 M759876 750 3/56 EC145

311/1—Llanelli (Town Hall Square) and Carmarthen (Lammas Street).
To revise fares in accordance with the following:

Proposed Fare Table

Llanelli (Town Hall)

4 Stradey Park Avenue

6 3 Furnace Square

7 5 3 Stradey Lodge

10 7 6 3 Cwmbach

1/2 1/- 11 10 7 Pantyllyn

1/4 1/4 1/2 1/- 11 5 Penymynydd

1/5 1/5 1/4 1/2 1/- 7 3 Waunffynonau Road

1/6 1/5 1/5 1/5 1/2 10 6 3 Trimsaran (Bird-in-Hand)

1/8 1/8 1/6 1/5 1/5 1/- 10 7 5 Llandyry Road

1/9 1/8 1/8 1/6 1/5 1/2 1/- 10 7 4 Trimsaran Road Station

1/10 1/10 1/9 1/8 1/8 1/5 1/2 1/- 11 7 5 Muddlescwm

2/- 1/11 1/11 1/11 1/9 1/6 1/5 1/5 1/2 1/- 10 7 Kidwelly (Borough Offices)

2/4 2/2 2/1 2/- 1/11 1/10 1/8 1/8 1/6 1/5 1/4 1/1 9 Corporation Arms

2/6 2/6 2/4 2/2 2/1 1/11 1/11 1/9 1/8 1/8 1/5 1/5 1/- 6 Glanmorlais

2/10 2/6 2/6 2/6 2/6 2/1 1/11 1/11 1/11 1/9 1/8 1/6 1/5 11 7 Llandefeilog

2/10 2/10 2/10 2/8 2/6 2/4 2/1 2/- 1/11 1/11 1/10 1/8 1/5 1/2 10 6 Upland Arms

3/- 3/- 2/10 2/10 2/10 2/6 2/4 2/2 2/- 1/11 1/11 1/10 1/8 1/5 1/1 9 5 Rama

3/- 3/- 3/- 2/10 2/10 2/6 2/6 2/4 2/2 2/- 1/11 1/11 1/8 1/5 1/2 11 7 3 Finger Post

3/2 3/2 3/- 3/- 3/- 2/8 2/6 2/6 2/4 2/2 2/- 1/11 1/10 1/6 1/5 1/1 10 7 5 Idole

3/2 3/2 3/2 3/2 3/2 3/- 2/10 2/8 2/6 2/6 2/4 2/2 1/11 1/9 1/8 1/5 1/4 1/- 11 7 Cwmffrwd (Black Lion)

3/4 3/4 3/2 3/2 3/2 3/- 2/10 2/10 2/8 2/6 2/6 2/2 2/- 1/10 1/8 1/5 1/5 1/2 1/- 10 4 Cwmffrwd (Bethel Chapel)

3/4 3/4 3/4 3/4 3/2 3/2 3/- 3/- 2/10 2/10 2/6 2/6 2/2 1/11 1/10 1/8 1/6 1/5 1/4 1/1 9 6 Tycoch

3/6 3/6 3/6 3/6 3/4 3/2 3/2 3/- 3/- 2/10 2/10 2/6 2/6 2/- 1/11 1/9 1/8 1/6 1/5 1/4 11 10 5 Pensarn

3/8 3/6 3/6 3/6 3/6 3/4 3/2 3/2 3/2 3/- 3/- 2/10 2/6 2/2 2/- 1/11 1/9 1/8 1/8 1/5 1/3 1/2 9 6 Carmarthen (Lammas St.)

SPECIAL FARES—3d. SINGLE: Star Square—Bryncaerau (Trimsaran) and Plough Inn—Castle Garage (Kidwelly).
SPECIAL FARES—4d. SINGLE: Kidwelly—British American Optical Factory (Mynyddgareg).
CHILDREN'S FARES: Children over 4 years and under 14 years of age, half-fare, with a minimum fare of 1d., fractions of 1d. to be charged as 1d.

Kidwelly

7 Mynyddygarreg (Penygroes)

10 4 Glyn Road

1/1 9 6 Four Road

Llanelli (Town Hall)

1/6 Trimsaran (Bird-in-Hand)

2/- 1/2 Kidwelly

2/4 1/6 9 Llansaint

Above: This attractive Harrington 'Cavalier' C51F bodied AEC 'Reliance' 2U3RA, found a new home at Trimsaran in March 1968. New in 1962 to Hawkey of Newquay, Cornwall, it was registered **799 OCV.**

Above: Numerically the first *new* AEC in the fleet, **JTH 92F** was one of three AEC 'Reliances' delivered in May 1968. This was a 6MU3R model with the smaller 505 engine, and Duple 'Commander III' C45F coachwork.

Above: The other two AEC 'Reliances' delivered in May 1968 were registered **JTH 424/425F**. Their chassis types were 6U3ZR and 6MU3R respectively, and both were fitted with Plaxton 'Panorama I' coachwork which seated 51 and 43 respectively. *(John Jones collection).*

Above: JTH 424F the AEC 'Reliance' 6U3ZR fitted with a larger 691 engine and 51 seat Plaxton 'Panorama I' coachwork is captured here at Tenby Coach Park on an excursion.

Above: The first 'Grant Aided' vehicle was delivered in July 1969 as **LBX 548G**. It was a Leyland 'Leopard' PSU3/3R, with Willowbrook DP49F body. *(V. Morgan).*

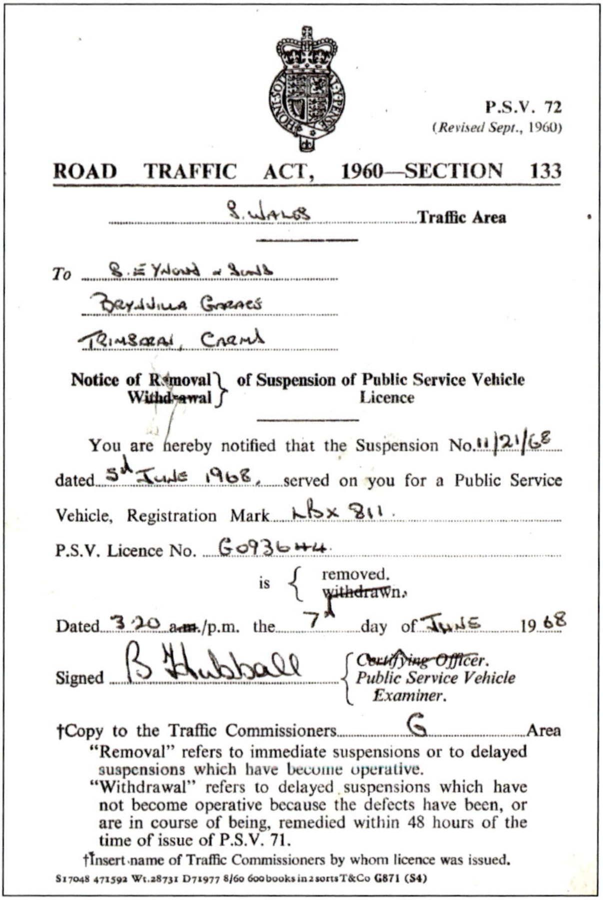

P.S.V. 72
(*Revised Sept.*, 1960)

ROAD TRAFFIC ACT, 1960—SECTION 133

S. WALES Traffic Area

To B. EYNON & SONS
BRYNVILLA GARAGES
TRIMSARAN, CARMS

Notice of ~~Removal~~ / Withdrawal of Suspension of Public Service Vehicle Licence

You are hereby notified that the Suspension No. 11/21/68 dated 5th June 1968, served on you for a Public Service Vehicle, Registration Mark LBX 811.

P.S.V. Licence No. G093644.

is removed. / ~~withdrawn~~.

Dated 3.20 ~~a.m.~~/p.m. the 7th day of JUNE 1968

Signed B Hubball ~~Certifying Officer.~~ *Public Service Vehicle Examiner.*

†Copy to the Traffic Commissioners G Area

"Removal" refers to immediate suspensions or to delayed suspensions which have become operative.

"Withdrawal" refers to delayed suspensions which have not become operative because the defects have been, or are in course of being, remedied within 48 hours of the time of issue of P.S.V. 71.

†Insert name of Traffic Commissioners by whom licence was issued.

S17048 471592 Wt.28731 D71977 8/60 600 books in 2 sorts T&Co G871 (S4)

Left: A copy of the notice issued by the Ministry of Transport's vehicle examiner, lifting the 'Suspension Order' issued to one of the company's vehicles LBX 811.

In February 1970, the South Wales Transport Company withdrew their two stage carriage services operating to the British American Optical Factory at Mynydd-y-garreg. The services; Llanelli to Mynydd-y-garreg via Burry Port and Kidwelly, (TGR421/32) and Cross Hands to Mynydd-y-garreg (BAOF) via Upper Tumble, Pontyberem, Ponthenry, Pontyates, Meinciau and Four Roads (TGR421/339), were quickly picked up by Eynon's as contract services, and were altered to accommodate a two shift pattern daily. This was in addition to the two contract services already operated for the B A O Factory serving Carway, Trimsaran, Kidwelly, and Llansaint.

In 1970, there was a large intake of vehicles, including four ex London Transport AEC RT's, (RT 190 / 1545 / 3106 / 3742), a Bedford VAL fitted with Duple Viceroy body - HOD 691E, and FCH 28, a Leyland 'Tiger Cub'/ Weymann. The 'new' arrival for 1970 came in November and was a 'showpiece' built by the Portuguese bodybuilder Salvador Caetano of Lisbon and marketed through Alf Moseley & Sons of Loughborough under the name 'Moseley Continental'. Registered as OBX 1J, its superb Caetano 'Lisboa' 51 seat coachwork was fitted to a Leyland 'Leopard' PSU3A/4R chassis, with the Leyland 0.680 engine coupled to a pneumo-cyclic (semi-automatic) gearbox. Finished in a non-standard livery of two-tone blue, with blue moquette seating and blue tinted interior lights, it was purchased direct from the 1970 Commercial Motor Show stand at Earls Court, London.

By now there was a fleet of nineteen vehicles, made up of 11 Leyland's, 7 AEC's and 1 Bedford.

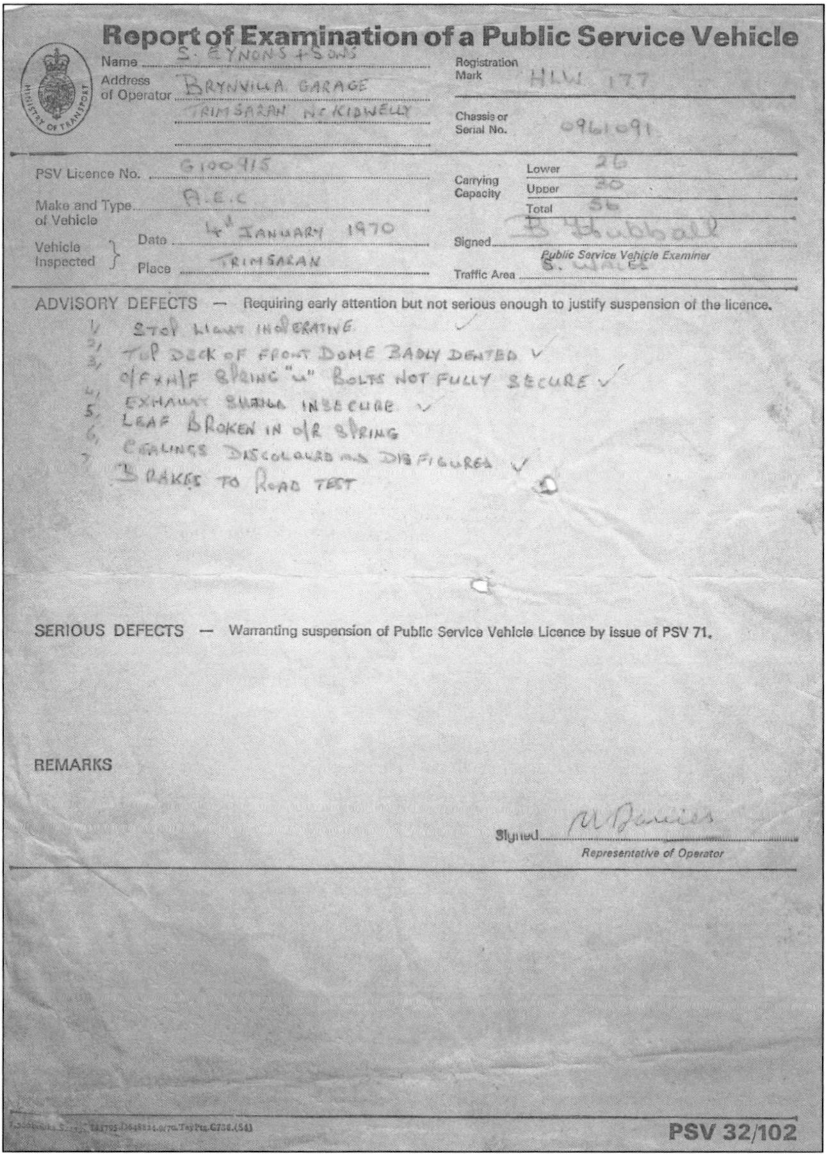

Report of Examination of a Public Service Vehicle

MINISTRY OF TRANSPORT

Name: S. EYNONS + SONS

Address of Operator: BRYNVILLA GARAGE, TRIMSARAN NR KIDWELLY

Registration Mark: HLW 177

Chassis or Serial No.: 0961091

PSV Licence No.: G100915

Make and Type of Vehicle: A.E.C

Carrying Capacity: Lower 26; Upper 30; Total 56

Vehicle Inspected: Date 4th JANUARY 1970; Place TRIMSARAN

Signed: B. Hubball — *Public Service Vehicle Examiner*

Traffic Area: S. WALES

ADVISORY DEFECTS — Requiring early attention but not serious enough to justify suspension of the licence.

1. STOP LIGHT INOPERATIVE ✓
2. TOP DECK OF FRONT DOME BADLY DENTED ✓
3. O/F & N/F SPRING "U" BOLTS NOT FULLY SECURE ✓
4. EXHAUST SHIELD INSECURE ✓
5. LEAF BROKEN IN O/R SPRING
6. CEILINGS DISCOLOURED AND DISFIGURED ✓
7. BRAKES TO ROAD TEST

SERIOUS DEFECTS — Warranting suspension of Public Service Vehicle Licence by issue of PSV 71.

REMARKS

Signed: M Davies — *Representative of Operator*

PSV 32/102

01 994 3641
Ext 292

LONDON TRANSPORT BOARD

21st January, 1970

Telephone : 01-994 3641 Ext. 274
Telegrams : CHISWORKS LONDON W.4

566 Chiswick High Road. London W4

566 CHISWICK HIGH ROAD, LONDON W.4

Samuel Eynon & Sons,
Bryn Villa Garage,
Trimsaran,
Near Kidwelly,
Carmarthenshire.

SALES ORDER No.
4936
A.W.C.A. 9341/156
To be quoted on all correspondence

SALES ORDER

Dear Sirs,

The undermentioned material will be ~~despatched to you by rail, carriage forward.~~ handed over to you upon presentation of this authority. to the Engineer.

A signature for the receipt of the goods will be required.

for A. G. DAY
PURCHASING OFFICER ~~CONTRACTS OFFICER~~

Material must be collected from	Arrangements for collection to be made with
Garage as detailed below.	between the hours of and on

QUANTITY No.	Weight approx. Tons	cwt.	qr.	lb.	Description
2					Second-hand Double Deck Bus Nos. RT 1545 - Poplar Garage, RT 190 - West Ham Garage. With Part worn tyres. With 3 year Certificates of Fitness. Each vehicle £575 (Ex London garage)

This vehicle is sold in accordance with the special conditions enclosed.

PLEASE NOTE: In most buses synthetic oil is used in the differential gears and rear hubs (where oil lubricated). These units should not be "topped up" with mineral based rear axle oil. When the oil level falls to the minimum the units should be drained COMPLETELY, refilled with mineral based oil, operated for 500 - 1,000 miles, re-drained and refilled with mineral based oil and operated 500 - 1,000 miles and again re-drained. Mineral based rear axle oil can be used in the normal manner.

NOTE: Loading is allowed Monday to Friday only. Loading is not allowed on Saturday.
Each time a collection is made the lorry driver must be provided with an authority certifying that the material is being removed on behalf of the person to whom this order was issued.

102/8 (1)
10M 2/68 530 Stock)

Above: This is a copy of the sales invoice/collection note given to Eynon's by the purchasing officer at London Transport in January 1970 for 2 x RT type AEC 'Regents' RT 190/1545, both with 3 year Certificate of Fitness at £575 each. Although dated 21/1/70, RT 190 received its M o T examination at Trimsaran on 4/1/70, see the report on the previous page.

Above: Seen here at Llanelli bus station still wearing its London Transport red livery, with Eynon's cream added to its upper deck is **HLW 177** formerly RT190, one of the two referred to on the sales invoice opposite. The registration number **HLW 177** is now fitted to another AEC - RT preserved at Cobham Bus Museum. See page 225 for details.

Above: Seen here at the Carmarthen bus terminus (Lammas St.) still in LT red, with Eynon's cream added to the upper deck is **KGU 414** formerly RT 1545. This is the other 'RT' referred to on the sales invoice opposite purchased for £575 each. Note the odd near-side headlamp fitted to the bus and a nice piece of street furniture - the straightforward Eynon's time-table visible on the shop wall of Sheffield House.

Above: This Weymann bodied Leyland 'Tiger Cub' PSUC1/1, **FCH 28** dating from 1954 was acquired in May 1970 from R. I. Davies, Tredegar. Its stay at Trimsaran was very brief – just 12 months. *(John Jones collection).*

Above: Only one roof box type London vehicle was acquired by Eynon's. It was 1950 Saunders bodied (RT 3106) **KXW 215** seen here at Eynon's depot in 1971, still running in full LT livery including the 'Round London Sightseeing Tour' advertisement, which was priced at just six shillings (6/-) an absolute bargain!

Above: Captured here outside T. P. Hughes' shop, incidentally named 'London House' in Carmarthen, is former London Transport RT 3742, **NLE 849** and again only 50% painted in Eynon's livery. This RT was affectionately called 'Nellie' by the staff, a name again derived from its registration number.

Above: 'Flagship' of the Eynon's fleet in the early 1970's was this Portuguese bodied Leyland 'Leopard' PSU3A/4R, purchased direct from the Commercial Motor Show at Earl's Court, London in October 1970. Registered with cherished number **OBX 1J,** it remained in this two-tone blue metallic livery throughout its three and a half year presence at Trimsaran, and had blue moquette seating matching the superb paintwork of its Caetano 'Lisboa' coachwork, which seated 51 passengers. *(D. I. Lodwick).*

Public Passenger Operators
and Coach Proprietors

Telephone: TRIMSARAN 244 C005301

SAMUEL EYNON & SONS

BRYN VILLA GARAGE, TRIMSARAN
KIDWELLY, DYFED

M.. 197....

V.A.T. Registration No. 122 7470 88

DATE		CHARGE		V.A.T. RATE	V.A.T.	
	V.A.T.					
	TOTAL					

Above: This is a Samuel Eynon chrome plated cap badge / lapel badge.

EXPANSION

An interesting development in 1971 was the take-over of Western Welsh Omnibus Company's Carmarthen to Llanelli via Pontyberem service 401. After giving the mandatory notice, Western Welsh a subsidiary of the newly formed 'National Bus Company' abandoned the service on Saturday 9th January 1971 after Carmarthenshire County Council refused to give funding for the 'un-remunerative service' through the new 'Rural Bus Grant Scheme' introduced with the afore-mentioned 1968 Road Traffic Act. At a council meeting, councillors said services should not be subsidised from the rates, they should be subsidised with funding from the 'National Exchequer' – central government.

In the meantime, the local authority approached Eynon's with a view to take over the controversial service and consequently a service reduced by two journeys daily was agreed upon to operate *without* council funding.

A syndicate of Western Welsh employees had also applied for the above Road Service Licence but it was refused.

A temporary licence was issued to Eynon's for a trial period beginning 11th January 1971, and ending 26th June 1971. The service commenced without any disruption on Monday 11th January 1971 and ironically two months later was operated with two former Western Welsh vehicles; LKG 225 a Leyland 'Olympian' and MUH 131 a Leyland 'Tiger Cub' purchased directly from Western Welsh and collected from their Neath depot.

The special short-term licence issued for an 'unforeseen service' from 11th January 1971 to 26th June 1971 was:-

TGR 311/Sp/6: Llanelli (Town Hall) to Carmarthen (Lammas Street),
via: Felinfoel, Llannon, Pontyberem, Bancffosfelen, Llangendeirne and Cwmffrwd.
To operate stage carriage service daily Monday to Saturday.

The full term licence to operate this service was applied for on 3rd March 1971 and granted on 12th May 1971 under application number:-

TGR 311/15: Llanelli (Town Hall) to Carmarthen (Lammas Street),
via: Felinfoel, Llannon, Pontyberem, Bancffosfelen, Llangendeirne and Cwmffrwd.
To operate stage carriage service daily Monday to Saturday.

Several members of Western Welsh staff transferred to Eynon's with the service, which was another very arduous hilly route running through the two Gwendraeth Valleys. From Llanelli, the route followed the A476 to Llannon some 720ft above sea level, joining the B4306 at Llannon and descending into Pontyberem in the Gwendraeth Fawr valley, then climbing steeply to Bancffosfelen and Crwbin before descending into Llangendeirne in the Gwendraeth Fach valley. Climbing steeply again out of Llangendeirne the route eventually descended into Cwmffrwd before finally reaching Carmarthen. Double-decker buses were not permitted on this service.

Above: Former Western Welsh 1225, **LKG 225** a 1956 Leyland 'Olympian' LW2 was purchased directly from Western Welsh in February 1971, to operate the Llanelli-Pontyberem-Carmarthen service, which had been inherited from Western Welsh a month earlier. It's captured here at Carmarthen working the Pontyberem service in 1971. The integrally built 'Olympian' was quite a unique vehicle, only sixty were built.

Above: **MUH 131** was another vehicle purchased directly from Western Welsh in February 1971 to work the former Western Welsh 401 service, Llanelli-Pontyberem-Carmarthen. This was a 1956 Leyland 'Tiger Cub' with Weymann 'Hermes' B44F body, and is seen here at the original Carmarthen bus terminus at Lammas Street in 1972.

Consequently, further cuts were made by Western Welsh on 30th April 1971 when they closed their Carmarthen depot and Laugharne outstation abandoning their remaining Carmarthenshire services which were absorbed by local independent operators. Pontyberem outstation had already closed on 9th January 1971 with the abandonment of its only service - 401.

Activity at the Eynon's establishment was now escalating. This prompted the two cousins David Eynon and Thomas-John Eynon, grandsons of the founder to relinquish their full time employment at the Trostre Tinplate Works in 1971 to join the family business. They had previously worked in the business between shifts at Trostre works doing school contracts, and also helped out on their rest days, holidays and at weekends.

During the 1970's, there were numerous vehicles added to the fleet, new and second-hand, in fact too many to mention individually, but 1971 saw no less than twelve second-hand Leylands arrive at Trimsaran, amongst them were ex Plymouth 'Titans' 39/41/46/47/54; LCO 839/41/46/47/54. In 1972, South Wales Transport AEC 'Regent' V's, 701/2/4/23; RCY 343/4/6/65 were taken into stock, the first two 701/2 having spent all their working life operating locally from their Llanelli depot. One of them, RCY 346 carried an all over advertising livery from March 1974 to May 1975 (basically red, white and green) for the 'Eisteddfod Genedlaethol Yr Urdd' (The Urdd National Eisteddfod) held at Llanelli 27-31 May 1975. It returned to fleet livery in May 1975. At this time, all over advertising on buses had become commonplace, and sister vehicle RCY 344 was next to receive an all over advertising livery, in this case an advertisement for 'Pinged Hill Garage Ltd, Kidwelly' the local Renault dealers in October 1974. There were other all over adverts in later years including one for 'Richards Travel' a local travel agent that worked in alliance with Eynon's, and one to advertise the Llanelli, Kidwelly and Carmarthen Job Centres!

Above: Two former S E L N E C, Leyland 'Tiger Cubs' with Park Royal bodies were acquired in early 1971 for the increased workload. One of the pair, **9747 NA** is seen here at Pontyberem Station

Above: This Leyland 'Tiger Cub' **9750 NA** with Park Royal DP40F body, was new to Manchester C T in 1961 for their airport service. It passed to Eynon's in April 1971 via the newly formed **S**outh **E**ast **L**ancashire **N**orth **E**ast **C**heshire PTE (S E L N E C).

Above: UWU 521F a 1968 Willowbrook DP41F bodied Leyland 'Leopard' PSU4/3R arrived at Trimsaran in June 1971 from Tetley, Leeds. This was another vehicle that regularly worked the tortuous Pontyberem service.

Above: Acquired from Bowen, Birmingham in June 1971 was this excellent Leyland 'Leopard' PSU3/3R, registered **6911 HA** and fitted with Harrington 'Crusader' C49F coachwork. It was new in 1963. *(R. F. Mack).*

Above: The first 'coach' purchased with the new 'Bus Grant' scheme was **PBX 700J,** this AEC 'Reliance' 6MU4R with Plaxton 'Panorama Elite Express II' coachwork which was delivered to full grant specification in July 1971. If they had waited a couple of weeks it could have had a K suffix registration.

Above: Eynon's bought five former Plymouth CT Leyland 'Titan' PD2/12's with Metro-Cammell 'Orion' bodies, LCO 839/41/46/47/54 in September 1971, to replace the last five Leyland RTL's. They remained in 'blanked out' Plymouth livery throughout their stay at Trimsaran, as displayed by **LCO 847** and **LCO 841** here at the depot.

Above: Leyland 'Titan' **LCO 854** is captured here at Kidwelly still wearing its Plymouth CT livery.

Above: Captured here turning around at Bryn Edda, Llansaint, for its return journey on unclassified single-track road to Kidwelly, is former East Yorkshire M S (672) **VKH 672,** a 1957 Leyland 'Tiger Cub' PSUC1/1 with Park Royal B39F body. Llansaint village is situated some 500ft above sea level, overlooking picturesque Carmarthen Bay and the south Pembrokeshire coast, with an exceptionally steep gradient out of Kidwelly town to reach the ancient village.

Above: **RBX 760K** seen here at Carmarthen, was the last 'bus' bodied vehicle purchased by Eynon's under the 'Bus Grant' scheme. Subsequent 'grant aided' purchases (twelve in all) were all coach bodied vehicles. This Willowbrook dual-purpose bodied 49 seater Leyland 'Leopard' PSU3B/4R entered service in January 1972, and was a regular performer of the Llanelli-Trimsaran-Kidwelly-Carmarthen service as seen here.

Above: Pictured here at Pontyberem Station in 1973, still wearing its South Wales Transport livery, is **NNY 58** a 1954 Leyland 'Tiger Cub' PSUC1/1 with Weymann 'Hermes' B44F body. It was new to BET subsidiary Thomas Bros, Port Talbot in 1954, passing to SWT upon formation of the National Bus Company.

Above: Former East Midland 1958 Leyland 'Tiger Cub' PSUC1/2, **XRR 539** with Willowbrook DP41F body, spent just 2 years at Trimsaran before being scrapped. *(John Jones collection).*

Above: **STH 555K** was another new 'Grant Aided' Leyland 'Leopard' PSU3B/4R and arrived in June 1972, fitted with Plaxton 'Panorama Elite Express II' coachwork. I photographed this working stage carriage service at Old Castle Road, Llanelli on 18th April 1978, whilst the driver took his tea break in 'Dai's Café' here at Old Castle Road.

Above: The driver and conductor have a cigarette break here at Llanelli bus station (Town Hall Square) before setting off for Llansaint with their former South Wales Transport AEC 'Regent V' **RCY 343** a Weymann bodied example. It remained in the SWT livery, complete with SWT fleet No 701 throughout its 2 year stay here. Four of these SWT Regent's RCY 343/4/6/65 were acquired in October 1972 to replace the last four London Transport vehicles in the fleet, some ageing AEC RT's.

Above: One of the quartet acquired from South Wales Transport in 1972 was this 1958 AEC 'Regent V' **RCY 344** seen at Carmarthen, repainted into an all-over advertising livery for Pinged Hill Garage (Gravell's) the local Renault dealer. RCY 343/4 had previously only worked from SWT's Llanelli depot, so were on home ground with Eynon's.

Above: **RCY 346** was another 'Regent V' acquired from SWT in 1972; where it had run for several years un-painted as an experiment. In 1974 it received this all-over advertisement for the 'Eisteddfod Genedlaethol yr Urdd' held in Llanelli 1975, reverting to the Eynon's livery in May 1975.

Above: **RCY 365** was numerically the last AEC 'Regent V' acquired by Eynon's and was one of the quartet mentioned opposite. They were the first 'modern type' front entrance double-deckers in the Eynon's fleet. RCY 365 is seen here at Blue Street, Carmarthen nearing its terminus at Lammas Street in 1972. *(R. F. Mack).*

'Bristol' chassis were favoured by numerous operators but were certainly un-liked by the Eynon's concern. Former Red & White Services, MAX 133, a Bristol LS6G had a very short stay of six months at Trimsaran in 1973, when it was exchanged for WWV 564; ex Wilts & Dorset Leyland 'Leopard' L1, which had originated from the fleet of 'Silver Star' at Porton Down, Wiltshire. The only other Bristols operated were a pair of Lodekka FLF6B's hired from Lister the dealer in September 1978, and two Bristol RELH's acquired in March 1984 and March 1987 respectively.

After modification of the aforementioned 'New Bus Grant' scheme in 1970, no less than twenty-one new vehicles arrived in the first decade, consisting of nine Leyland, eight AEC and four Bedford. Only fourteen of these were acquired through the grant scheme, seven were acquired without a grant! Nevertheless, one of the Leylands acquired in June 1973, VTH 655L a PSU3B/4R with Duple 'Dominant' Express body was licenced to D I Lodwick T/A: Samuel Eynon & Sons on a separate operator licence. This was purely in order to gain an extra licence.

Furthermore, one of the new coaches delivered in October 1973 was an extremely rare combination of chassis and body. The vehicle concerned, WTH 255M had a twelve metre Leyland 'Leopard' PSU5/4R chassis fitted with Caetano 'Lisboa II' 57 seat coachwork finished in a non-standard livery of cream and gold. This coach was not a 'Grant Aided' vehicle and left the fleet in February 1977.

Above: Captured here working private hire with the choir - 'Cor Meibion Mynydd Mawr' is another Leyland 'Leopard' PSU3B/4R, with Caetano 'Lisboa II' coachwork seating 51. The PSU3B/4R had a Leyland 0.680 engine coupled to the Pneumo-cyclic gearbox, air brakes and power steering as standard. New in October 1972, **TTH 500L** had been exhibited at the 1972 Commercial Motor Show, Earls Court, London prior to delivery.

Above: Delivered in December 1972 to full 'Bus Grant' specification was this Leyland 'Leopard' **UBX 55L,** with an identical PSU3B/4R chassis to the Caetano Lisboa bodied example above. The 11 metre coachwork was built by Plaxton to the 'Panorama Elite Express III' layout seating 51. It was part exchanged for four double-deckers in May 1983. The view was taken at Ferryside 12th March 1978.

Right: The first 'Bristol' chassis in the fleet arrived at Trimsaran in late 1972. New in February 1954 to Red & White Services, Chepstow, it was a Bristol LS6G with ECW C39F coachwork, and registered **MAX 133.** It was purchased as a temporary stop-gap from a Scottish operator Irvine of Law. This coach with a 'crash gearbox' was not liked by the staff and was exchanged for a Leyland 'Leopard' after very little use just six months later. Its replacement, WWV 564 is seen below. *(John Jones).*

Above: This 1960 Leyland L1 'Leopard' **WWV 564** was a replacement for the 'Bristol' LS6G MAX 133 pictured above. New to Shergold & White, T/A: 'Silver Star Motor Services' of Porton Down, Wiltshire, it was fitted with this Harrington Cavalier body complete with rear dorsal fin. The body however was extensively rebuilt by its second owners, Wilts & Dorset, who rebuilt the rear end after an accident, removing the stylish dorsal fin, re-styled the front panel, fitted bus seats and converted it to 'One Man Operation' **or** One Person Operation with 39 seats. Eynon's purchased this 'Leopard' from Wilts & Dorset (909) in April 1973. *(V. Morgan).*

Above: Another 'Grant Aided' Leyland 'Leopard' PSU3B/4R arrived in May 1973. It was registered **VTH 5L** and was again fitted with a Plaxton 'Panorama Elite Express III' body which this time seated 53. It's seen here at the depot about to depart for the Pontyberem service. VTH 5L had a sad end in November 1979, when it was completely burnt out in a fire at the depot yard, along with Bedford DHN300H and Leyland PD3A, FKY250E.

Above: **VTH 655L** was also a 'Grant Aided' Leyland 'Leopard' PSU3B/4R, but this was fitted with a Duple 'Dominant' Express C51F body. It was delivered in June 1973 and licenced to D I Lodwick T/A: Samuel Eynon & Sons, in order to gain an extra licence. Mr Lodwick was a partner and General Manager of the business. This view was taken on 19th February 1977, at Causeway Street, Kidwelly, close to the Borough Offices.

(Vernon Morgan).

<u>Above:</u> Another 'first' came with the purchase of **WTH 255M** in October 1973. It was not only the first 12 metre coach in the fleet but was an extremely rare combination of chassis and body. The chassis, a Leyland <u>PSU5/4R</u> 'Leopard' was fitted with this Caetano 'Lisboa II' 57 seat body, finished in this non-standard livery of cream and gold. After a comparatively short stay at Trimsaran it was sold to a dealer in February 1977.

<u>Above:</u> The first 'midi-coaches' in the fleet, were a pair of Bedford VAS5's, which arrived in October 1973. Pictured here is one of the pair **KNK 350G** a 1969 Bedford VAS5 with Duple 'Vista 25' C29F body. The other Bedford VAS with Plaxton bodywork, DHN 300H is pictured overleaf.

Above: The second 'midi-coach' acquired was another Bedford VAS5: **DHN 300H** which dated from 1970. This Bedford had a Plaxton 'Panorama' C29F body, and came to a sad end on 29th November 1979 when it was destroyed by fire at the depot, taking with it VTH 5L, a Leyland PSU3B/4R and FKY250E, Leyland PD3A.

Above: No less than six vehicles were purchased from Barton of Chilwell (Notts) in early 1974. Seen here at Blue Street, Carmarthen is ex Barton (678) **RNN 266** a 1954 Leyland 'Tiger Cub' PSUC1/2 with a rather unusual looking 'Scottish Bus Group' style Alexander DP45F body. The Barton vehicles were all withdrawn after just 13 months use. This particular one is being driven by a former Western Welsh driver 'Dai titch'. *(R. F. Mack)*

Above: **RNN 617** was another Leyland 'Tiger Cub' PSUC1/2 with 'Scottish Bus Group' style Alexander DP43F body acquired from Barton Transport (679) in January 1974. It's seen here still in Barton livery about to depart from 'Star Square' Trimsaran on a school contract, with Eynon's garage visible in the background.

Above: Eynon's acquired three of these uncommon Yeates 'Europa' bodied AEC 'Reliance' coaches from Barton Transport in January/February 1974. Last to arrive: **945 MRR** above, was a 4MU3RA model with the AH590 engine, joining sister vehicles **946/7 MRR**, (2U3RA models) that had arrived a month earlier in January. After sale to a dealer in 1975, this one saw further service with Runnalls. Townshend, Cornwall. *(R F Mack).*

Above: The sixth former Barton vehicle at Trimsaran was **864 HAL** a 1961 AEC 'Reliance' (2MU3RV) with an early Plaxton 'Panorama' C41F body. It's captured here at Heol Waun-y-clun, Trimsaran, just up the street from the depot, still wearing its Barton livery – a livery which it retained throughout its stay at Trimsaran.

On the 1st April 1974, Carmarthenshire County Council amalgamated with the neighbouring counties of Pembrokeshire and Cardiganshire to form one county renamed 'DYFED'. During the re-organisation of the councils, the vehicle licensing office for Carmarthenshire, located at Carmarthen County Hall closed down, transferring all its vehicle licensing business to the newly opened DVLA at Morriston (Swansea) together with the Carmarthenshire registration marks of BX and TH. Haverfordwest and Aberystwyth vehicle licensing offices remained open under full control of the DVLA at Swansea, retaining their registration marks of DE and EJ respectively.

After this major change, east Dyfed area companies registered their new buses at Swansea, or as in Eynon's case had the dealer to register their vehicles, such as HFP 118/9N, NAY 393P and OAY 438P. On the other hand, Eynon's had ordered a new vehicle with a Swansea registration: GCY 74N, a Leyland 'Leopard' PSU3B/4R, chassis number 7400391 with Plaxton 'Panorama Elite Express III', C53F body, but it was diverted to West Wales Motors at Tycroes in full Eynon's livery in October 1974. Eynon's then took delivery of GNY 431N, an identical 'Leopard' with consecutive chassis number 7400390 and an identical Plaxton 'Panorama Elite Express III' C53F body in November 1974. This was also a diverted order – from Dorothy June Vowles of Merthyr Tydfil, Mid-Glamorganshire, and was delivered in Vowles' livery of white with blue relief. Eynon's however, quickly applied red relief to both sides of its grant specification body.

Above: Another rare combination of chassis and body types are depicted here with **XTH 944M**, which was new to Eynon's in May 1974. It's Caetano 'Lisboa II' C53F coachwork, with doors conforming to bus grant specification, was fitted to an AEC 'Reliance' 6U3ZR chassis. Only twenty-three vehicles of this combination were built.

Above: The third Bedford VAS5 in the fleet **CKP 441K** arrived in June 1974. New in 1972, it was fitted with Duple 'Vista 25' coachwork seating 29 and was sold to a dealer in September 1977.

Above: OCO 512 was one of five ex Plymouth CT Leyland 'Titan' PD2/40's acquired in July 1974. New in May 1958 they were registered OCO 511/2/4/6/9 and had Metro-Cammell 'Orion' H30/26R bodies. OCO 512 is seen here at 'Star Square' Trimsaran picking up passengers for a journey into Llanelli town centre.

Above: Bunched together here at Eynon's yard in October 1974, is another former Plymouth CT Leyland 'Titan' PD2/40 with Metro-Cammell 'Orion' H56R body, registered **OCO 516**. Compared to the earlier 'Titans' Eynon's received from Plymouth, this five didn't give a lengthy service; the best one OCO 514 lasted just two years.

Right: Former Trent MT Leyland 'Titan' PD2/12 **JCH 265** was acquired in July 1974 via Whippet of Hilton, Cambridge. New in 1956 it was fitted with this 'classic' looking Metro-Cammell 'Orion' high-bridge type body which seated 33 on the upper deck and 26 on the lower, with the extra comfort of rear platform doors. **JCH 265** is seen here parked up at Eynon's 'new' yard, which had previously been a field, located to the rear of Bryn Villa Garage. The field, acquired in 1975 was desperately needed after a compulsory purchase order had been issued on the existing yard in front of the garage for a road improvement. See photo on page 64.

Above: Eynon's had a 'Penchant' for the Leyland 'Tiger Cub' as they were cheap to buy and very economical, returning an average fuel consumption of 13.6 m.p.g. from their 5.7 litre engines. Captured here at Lammas Street, Carmarthen is former Western Welsh (1273) **UKG 273** a 1961, PSUC1/2 model with Metro-Cammell DP41F body, which arrived at Eynon's in 1974 via Wylie of Thorne, South Yorkshire.

Above: This Leyland 'Leopard' PSU3B/4R with Plaxton 'Panorama Elite Express III' body registered **GCY 74N** was ordered by Eynon's but delivered to West Wales Motors, Tycroes in October 1974, in full Eynon's red and cream with gold waist band livery, to which West Wales added their dark grey livery to the lower panels.

Above: This Leyland 'Leopard' PSU3B/4R with Plaxton 'Panorama Elite Express III' body registered **GNY 431N** was a diverted order from D J Vowles of Merthyr Tydfil in November 1974, replacing GCY 74N pictured above, which had been diverted from Eynon's to West Wales Motors a month earlier. **GNY 431N** was delivered to Eynon's in Vowles' livery of white with blue waist band, to which Eynon's added the red. They were identical vehicles with consecutive chassis numbers, but GNY 431N had been fitted with this replacement front grille by 12th February 1978 when I photographed it here at Trimsaran. *(V. Morgan).*

Above: The first fully fronted double decker was **PBN 657** acquired in November 1974. It was a 1961 Leyland 'Titan' PD2/27 with an unusual looking Metro-Cammell 'Orion' FH35/27F body, which incorporated this 'Midland Red' style front grille and a front entrance with manually operated sliding door. It was new to Bolton CT (139).

Above: Seen here when new in February 1975 is dealer registered **HFP 118N**, a Bedford YRQ with Plaxton 'Panorama Elite III' C45F coachwork. This coach and its twin sister, HFP 119N were not 'Grant Aided' vehicles.

Above: The Bedford VAL's Eynon's purchased new in the 1960's were disposed of after a very short time, as they were not very happy with the braking system on them. In April 1975 however, this VAL14, **JXD 548D** with Plaxton 'Panorama' C52F body joined the fleet, followed a month later by another second-hand VAL pictured below.

Above: XUP 457F a 1968 Bedford 'VAL70' with Plaxton 'Panorama II' C52F coachwork was purchased in May 1975 from Martindale, Ferryhill, Durham and is captured here working stage service at Llanelli Town Hall.

Above: This Leyland 'Tiger Cub' PSUC1/2 with Weymann DP41F body, **SCG 856** was new in 1957 to the much loved company King Alfred Motor Services (R Chisnell) Winchester. It passed to Hants & Dorset Motor Services, (National Bus Co) with the King Alfred business in April 1973, and was purchased by Eynon's in May 1975. It's seen here at Kidwelly still carrying the Hants & Dorset - NBC poppy red and white livery it arrived with.

Above: **TRN 739** was one of four identical Leyland PSU3/3RT 'Leopards' purchased from Ribble Motor Services in May/June 1975. They were 11 metre Plaxton 'Panorama' C49F bodied TRN 733/5/9/59 followed later by TRN 743/753 which had seen service with Edmunds, Rassau and Lewis, Morriston respectively. I took this photo on 19th February 1977 when it was laid up due to engine failure – Note the towing eye screwed into its front end.

To eliminate traffic congestion at Carmarthen's Lammas Street - the town's main bus terminal, the newly formed Dyfed County Council built a new bus station at Blue Street, to centralise all bus services operating into the town including Eynon's. The new bus station opened on 3rd August 1975 and ironically was still congested on market days, as several market day only services converged on the town together with numerous touring coaches. Carmarthen is a popular destination for day trippers and holidaymakers visiting west Wales.

Above: This view of Carmarthen bus station taken on Wednesday 28th March 1990 shows clearly the chaos 21 PSV's can cause when converged into a confined area. The bus station has since been re-developed making it smaller, but nowadays buses are only allowed to drop off and pick up. A waiting time of 10 minutes only is allowed in the bus station.

On 22nd October 1975, Eynon's applied for the Express Carriage licence previously held by John Evans & Sons Ltd, of Als Garage, Bancffosfelen, Pontyberem. John Evans & Sons however had ceased operating PSV's since June 1974; that part of their transport business, together with the three buses had passed to Williams Bros, Upper Tumble. Williams Bros had been operating the 'National Coal Board' Express Service to Cynheidre Colliery using John Evans' licence; TGR 1254/12. Eynon's licence application for this service was:

TGR 311/16: Drefach (Square) to Cynheidre Colliery (Shaft No3)
via Capel Sion, Mynydd-Cerrig, Bancffosfelen and Pontyberem.
Fares will be subsidised by the National Coal Board.
Only NCB personnel employed at Cynheidre Colliery to be carried.
The service is to run on working days only throughout the year.

The licence was granted on 28th January 1976 and operated for a period of three years only.

Above: In 1975 Eynon's bought two of these unusual looking fully fronted double-deckers from Ribble Motor Services. Built in 1957, they were Leyland 'Titan' PD3/4's with Burlingham FH41/31F bodies. The bus crews at Ribble were quick to apply the name 'Sabrina' to their revolutionary new 72 seaters – Sabrina was a 1950's English glamour model! Pictured here at Eynon's yard just one month before its withdrawal in February 1978 is **KCK 866.**

Above: The other identical 'Sabrina' acquired in 1975, **KCK 854** entered service in February 1976 painted in this all-over advertising livery for a local travel agent 'Richards Travel', who worked in alliance with Eynon's.

Above: In August 1975, Eynon's bought **UBN 904** which is seen here at the new Carmarthen bus station. Acquired from Shennan, Drongan along with UBN 907, they were Leyland 'Titan' PD3A/2's with East Lancs FH41/32F bodies, fitted with 'St. Helens' style front grilles, and new to Bolton CT in 1962. This one saw 5 years of service at Trimsaran.

Above: Ex Ribble Motor Services **TRN 743**, a 1963 Leyland 'Leopard' PSU3/3RT with Plaxton 'Panorama' C49F coachwork, joined four other similar 'Leopards' from Ribble (733/5/9/43) when it was purchased from Edmunds of Rassau, Gwent in September 1975. This one outlasted all the others including 753 which arrived in August 1978.

Above: This Leyland 'Tiger Cub' PSUC1/1 registered **WCG 104**, with Weymann B45F bodywork was new to King Alfred Motor Services, Winchester in 1959. It was acquired by Hants & Dorset (2704) with the 'King Alfred' business in April 1973, and sold to Eynon's in September 1975 where it worked intermittently until July 1981. After withdrawal it was sold to 'Friends of King Alfred Preservation Group' Winchester in October 1981, and is now fully restored into the livery of its original operator - King Alfred Motor Services, and operates at open day events.

At around the same time in February 1976, the South Wales Transport were re-organising services in west Wales, and part of their service 129 from Ammanford to Burry Port was regarded as un-remunerative and abandoned. It was a route previously operated by J James & Sons Ltd of Ammanford (Ammanford – Cross Hands – Pontyberem – Pontyates – Trimsaran – Pembrey and Burry Port). The service had passed into SWT ownership with the acquisition of James' business in 1962, and the section abandoned was Pontyates (Station) to Burry Port (Railway Station).

The new authority, Dyfed County Council approached Eynon's inviting them to tender for the abandoned service with a subsidy, which the company immediately agreed to, and applied for the RSL on 25th February 1976 with the following application number:

TGR 311/17: Pontyates (Railway Station) to Burry Port (Railway Station).
via Carway, Trimsaran (Trilwm), Pinged and Pembrey.

South Wales Transport immediately objected to the application on grounds of encroachment between Pembrey and Burry Port. This resulted in a public hearing held at the Council Offices, Spilman Street, Carmarthen, on 23rd April 1976, and in the meantime the Ministry of Transport issued Eynon's with the following special licence for unforeseen service of stage carriage, allowing them to operate the disputed service:

TGR 311/Sp/7: Pontyates (Railway Station) to Burry Port (Railway Station).
via Carway, Trimsaran (Trilwm), Pinged and Burry Port.
Period of operation: 29/2/76 to 24/4/76

After the public hearing, the licence TGR 311/17 was finally granted on 19th May 1976, allowing the company to operate the abandoned service along the disputed 2 mile section of SWT's route 173/4 between Burry Port (Station) and Pembrey (Butchers Arms). This new service, designated route number 195 by the local authority, served the villages of Carway and Trimsaran with ten journeys daily from Pontyates, alternate journeys only continued to Burry Port. The numbers of passengers carried on off peak journeys were so low it necessitated a smaller vehicle on the route, which eventually led to the purchase of the company's first mini-bus in 1979.

Throughout the years Eynon's had developed a close business relationship with Gravell's of Pinged Hill Garage, Kidwelly, and took the opportunity in April 1976 to acquire Pinged Hill Garage's last remaining public service vehicle; BUX 236L a Bedford YRQ with Duple 'Dominant' 45 seat coachwork, along with his 'O' licence and National Coal Board – 'Express Carriage' to Cynheidre Colliery. Eynon's operated the NCB service using the Road Service Licence of Pinged Hill Garage (TGR4917/1) until it expired, before applying for its transfer in November 1978 on application number TGR 311/22. See page 117.

Above: This 1973 Bedford YRQ with Duple 'Dominant' 45 seat coachwork, **BUX 236L** was acquired with the operator licence of Pinged Hill Garage Ltd, Kidwelly in April 1976. It was sold in July 1977 still in this green and white livery.
(G. Courtnage).

The Eynon's partnership however were always looking out for a bargain when they bought additional vehicles. This led to the purchase of a repossessed two year old Ford R1014 with

Willowbrook 'Expressway' DP45F body in June 1976. This became another 'first' in the fleet, the first Ford PSV chassis. Registered RUH 656M, it had previously operated for the defunct Tri-Afon Motors Ltd (formerly Peter Smith) Garnswllt, and came to Eynon's initially for storage. After all the legalities relating to the 'New Bus Grant' had been resolved, the deal was finalised and the bus overhauled before entering service in January 1977.

In October 1976, a local factory - Avon Inflatables Ltd, decided to provide subsidised transport for their employees on a trial basis. Four special short term RSL's had to be applied for, and were issued to start on 14th October 1976 and expire on 8th December 1976. These special short term 'Express Carriage' licences issued were as follows:

TGR 311/Sp/8:	Trimsaran	to	Dafen	(Avon Inflatables Ltd)
TGR 311/Sp/9:	Penyfan	to	Dafen	(Avon Inflatables Ltd)
TGR 311/Sp/10:	Llanelli	to	Machynys	(Avon Inflatables Ltd)
TGR 311/Sp/11:	Pontarddulais	to	Llanelli	(Avon Inflatables Ltd)

The full term 'Express Carriage' licences were applied for in December 1976 as follows:-

TGR 311/18: Llanelli to Machynys, via Felinfoel and Llwynhendy
Starting at Felinfoel Co-operative, Felinfoel RFC, Bryngwyn School, Dafen, Llwynhendy, Penallt, Robinson Street (Llanelli) and Station Road.

TGR 311/19: Trimsaran to Dafen,
via Burry Port, Pwll, Llanelli, Llanerch, Maestref, Capel Road and Havard Road.

TGR 311/20: Penyfan to Dafen,
via Morfa and Felinfoel.

TGR 311/21: Pontarddulais to Llanelli,
via Llangennech and Dafen.

All the services will be subsidised by Avon Inflatables Ltd.
The services are for employees of Avon Inflatables Ltd, only.

There were no objectors to the applications, and the licences were all granted on 9th March 1977.

Until this point in time, route numbers had never been used by the company, but the local authority were now allocating route numbers throughout the county, as a means of identifying the services they were subsidising. The route numbers allocated to Eynon's, but still not displayed were as follows:

195 – Pontyates – Burry Port.
196 – Llanelli – Pontyberem – Carmarthen.
197 – Kidwelly – Four Roads.
198 – Kidwelly – Llansaint.
199 – Llanelli – Trimsaran – Carmarthen.

Above: Another 'Grant Aided' coach purchased in March 1976 was **NAY 438P,** pictured here at the depot on 8th October 1980. This was an AEC 'Reliance' 6U3ZR with 760 engine coupled to a 6 speed manual ZF gearbox, and Plaxton 'Supreme' Express C53F coachwork. It passed to Mansel David, Pontycymmer, Mid-Glam, in May 1983. *(V. Morgan).*

Above: Another dealer registered coach purchased under the 'Bus Grant' scheme in June 1976, was **OAY 393P.** It was identical to NAY438P above, another AEC Reliance 6U3ZR with Plaxton 'Supreme' Express C53F body. *(V. Morgan).*

Above: Eynon's had a penchant for exotic styles of coaches, and purchased another vehicle with a rare combination of chassis and coachbuilder in June 1976. **RFF 118L** seen here at the depot in February 1977, had an AEC 'Reliance' 6U3ZR chassis, and was one of only six Van-Hool 'Vistadome' bodied AEC Reliance's built. It was built in 1973 by Van-Hool's subsidiary McArdle in Ireland. *(V. Morgan).*

Above: Another coach that never received fleet livery was this 1973 Bedford YRQ registered **BGV 238L**. It was fitted with a Caetano 'Cascais II' Express type body seating 45, with doors and the like conforming to bus grant specification, and arrived from Beeston of Hadleigh, Suffolk in June 1976. This attractive little Bedford YRQ was part exchanged for a new Bedford YMT/Duple 'Dominant' 53 seat coach in July 1977.

Above: Captured here at Cathedral Road, Cardiff on 15th January 1977 is the first Ford PSV in the Eynon's fleet, **RUH 656M** a 1974 Ford R1014 with Willowbrook 'Expressway' C45F body. Built to the 'New Bus Grant' specification, it was acquired after the collapse of Tri-Afon Motors (Peter Smith) Garnswllt near Ammanford, an ambitious operator who invested in too many 'New Bus Grant' vehicles. *(V. Morgan).*

Above: Another Willowbrook 'Expressway' purchased in September 1976 was **HGE 469L** on a 1973 Bedford YRQ chassis. It's seen here at Eynon's yard on 8th October 1980 parked alongside a recent addition to the fleet, RBO119G a Bedford J2SZ10 from Williams. Llansamlet, West Glamorgan. *(V. Morgan).*

In 1977, the company invested in two new coaches without the aid of the 'New Bus Grant'. They were a pair of Bedford YMT's with identical Duple 'Dominant II' C53F bodies as seen above and below. First to arrive just a month before the registration number year suffix changed from R to S was **PTH 647R** which was licenced in July 1977. Its partner arrived later that month but wasn't licenced until August gaining the 'S' registration suffix.

<u>**Above:**</u> As mentioned above, **RTH 130S** was the second Bedford YMT delivered in July 1977. It wasn't taxed until 1st August gaining the new registration number year suffix of 'S' - RTH130S, but was used before August 1st. They both had a very short stay and left the fleet in August 1978, together with AEC/Caetano XTH 944M.

On 10th May 1977, the company's Caetano bodied AEC 'Reliance' coach, XTH 944M was involved in a serious accident opposite Llanelli library. A Leyland National bus owned by the South Wales Transport Co, ran into the back of a car, developed a fault and out of control went into reverse at full speed hitting the coach, and pushing it into a bus shelter. Damage to the coach was extensive and had to be sent to the Caetano dealer, Moseley for repair, with a Caetano 'Cascais' bodied Ford R192, DBC263K operating on loan from the dealer in May/June 1977.

For the start of the new academic year in September 1977, the company bought their first Leyland 'Atlanteans'. The three Alexander bodied PDR1/1 (Mk1) 'Atlanteans' SGD 610/21/35 from Greater Glasgow PTE (LA32/43/57) were very unreliable, suffering from over-heating and engine problems, in-fact they were continually on stop and the management stated that they would certainly not buy any more rear engine buses! This was soon after they'd received three rear engine Leyland 'Panthers' from Lincoln CT, EVL550/2/3E which suffered similar problems and were sold off after 21 months. In comparison, the company favoured the conventional layout Leyland PD2/PD3 'Titans' and soon replaced the 'Atlanteans' with more 'Titans'. 'Atlantean' SGD 610 was in-fact the only one to be painted, receiving an all-over orange livery advertising the Llanelli, Kidwelly and Carmarthen Job Centres in December 1978.

On the other hand, mention should be made here about an incident that occurred with a Leyland PD2, when the driver was pulled over by an overtaking motorist, and told that something had fallen off the bus and that the bus was trailing oil. The problem was that a con-rod had smashed through the side of the engine – and he was still merrily driving along unconcerned. He was not even disciplined!

Above: **SGD 635** was one of three 1962 Leyland 'Atlantean' PDR1/1's with Alexander H44/34F bodies purchased in September 1977 from Greater Glasgow PTE. They were a major source of trouble to the company during their difficult times. It's captured here on 28th January 1978. *(V. Morgan).*

Above: This former Greater Glasgow PTE, Alexander bodied Leyland 'Atlantean' PDR1/1, registered **SGD 610** was the only one of the three to receive a coat of paint at Trimsaran. It received this all-over orange livery and advertisement for the local Job Centre's of Carmarthen, Kidwelly and Llanelli in December 1978. I photographed it here at the depot on 20th Oct. 1979, just weeks before its substitution by a former Brighton C T Leyland 'Titan'. *(V. Morgan).*

Above: Throughout the years several former Ribble Motor Services Leyland's found a home at Trimsaran. This early 1963 PSU3/1R type 'Leopard' **TCK 459** with Marshall B53F body, had arrived in September 1977 and was withdrawn in December 1980. I photographed this at the depot in March 1978. *(V. Morgan).*

Above: Former Ribble M S (462) **TCK462** was another Leyland 'Leopard' PSU3/1R with 4 speed synchromesh gearbox and 11 metre Marshall B53F body. It was looking rather tired here on 20th January 1981, just two months before its fate, sold for scrap. *(V. Morgan).*

Above: This 1961 Leyland 'Atlantean' PDR1/1 with Metro-Cammell H44/33F body was purchased just two months after the Glasgow 'Atlanteans' had arrived – before Eynon's had decided not to buy anymore rear engine buses. Although, this former Wallasey 'Atlantean' **JHF 821**, which was acquired via Godfrey Abbott Group, of Sale, Greater Manchester, was a far better buy, and used regularly crew operated on the arduous Llanelli-Trimsaran-Kidwelly-Carmarthen service until April 1980. It's seen here on 28th January 1978. *(V. Morgan).*

Above: Seen at Carmarthen bus station in August 1978 is **FKY 250E** a Leyland 'Titan' PD3A/2 with St Helens type front and a Neepsend H40/30F body. New in 1967 to Bradford C T it was acquired via West Yorkshire PTE in February 1978, and was completely burned out in a fire at the depot yard on 29th November 1979.

Above: **TRN 753** was the fifth former Ribble, Leyland 'Leopard' PSU3/3RT with Plaxton 'Panorama' body to be acquired. This one had previously operated for John Lewis Coaches of Morriston, Swansea, where it was out of service by March 1978. It was acquired by Eynon's and licenced to them in August 1978. *(V. Morgan).*

Towards the end of the decade, Eynon's coach fleet had become the envy of some local competitors, as the fleet consisted of four attractive Caetano bodied coaches together with several Plaxton and Duple bodied examples which had all been acquired new. This however sparked off a price war between the operators, resulting in financial problems at Eynon's in early 1978. This was at a time when Britain was suffering from a high annual inflation rate combined with rising costs and the price of new vehicles was ever increasing.

S. EYNON + SONS
JAMES MAURICE EYNON
+ DAVID IEUAN LODWICK

LICENCE NOT TRANSFERABLE — ROAD TRAFFIC ACT 1960

P.S.V. LICENCE G 149276

REGN. MARK RTH 130S

EXPIRES 31-7-78

CHASSIS No. 451411

SEATING CAPACITY

LOWER DECK 53

UPPER DECK —

Above: A rear end view of Bedford YMT/Duple 'Dominant II' **RTH 130S** displays the Gothic style lettering applied to the rear of Eynon's Coaches. This picture was taken on 9th April, 1978 when the coach was on stop awaiting attention to its engine – under warranty. *(V. Morgan).*

Left: The first PSV licence disc issued to RTH 130S (pictured above) in August 1977 is reproduced here. It was a legal requirement to display each vehicle's PSV licence disc on the vehicle's windscreen, displaying the name of the licence holder and the vehicle's identification details. This style of licence was discontinued under the 1980 Road Traffic Act, in favour of the coloured operator discs of today which are transferable between vehicles.

TURBULENT TIMES

Unfortunately the company's finances seriously deteriorated in mid-1978, and financial assistance was given to the unstable company by a prominent local businessman, keeping the 'unlimited' company operational, yet the shareholders still insisted on keeping the establishment unlimited.

Four front line coaches were disposed of during the troubles, XTH 944M, GNY 431N, PTH 647R and RTH 130S, which were replaced by three hired double-deckers in the interim period before three aging Leyland 'Panthers' arrived. Additional help was given by brothers Derrick and Maldwyn Williams of Gwyn Williams & Sons Ltd, Lower Tumble (local competitors). They bought a 1964 Leyland 'Leopard' 217 HUM, with Plaxton 'Panorama' coachwork, painted it into Eynon's fleet livery and donated it to the company as a goodwill gesture in October 1978.

If all this were not enough, one evening in October 1978 a local young man decided to take one of the company's buses for a joy ride. The bus sustained considerable damage upon leaving the premises but this didn't deter him – he carried on until a suspicious policeman stopped him 30 miles away at Pyle. He was fined £50 and ordered to pay the company £250 damages.

Above: This Leyland 'Leopard' PSU3/3R with Plaxton 'Panorama' C49F body, **217 HUM** was given to the company as a goodwill gesture in October 1978. New in 1964 to Wallace Arnold (Devon) with a centre entrance doorway, it was converted to front entrance layout before entering service with West Wales Motors of Tycroes. *(V. Morgan).*

As already mentioned, Eynon's took over the PSV business of Pinged Hill Garage, Kidwelly back in April 1976 but had continued to operate the National Coal Board's 'Express Carriage' service on Pinged Hill Garage's licence (TGR 4917/1) until November 1978, when a transfer was finally applied for. This transfer was granted on 21st March 1979, as follows:

TGR 311/22: Kidwelly to Cynheidre Colliery (Shaft 1&2),
via Four Roads, Meinciau, Pontyates and Ponthenry. Three shifts daily.
To operate Mon – Sat inclusive, only when Cynheidre Colliery is working.
Only National Coal Board employees to be carried.

It was later modified to start at Pwll (Graig Comprehensive School).

Above: Captured here at Queen Elizabeth Cambria School, Carmarthen on 26th September 1978 is **VCS 431,** one of three buses hired in from Lister (dealer) due to a vehicle shortage. It was an Albion LR1 'Lowlander' with Alexander 'C type' body, built to H40/31F layout incorporating a Leyland 'St Helens' type front. This was new in 1964 to Western SMT (N1877) in Scotland. *(T. S. Powell).*

Left: This 1962 Bristol 'Lodekka' FLF6B **527 VRB** with an Eastern Coachworks H38/32F body was also hired from Lister (dealer) in September 1978 for a period of two months due to the vehicle shortage. It had previously operated with NBC subsidiary Trent M T (688). I captured this at the depot on 24th September 1978, alongside UBN904. *(V. Morgan).*

<u>Above:</u> 528 VRB, was another former Trent MT (689) Bristol 'Lodekka' FLF6B with ECW H38/32F body, and the third vehicle hired from Lister (dealer) during the company's troubled times of September 1978. This 'Lodekka' was also photographed at Trimsaran, on Sunday 24th September 1978, alongside Leyland 'Atlantean' JHF 821.

<u>Above:</u> Three former Lincoln C T Leyland PSUR1/1R 'Panthers' with 49 seat bodywork by C H Roe were purchased from Lister (dealer) releasing the three hired double-decker's in October 1978. **EVL 550E** seen here at Station Road Kidwelly on 1st December 1979, was numerically first of the trio; EVL 550/2/3E dating from 1967. They were not very successful and returned to Lister in July 1980. *(V. Morgan).*

Soon after the financial crisis had passed, the garage foreman decided to leave and move on to pastures new, giving the management another problem – finding a suitable person for the post. After some considerable thought and time the position was filled in late 1979 by a new 'fleet engineer' responsible for all engineering issues within the business.

Meanwhile, in an attempt to economise, Eynon's purchased their first ever mini-bus, NCR 268M a Ford Transit in February 1979, to operate the council supported 195 service – Pontyates to Burry Port, which only carried a handful of passengers. Additionally, in the evenings it was used for private hire - work that had previously been contracted out or worked with a full size vehicle. It was soon followed by a few other 29 seat Bedford VAS and a Bedford J2SZ10/Plaxton 20 seater.

Above: This 1973 Ford Transit 12 seater with Bristol Street Motors conversion **NCR 268M,** was the first mini-bus ever owned by Eynon's. It was purchased for the local authority supported service 195, Pontyates to Burry Port.

In1979, after the announcement of the AEC works' closure, and with a fresh injection of cash, no less than four AEC 'Reliance' coaches were hurriedly ordered to 'Bus Grant' specification - which was supposedly ending in August 1980. As previously mentioned, the grant scheme was extended by four years in November 1979, and was finally axed by a Tory government in March 1984!

The first two 'Reliances' XBX 830/1T arrived in June 1979 fitted with Plaxton 'Supreme Express IV' C53F bodies, AH760 engines and 6 speed synchromesh gearboxes. The second pair; BTH 364/5V had the same mechanical layout, but had Duple 'Dominant Express II' C53F bodies and were licenced in Oct/Nov 1979 respectively. These AEC's soon became regular performers of the company's *new* London 'Express Service' terminating at Marble Arch, which began in October 1980 after the 1980 Road Traffic Act lifted the licence restriction on Express Carriage Services. The service which initially operated on Saturdays only, became enormously popular with day trippers at only £3.00 per person (pre-booked) day return, and sometimes required two coaches.

XBX 830T **above** and **XBX 831T** **below** were both received in June 1979 with the aid of the 'Bus Grant' scheme and built to full grant specification. They were identical AEC 'Reliances' with identical Plaxton 'Supreme Express IV' coachwork seating 53. XBX 830T is seen here outside Bryn Villa, Trimsaran on 9th January 1981, all prepared for its 'Express Service' to London the following morning at 07 00 from Llanelli Town Hall. *(V. Morgan).*

Above: XBX 831T was identical to XBX 830T when new. They were regular performers of the Kidwelly/Llanelli to London 'Express Service' which began in October 1980. **XBX 831T** is seen here in March 1986 with the new style 'Supreme IV' front grille, which it received during a front end rebuild in late 1985, after a major accident. *(V. Morgan).*

Above: I took this view of **BTH 364V** on 3rd November 1979 when it was just 4 weeks old. It had the same AEC 'Reliance' 6U3ZR chassis as XBX 830/1T delivered five months earlier, but this had a Duple 'Dominant Express II' C53F body built to 'Grant Specification' and identical to its twin pictured below BTH 365V. It received considerable damage in May 1984 when a lorry collided with it on the M4 Motorway. Its repairs took 16 months.

Above: BTH 365V was the last *new* AEC 'Reliance', and the last 'Grant Aided' vehicle purchased by the company in November 1979. It was identical to its twin, BTH 364V seen above, and worked very hard on both stage and express carriage services together with continental tours to Paris. This coach is now owned by a preservation group in South Wales, and at the moment is sadly not in the livery of Eynon's. It's seen here at the Eynon's depot on 3rd November 1985.

The success of the London Express service was astonishing. This prompted management to modify the service to operate on Tuesdays and Saturdays and to start from Kidwelly, and within a short while modified again to run on Tuesday Thursday and Saturdays, with an added incentive the introduction of period returns and 2/3 day mini-breaks with accommodation at Paddington.

It was a 210 mile trip to central London, which would usually take 4 hours from Llanelli in the days before speed limiters and the prohibition of coaches from the third lane of motorways!

Bearing in mind that fifteen years earlier Eynon's were predominantly Leyland users, the switch to AEC's for their six front line coaches was quite intriguing – especially after the announcement of AEC's closure.

Above: Eynon's took this ageing 1964 AEC 'Reliance' 2U3RA, **4991 VT** in part exchange for a newer 1971 AEC 'Reliance', PBX 700J in August 1979. It was fitted with a Duple 'Commander' C49F body, and served the company for just 5 months before it died. The photograph was taken at Old Castle Road, Llanelli on 27th November 1979, whilst the driver took his break in 'Dai's Café' here at Old Castle Road – a popular venue for Llanelli bus drivers.

September 1979 saw the arrival of the last London Transport vehicles in the fleet. A pair of well-worn AEC 'Regal IV' RF type buses, MLL 934/MXX 489 (RF516/512) were bought for a new school contract to Coedcae Comprehensive School in Llanelli. They both suffered from overheating and cylinder head gasket problems after climbing the 'Trimsaran' mountain, and subsequently RF516 was withdrawn after only two months and used for spare parts. RF512 worked for seventeen months before being laid up and eventually sold for preservation in May 1987.

The company however had more than their share of serious problems throughout their existence, and on the evening of 29th November 1979, three vehicles were totally destroyed in a fire at the depot yard. The theory was that an electrical fault had developed on Plaxton bodied

Bedford VAS, DHN 300H, causing the fire which quickly spread to a Plaxton bodied Leyland 'Leopard' coach, VTH 5L and a Leyland 'Titan' PD3A, FKY 250E that were parked adjacent to each other. Furthermore, a Willowbrook bodied Bedford YRQ, HGE 469L was slightly scorched by the fire, which resulted in vehicles being borrowed from other operators. Two ex Crosville Bristol MW's and a former Cardiff PD3 (405 CKG) were hired from Morris Bros, Swansea until replacement buses were bought. The replacement buses were two former Brighton Corporation Leyland 'Titan' PD2/37 deckers BUF 528/9C which had latterly operated for Warrington B T, as their 98/99.

Above: This photograph depicts the extent of the damage caused by the fire at Eynon's depot on 29th November 1979. The fire which broke out in the Bedford VAS (**DHN 300H**) on the left quickly spread to the Leyland 'Leopard' (**VTH 5L**) in the centre and to the Leyland 'Titan' (**FKY 250E**) on the right. The Bedford YRQ that was scorched (HGE 469L) was easily repaired and put back into service. *(V. Morgan).*

Above: Another view taken from a different angle, of the three burnt out vehicles **FKY 250E, VTH 5L** and (hidden behind VTH 5L) **DHN 300H** taken at Eynon's yard on 1st December 1979. *(V. Morgan).*

Right: This former Greater Manchester Leyland 'Atlantean' (5143) **GBU 143D**, didn't quite make it to Eynon's. On route to Trimsaran in September 1979 from the dealer Lister of Bolton, the driver took a wrong turning for Trimsaran at Pen-y-bedd, Pembrey. The lane subsided with the weight of the bus and it ended up in this ditch. The company had intended to replace a Greater Glasgow 'Atlantean' SGD 621 with GBU 143D, but it was inspected and returned to Lister. *(M. A. Morgan).*

Below: The company's fondness of former London Transport vehicles led to the purchase of two RF class AEC 'Regal' IV's when they came out of service in September 1979. One of the pair, (RF512) **MXX 489** is seen here on 8th October 1980 at Trimsaran with my trusty old Singer Gazelle IIIC parked behind it. This particular RF dating from March 1953, with Metro-Cammell B39F body was finally withdrawn from service in February 1981, and kept intact until May 1987 when it was sold for preservation. The second RF, pictured on page 125 only worked for two months at Trimsaran – giving lots of problems it was withdrawn for a source of spares.
The die-cast model makers EFE brought out a limited edition 1/76th scale model of this particular Eynon's bus in April 2002. (See page 238). *(V. Morgan).*

Above: Still bearing its London Transport livery at Eynon's yard when I took this view on 1st December 1979 is former RF516, **MLL 934** dating from September 1952. This bus was a replacement for RF520, which had broken down upon leaving London for Trimsaran in September 1979. This one also suffered overheating problems, and was withdrawn after just two months use in November 1979, but retained as a source of spares for the other RF, MXX489 (RF512).

Above: **HEO 278** was a 1961 Leyland 'Titan' PD2A/27 bodied by Massey Bros, of Wigan to H37/27F layout. Fitted with a St Helens style front grille, it arrived in September 1979 from Barrow-in-Furness CT (108) and despite its age gave five and a half years' excellent service. Far better than the Mk I 'Atlanteans' from Greater Glasgow. *(V. Morgan).*

Replacement buses for the fire damaged vehicles of 29th November 1979 were two 1965 Leyland 'Titan' PD2/37's **BUF 528/9C (<u>Above and Below</u>)** with Weymann H37/27F bodies, which had been new to Brighton Corporation (28/9). They had been converted to OMO by Brighton but were crew operated at Eynon's, Latterly operating for Warrington BT (98/9), they arrived at Trimsaran in January 1980, with 528 giving the company eight years' service! *(V. Morgan).*

Above: This is typical rural scene captured on Eynon's service to the village of Llansaint, some 500 feet above sea level, overlooking the picturesque Carmarthen Bay. This former Brighton Corporation (29) Leyland PD2, **BUF 529C** is seen pulling hard up the steep hill out of Kidwelly, which is seen in the backdrop. It was essential to have a bus with a good engine and good brakes on this scenic route.

Towards the end of October 1979, another new Excursions & Tours licence was applied for:

TGR 311/23: Excursions & Tours starting from Kidwelly (Borough Offices)
Picking up at Trimsaran (Bird-in-Hand) and Carway (Brongwendraeth).
Period of operation May to August annually.
Max number of vehicles to be operated on any one excursion and tour on any one day to be one.

There was one objector to this application: Jenkins Tours, Llanelli.
After a public hearing the licence was granted on 19th March 1980.

An interesting development in November 1979 was the announcement of the 1980 Road Traffic Act by the Minister of Transport, Mr Norman Fowler. The Act which came into effect on 1st October 1980 was basically the beginning of deregulation, allowing Express Carriage Services over 30 miles in distance to be freed from licensing regulations, and Excursions & Tours would not require licensing at all, and the restriction of advertising E&T's, which had previously applied to Eynon's were lifted. The Act also abolished the licensing of bus conductors, and brought about the new 'coloured' operator licence discs. At the same time operator licence numbers were changed from TGR xxx prefix to PG xxx prefix (in the SWTA), with other traffic areas following suite with *their* appropriate Traffic Area letters. The Minister also announced that the 'New Bus Grant' scheme would cease by 31st March 1984.

Relaxation of the licensing system introduced in the above Act permitted Eynon's to inaugurate a Saturdays only Express Service from Llanelli to London (Marble Arch) as mentioned on pages 119/122, and prompted them on 1st October 1980 to apply for modification of their RSL (TGR 311/17), revising the time-table to incorporate an extension of the service to Pontyberem, and improve connections at Trimsaran for Llanelli & Carmarthen. This was granted on 1st April 1981.

At the same time Dyfed C C introduced a route numbering system for all stage carriage services operating within the county. Unfortunately not many operators used their allocated route numbers as it wasn't a mandatory requirement until several years later.

As already mentioned, the start of each school year brought with it complications, and in turn modifications of school contracts, and after buying four new AEC 'Reliances' a year earlier in 1979, the company were again experiencing cash flow problems at the start of the 1980/1 academic year when an extra vehicle was required. Surprisingly, an extra vehicle was provided by the company's new fleet engineer, and painted into Eynon's fleet livery. It was a 1965 Bedford SB5 with Duple 'Bella Vega' C41F body registered HRO 659C, and was leased to the company. It operated on Eynon's licence disc and was fuelled, maintained and driven by Eynon's personnel. The engineer later bought more of his own buses, and consequently added them to the Eynon's fleet, as shown in the fleet list on pages 217-226.

From this point in 1980 the fleet became a menagerie, there was a massive influx of vehicles with a variety of marques, types and liveries, nothing was standard, besides there were a lot of elderly vehicles brought in from Joe Sykes the Barnsley dealer for re-certification. Furthermore, all dealings for the purchase or sale of second-hand buses were left to the engineer as he was some sort of a dealer himself - buy or sell anything from an air compressor to a car, van or a bus!

Above: With a preference to the conventional type Leyland double decker, the company continued to buy this type of bus until their availability became extinct. **JRJ 272E** seen here at Llanelli Bus Station on 17th October 1981 was one of three former Greater Manchester PTE, Metro-Cammell 'Orion' bodied Leyland PD2/40's purchased in 1980. Registered JRJ 261/72/7E they were all new to Salford Corporation in 1967.

Above: **JRJ 261E,** was ano former Greater Manchester Leyl PD2/40 with Metro-Cam 'Orion' H64F body which was in April 1967 to Salford C T. It purchased in July 1980 photographed in October that alongside Leyland 'Titan' PD2 BUF529C. *(V. Morga*

Left: This Leyland 'Titan' PD3 **TRN 387** fitted with Me Cammell 'Orion' H39/31F b and St Helens type front grille, new to Preston BT No 85 November 1963. It was purcha by Eynon's in May 1980 and sold to a dealer in March 1981, continued use - on contract hir Knowsley Safari Park. They r have had a favourable price for very tidy vehicle. I photograph here in October 1980, still in Preston blue and cream livery never received the Eynon's live *(V. Morg*

Above: This 1965 Bedford SB5 with Duple 'Bella Vega' C41F body, **HRO 659C** was leased to the company by their fleet engineer. Painted in the Eynon's livery, it worked their contracts using the Eynon's licence discs throughout its fourteen month stay at Trimsaran. *(V. Morgan).*

Above: This neat little 1969 Plaxton 'Embassy' bodied Bedford J2SZ10, registered **RBO 119G** seated 20, and was in great demand for small groups of people – but was only operated for eighteen months. It arrived in October 1980, just in time for Christmas parties, and was sold for a caravan conversion in 1982. *(V. Morgan).*

Above: Added to the fleet in November 1980 was **BVJ 160B** a 1964 Bedford VAS1. This Bedford, acquired from Arthur Thomas, Gorseinon was fitted with a Plaxton 'Embassy' C29F body matching the little Bedford J2SZ10 acquired a month earlier. The view also shows part of Bryn Villa, Eynon's office (left) with my trusty old 1963 Singer Gazelle which has clocked up 300,000 miles, parked outside. *(V. Morgan).*

S. EYNON & SON

LONDON

DAY EXCURSION

RETURN FARE £3

Christmas Shopping Specials

Saturday

Dec. 6, 13, 20

Depart Llanelli Town Hall 7 a.m. Return approx. midnight

BRISTOL

DAY EXCURSION

Sat. Dec. 13

RETURN FARE £2

Depart Llanelli Town Hall 8 a.m. Return approx. 8.30 p.m.

Book at: Bryn Villa Garage, Trimsaran, Tel. 385, and Hourmont Travel Ltd., 23, Frederick St., Llanelli, Tel. 56501.

Left: Up until the passing of the 1980 Road Traffic Act, Eynon's were not allowed to advertise excursions and tours. The new Act relaxed the licensing laws for Express Carriage services and Excursions & Tours, and also lifted the restriction of advertising tours. This particular advertisement extracted from a local newspaper was the company's first ever 'tours' advertisement dated 29th November 1980. Furthermore, it was promoting their 'new' weekly Express Service to London which had been inaugurated after introduction of the new Act a month earlier.

It can be seen from the Tours Programme reproduced opposite, how popular Eynon's day excursions became in 1981. Some of their tours would fill two or three 53 seat coaches especially the Saturday trips to London (Marble Arch) at £3.00 per seat. These prices were far too low and certainly didn't help their financial situation. The fares on the 'London Express' service were deliberately kept low as there were two competitors on the route from its beginning. One competitor J James & Son of Central Garage, Burry Port vigorously challenged Eynon's for a short while, before changing to Continental Tours. The other competitor at the time, Jenkins Tours of Llanelli, regularly advertised London excursions, but they never ran – theirs were all cancelled through lack of support.

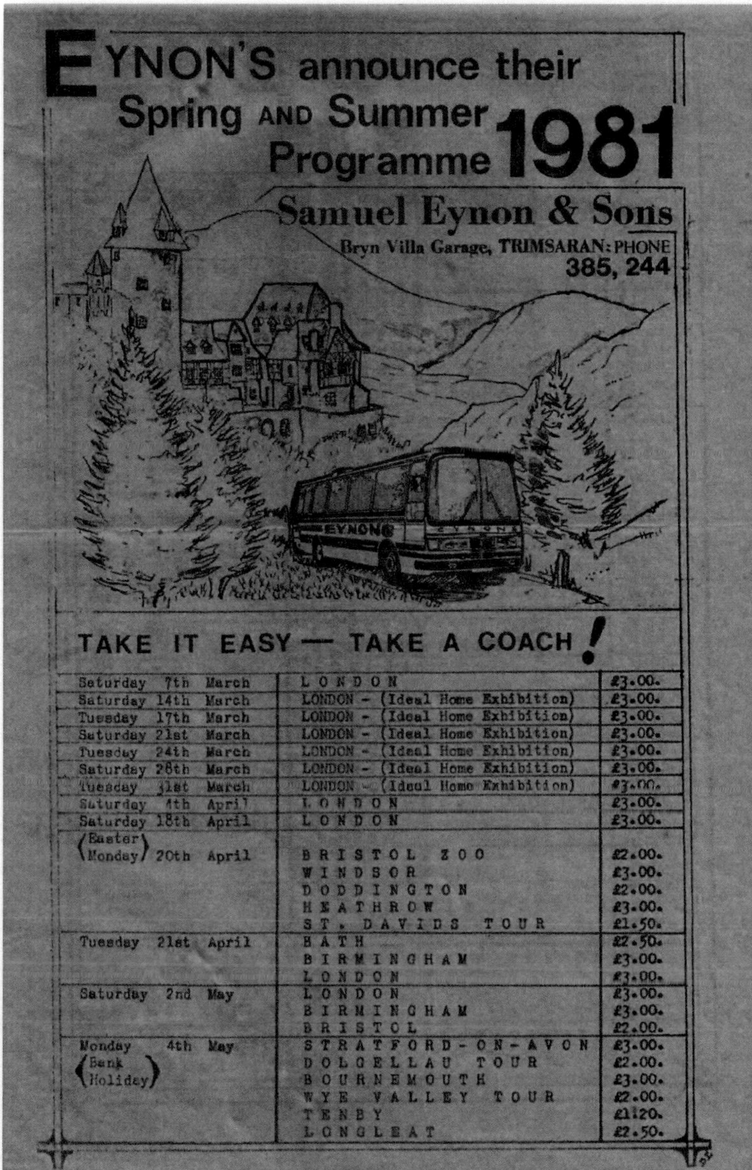

EYNON'S announce their Spring AND Summer Programme 1981

Samuel Eynon & Sons

Bryn Villa Garage, TRIMSARAN: PHONE 385, 244

TAKE IT EASY — TAKE A COACH !

Saturday 7th March	LONDON	£3.00.
Saturday 14th March	LONDON - (Ideal Home Exhibition)	£3.00.
Tuesday 17th March	LONDON - (Ideal Home Exhibition)	£3.00.
Saturday 21st March	LONDON - (Ideal Home Exhibition)	£3.00.
Tuesday 24th March	LONDON - (Ideal Home Exhibition)	£3.00.
Saturday 28th March	LONDON - (Ideal Home Exhibition)	£3.00.
Tuesday 31st March	LONDON - (Ideal Home Exhibition)	£3.00.
Saturday 4th April	LONDON	£3.00.
Saturday 18th April	LONDON	£3.00.
(Easter Monday) 20th April	BRISTOL ZOO	£2.00.
	WINDSOR	£3.00.
	DODDINGTON	£2.00.
	HEATHROW	£3.00.
	ST. DAVIDS TOUR	£1.50.
Tuesday 21st April	BATH	£2.50.
	BIRMINGHAM	£3.00.
	LONDON	£3.00.
Saturday 2nd May	LONDON	£3.00.
	BIRMINGHAM	£3.00.
	BRISTOL	£2.00.
Monday 4th May (Bank Holiday)	STRATFORD-ON-AVON	£3.00.
	DOLGELLAU TOUR	£2.00.
	BOURNEMOUTH	£3.00.
	WYE VALLEY TOUR	£2.00.
	TENBY	£1.20.
	LONGLEAT	£2.50.

The front page of Eynon's first ever Tours brochure in 1981. It was a home produced two page paper leaflet that was quite effective.

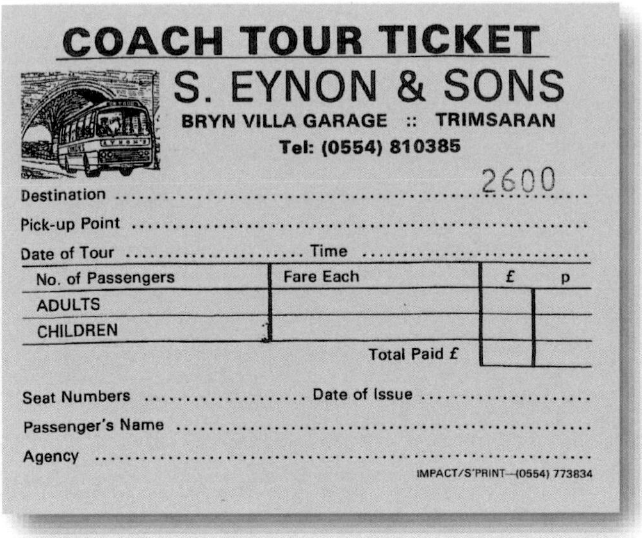

COACH TOUR TICKET

S. EYNON & SONS

BRYN VILLA GARAGE :: TRIMSARAN

Tel: (0554) 810385

2600

Destination ....

Pick-up Point ....

Date of Tour .... Time ....

No. of Passengers	Fare Each	£	p
ADULTS			
CHILDREN			
	Total Paid £		

Seat Numbers .... Date of Issue ....

Passenger's Name ....

Agency ....

IMPACT/S'PRINT—(0554) 773834

Left: This was the type of ticket passengers on coach excursions and the London Express service were issued with upon payment of their booking at the company's booking office, and their agency offices, or if required issued by the driver in the event of receiving extra passengers for the particular tour.

Jenkins Tours had latterly been the only operator in Llanelli to hold a licence to advertise Excursions & Tours but the 1980 Road Traffic Act had taken away that privilege resulting in Jenkins' slow decline.

Eynon's troubles however were not decreasing, adding to their list was the issue of vandalism which had become intolerable by November 1980, resulting in complete withdrawal of late night buses on Saturdays between Kidwelly and Carmarthen. That particular evening service was later withdrawn altogether, with their last bus leaving Carmarthen at 17.30 Mon-Sat.

Simultaneously, Llanelli was beginning to feel the effect of the Duport Steelworks closure in March 1981. The closure had a knock-on effect to every business in the surrounding area including public transport. Competitors, SWT made several cuts owing to lack of patronage, but Eynon's continued to run the same time-tables *and* still employed two conductors on their staff, running two crew operated buses on the Llanelli-Trimsaran-Kidwelly-Carmarthen service which by now had been allocated service number 199 by Dyfed County Council.

Furthermore, there were no inspectors (revenue protection officers) employed by the company, even though passengers had apparently reported members of staff that were not issuing tickets. Finally, a partner of the business caught two members of staff that hadn't issued tickets, and they were immediately dismissed. It was alleged that one person had 'pocketed' a lot of money. He'd been boasting in his local that he could 'make' the equivalent of a day's wages every day. Another OMO driver was caught using two ticket machines - the 'Setright Speed' type. This came to light after a ticket machine had 'gone missing' from the office.

The depot engineer on the other hand bought three more vehicles in 1981, two Ford R192's and another Bedford SB5, and again leased these to Eynon's on the same arrangement.

Above: This 1968 Duple 'Viceroy' C45F bodied Ford R192, **PFH 886F** arrived at Trimsaran in February 1981 from Brown & Simmonds, of Kingswood, Bristol. It operated on lease to Eynon's for three years from the fleet engineer, who eventually sold it to J. Sykes, the Carlton dealer in March 1984 for onward sale to a Jazz Band. (V. Morgan).

Above: Eynon's purchased numerous Greater Manchester PTE buses throughout the years, amongst them was this 1968 Leyland 'Leopard' PSU4/1R, **KDB 405F** with an East Lancs B43D body which was new to Stockport Corporation (405) in March 1968. It arrived at Trimsaran in March 1981 where it worked for the three years with the centre exit doorway fastened up and out of use. This view was taken on 23rd August 1981 at the depot yard. *(V. Morgan).*

Above: **HTJ 131F** was another Leyland 'Leopard' PSU4/2R fitted with East Lancs B43F body acquired from Greater Manchester PTE (6060) in March 1981. This one was new in April 1968 to Leigh Corporation (20) passing to the newly formed S E L N E C PTE in 1969; renamed Gtr. Manchester PTE in 1974. After seven years with Eynon's it passed to Davies Bros where it worked until July 1990, then laid up until sold for preservation in August 1996. It carried three different styles of livery with Eynon's - this was the last one it received on 16th April 1988 ready for its re-certification. It was a lovely little bus to drive, I drove it many times. *(V. Morgan).*

Above: New to Ramsbottom UDC (9) in November 1967 was this Leyland 'Titan' PD3/4 with East Lancs H41/32F body. Registered **FTF 703F** it quickly passed to S E L N E C PTE upon its formation in 1969, and under the local government reorganisation of 1974, S E L N E C was renamed Gtr. Manchester PTE. Eynon's acquired **FTF 703F** from Gtr. Manchester PTE (6409) in March 1981, but didn't licence it until December 1982. Fortunately, I took this view on 9th January 1983, as it left the stable 3 months later - part exchanged for three Leyland single-deckers with West Wales Motors of Tycroes, who were by now working in alliance with Eynon's. West Wales converted it to OMO and used it regularly on their lucrative Ammanford to Swansea route, but found it to be too slow and part exchanged it for a Leyland 'Atlantean'. *(V. Morgan).*

Above: Another vehicle new to Ramsbottom UDC (10) was **OTJ 334G** pictured here one foggy morning in April 1981 at Trimsaran. **OTJ 334G** was the penultimate Leyland 'Titan' PD3/4 built for the UK market in 1969 and was bodied H41/32F by East Lancs. The Ramsbottom fleet of 12 vehicles, passed to S E L N E C PTE in 1969, renamed Gtr. Manchester PTE in1974. Eynon's bought OTJ 334G from G M PTE in March 1981, selling it to a dealer in February 1984 it passed to a driving school as a PSV licenced driver trainer.

Above: In July 1981, an identical pair of Leyland 'Leopards' **TRK 5/6F** were purchased from Llynfi Motors of Maesteg (127/8). Seen here on 29th January 1982 is one of the pair, **TRK 5F** a 1968 PSU3A/2RT model with Plaxton 'Panorama' I, C51F body which looks quite smart in this style of Eynon's livery. Its partner TRK 6F however, never received a repaint into Eynon's livery, remaining in the boring Llynfi blue/black/cream livery until sold in June 1983. **TRK 5F** above was withdrawn in October 1982 after crashing into the rear end of Eynon's VTH655L on the B4308 road near 'The Farriers Arms', Cwmbach. It was later used for spares before its eventual sale to J. Sykes the Barnsley scrap dealer in 1983. *(V. Morgan).*

At around the same time the company made an association with a new travel agent that had arrived in Llanelli. The Cardiff based 'Hourmont Travel' promised Eynon's additional work from other branches across South Wales, and on the intensity of this extra work, three new coaches were sought after, but finance was only available for one. That vehicle was KTH 530X a Volvo B58-56 with Plaxton 'Supreme IV' coachwork which arrived in August 1981 and returned to Moseley the dealer in April 1982 due to financial problems. The other two coaches required for the Hourmont work were bought by Mr David Gravell of Pinged Hill Garage, Kidwelly, and were leased to Eynon's. These were also Volvo B58-56's, which were registered JBX 693/4X and fitted with Plaxton 'Supreme IV' and Duple 'Dominant II' bodies respectively, arriving in November 1981. The pair were returned to the lessor in May 1982 due to the loss of Hourmont Travel's work to another South Wales operator.

As a direct result of that problem, only a handful of 'elderly' buses were acquired during 1982, two 1965/6 Leyland 'Leopards', one 1970 Ford R226 which never ran as it needed too much work, one 1965 Leyland 'Titan' and one 1966 Leyland 'Atlantean', a marque that the Eynon's partnership said they would never buy again. The fleet engineer on the other hand bought an ageing AEC 'Reliance' with Duple 'Commander' body and leased it to Eynon's.

The establishment had been through a really bad winter both in terms of weather and work. The bad weather was to blame for the loss of revenue in January 1982, when a heavy snowfall closed several roads in the county, with huge snowdrifts that took snowploughs several days to clear. Nevertheless, when the road between Kidwelly and Carmarthen re-opened it had been cleared as a single track road with passing places, and in an attempt to look after their regular clientele on the Llanelli-Kidwelly-Carmarthen service, a Landrover was employed to travel ahead of the bus, stopping oncoming traffic and warning them of the approaching bus. This allowed the bus a clear passage along the single track road!

Above: **VWG 407** was a Bedford VAS1 acquired from James Bros, Llangeitho, Dyfed (Cardiganshire) in August 1981. Captured here on 23rd August 1981, it was new in 1963 to Alexander (Midland) MW269, and fitted with a Duple 'Bella Vista' C29F body with minor differences to 369 FGB opposite. *(V. Morgan).*

Above: **369 FGB** was another Bedford VAS1, but fitted with a rare 7ft 6inch wide Duple 'Bella Vista' C29F body. It was new in 1962 to Scottish operator David McBrayne (17), and was also acquired from James Bros, Llangeitho, Dyfed in August 1981, hence the Llangeitho destination blind displayed when I photographed it here on 23rd August 1981. *(V. Morgan).*

Above: In August 1981 the depot engineer bought another Ford R192 with Duple 'Viceroy' C45F body, **SDD 334G** from the same source as his previous purchases - Brown & Simmonds, Kingswood, Bristol. It was a very tidy coach for the year - 1969, and this was again leased to Eynon's on the same arrangement covering school contracts for three years, before being sold to a Jazz Band in Merseyside in July 1984. *(V. Morgan).*

Above: This 1971 Bedford SB5 with Duple 'Vega 31' C41F body **PTH 100K**, was another vehicle owned by the depot engineer and leased to Eynon's on the same odd arrangement. Purchased in November 1981 from competitors Gwyn Williams & Sons, of Lower Tumble, it had come from a good home, and is seen here at Cardiff working private hire on the occasion of Llanelli RFC's cup final day in May 1982. *(V. Morgan).*

Above: This Volvo B58-56 was one of three acquired in 1981 to fulfil the requirements of Hourmont Travel across south Wales. This particular Volvo, **KTH 530X** with Plaxton 'Supreme IV' C53F coachwork arrived in August 1981, and is seen here on 19th April 1982 displaying the Hourmont Travel vinyl stickers on the day before its departure from Trimsaran to Moseley (dealer) Cinderford and onward sale to Stone of Bath a month later. Behind the wheel is another Eynon family member, Hugh Bonnell, brother in law of James Maurice Eynon. *(V. Morgan).*

Above: Delivered incorrectly as JBX 293X in November 1981, **JBX 693X** was another Volvo B58-56 with Plaxton 'Supreme IV' C53F coachwork identical to KTH 530X opposite. This and JBX 694X below were leased from Gravell's (Pinged Hill Garage) Kidwelly, hence the 'G' placed between the 'EYNONS EXECUTIVE'. They were acquired for the 'Hourmont Travel' work which was lost to another operator in May 1982, resulting in their inevitable disposal. *(V. Morgan).*

Above: This Volvo B58-56, **JBX 694X** was also delivered with an incorrect registration number JBX 294X. New in November 1981, this Volvo had a Duple 'Dominant II' C53F body, and was leased from Gravell's for the 'Hourmont Travel' work, as was JBX 693X above. Both JBX 693/4X returned to their lessor in May 1982, who sold them both to Thomas of Clydach Vale, successor to Eynon's on the Hourmont work. Thomas used them in Eynon's livery as shown here on 7th August 1982, covering the Eynon's name with a vinyl 'Hourmont' advertisement. *(V. Morgan).*

Above: Another former Stockport Corporation Leyland 'Leopard' acquired via Gtr. Manchester PTE (5086) was **KDB 406F** seen here on 31st January 1982. This again had an East Lancs body that retained its centre doorway- a doorway not used by Eynon's. It arrived in November 1981 and was sold for scrap in June 1984. *(V. Morgan).*

Above: The old faithful Leyland 'Titan' PD2/37 **FEK 1F,** which was new in April 1968 to Wigan Corporation. Bodied by Massey Bros of Wigan to H37/27F layout it passed to Gtr. Manchester PTE (3290) in 1974, and came to Eynon's in November 1981, working regularly on stage carriage as seen here on 21st April 1982. It doubled as a driver trainer, with several drivers passing their driving test on it. Latterly used only for schools, it passed to Davies Bros with Eynon's business in 1988, and continued working schools until the loss of its contract in July 1990-when it was recertified and advertised for sale. In September 1991, I had the privilege of driving it to Haverfordwest DVLA office for visual inspection to have its 'cherished registration number' removed. It was then re-registered ODE 47F and sold in February 1992 for spares.

Above: Only one decker was missing from this line up at Eynon's yard on 31st January 1982 – BUF 528C. From left to right are: FEK 1F, BUF 529C, JRJ 272E, JRJ 277E, JRJ 261E, OTJ 334G, HEO 278 & NCR 268M Ford Transit. *(V. Morgan).*

The management and staff at Eynon's would do their utmost to keep services running in all circumstances. On the occasion of the heavy snowfall mentioned earlier, two coaches were returning from Austria with school children, to find the M4 motorway had been closed near Cardiff due to heavy snow. The drivers persuaded the Police to allow them to continue, resulting in a Police escort along the motorway. On another occasion a driver was given a ticking-off by management for allegedly 'wearing out' a new set of tyres by struggling to get a bus up the Trimsaran Mountain into Llanelli. This was before the days of salt spreading on our roads – the only assistance then would be a shovel and loose gravel. Normally, if conditions were so bad, the drivers would make a detour through Pembrey and Burry Port. However, Eynon's were noted for keeping going after the rest had stopped.

In 1983, a close association was formed with West Wales Motors Ltd, of Tycroes, at a time when they were also experiencing financial difficulties. The connection was initially made through Eynon's fleet engineer, and exchanging of vehicles soon became commonplace. It all started in April 1983 when Eynon's swapped two Leyland 'Titan' double-deckers' for West Wales' Leyland 'Tiger Cubs' YTE 952D / LBX 550G and Leyland 'Leopard' EPT615G. Apart from the exchanges with West Wales, there was still very little movement of second-hand stock, but they did buy five more deckers which included another Leyland 'Atlantean' FUS 168L from Strathclyde PTE, formerly Greater Glasgow PTE.

However, with financial assistance from a local businessman, Eynon's were able to purchase another new coach in May 1983. This was another 'first' for the establishment, the first DAF chassis and first LAG coachwork. Registered PBX 280Y it was a DAF MB200DKFL600 with Belgian built LAG 'Galaxy' C53F body supplied by Yeates of Loughborough, taking AEC 'Reliance' OAY 393P in exchange. Nine months later OAY 393P was re-acquired from Yeates.

Above: This Leyland 'Leopard' PSU3/3R, **JRC 254D** originated from the fleet of Trent Motor Services, and was bodied by Metro-Cammell on a Weymann shell to DP51F layout. It was acquired in June 1982 from Dean Forest Coaches, Joys Green, Gloucestershire, and was withdrawn in March 1984 after an accident. *(V. Morgan).*

Above: **WYB 741H** was another coach owned by the fleet engineer, and again operated on lease to Eynon's from June 1982 to April 1984. It was a 1969 AEC 'Reliance' 6U3ZR with Duple 'Commander IV' C51F body acquired in June 1982 from the same source as JRC 254D above - Dean Forest Coaches, Joys Green. Buy one get the second one at half price perhaps. *(V. Morgan).*

Above: Originally new to Ribble MS (599), **ARN 599C** was one of a pair of Leyland 'Leopard' PSU3/1R's with Weymann B53F bodies acquired from Waddon, Caerphilly in November 1982. The other one ARN 605C was used for spares.
(V. Morgan).

Above: Former Brighton CT, **DCD 19C** was a very tidy 1965 Leyland 'Titan' PD2/37 with Weymann H37/27F body acquired from Wood (Verwood Transport) Verwood, Dorset in December 1982. Surprisingly the fleet engineer sold it to West Wales Motors, Tycroes in exchange for two 'Tiger Cubs' and a 'Leopard'

Above: The driver of this former Bournemouth Corporation Leyland 'Atlantean' **HEL 203D** had total disregard to the law and the safety of his passengers – school children from Ysgol Gyfan Y Strade returning home to Trimsaran. This view taken at Denham Avenue, Llanelli on 12th July 1983 clearly shows the entrance doors wide open – a serious offence that doesn't bear thinking about especially whilst carrying children, and there are no prizes for spotting the driver smoking whilst driving a PSV (PCV) – another offence. A third offence, not wearing a PSV drivers' badge. This discerning driver should have had the competence to respect the safety of everyone - as he was after all the company's fleet engineer!

Left: A Road Fund Licence disc (Tax disc) from the Leyland 'Atlantean' pictured above: **HEL 203D**. The cost for six months duty in 1986/7 was £60.05. Road fund licence discs are now an item of a by-gone era.

As we have seen, back in 1979 the Eynon's management had stated that they wouldn't buy any more rear engine vehicles because of the problems they experienced with their Mk I 'Atlanteans' from Greater Glasgow PTE. However, **HEL 203D** was a Mk I 'Atlantean' PDR1/1 with Metro-Cammell H43/31F body, new in September 1966 to Bournemouth CT (203); to Thomas, Clydach Vale (Rhondda) 5/81; to Waddon, Caerphilly 9/82; to Eynon's, Trimsaran 11/82; to Davies Bros (Pencader) Ltd, 6/88 withdrawn 2/89, cannibalised and the remains to Wacton Bus (dealer) Bromyard for scrap 14/4/1990. Twenty-three years of service is not bad I would say!

Above: Captured here at the depot displaying destination boards for their newest 'subsidised' service: Tumble to Burry Port via Pontyates, in January 1984 is **YTE 952D** a 1966 Leyland 'Tiger Cub' PSUC1/12 with a rare Massey B45F body – only 17 'Tiger Cubs' were bodied by Massey Bros. First licenced in January 1967 to J Fishwick & Sons Ltd, Leyland, Lancashire, it arrived at Trimsaran in April 1983 from West Wales Motors of Tycroes, in exchange for a Leyland 'Titan'.

Above: **LBX 550G** was another Leyland 'Tiger Cub' PSUC1/12T taken in exchange for a Leyland 'Titan' from West Wales Motors (59) in April 1983. This had been West Wales' first 'Grant Aided' vehicle in April 1969, fitted with a Willowbrook DP45F body, and was one of the last Leyland 'Tiger Cubs' built for the home market in 1969. The two speed axle was fitted by West Wales Motors themselves. I took this photograph on 27th October 1985. *(V. Morgan).*

Above: **LSY 140J** was another Ford R192 with Plaxton 'Panorama Elite II' coachwork which the chief engineer purchased for his own collection in February 1983. It came from the same stable as Eynon's former Brighton 'Titan' DCD 19C purchased two months earlier. The engineer again, leased this coach to Eynon's for two years. *(V. Morgan).*

Above: This 1969 Leyland 'Leopard' PSU3/3R with Plaxton 'Derwent' B55F body, **EPT 615G** was the third of three single decker Leylands received from West Wales Motors of Tycroes in April 1983, in exchange for double decker Leyland 'Titans'. **EPT 615G** had been new in July 1969 to Summerson, West Auckland, Co Durham. It operated with Eynon until November 1986, when it had engine failure, and was sold for scrap in February 1988. This view was taken on 26th November 1983. *(V. Morgan).*

Above left: **EWS 804D** a former Lothian Regional Transport, Leyland 'Atlantean' PDR1/1 with Alexander H43/31F body was acquired in May 1983 but not operated. It was quickly sold on to West Wales Motors together with **ASC 654B (right)** a 1964 Leyland 'Titan' PD3/6 with Alexander H41/29F body, new to Edinburgh (Lothian RT) which had been acquired from Hewlett & Sutton, Morecambe in May 1983. **ASC 654B** with a Midland Red style front grille operated very briefly with Eynon's before its combined exchange for a 'Leopard' with West Wales Motors of Tycroes in June 1983 where it operated for just two months only in West Wales' livery. It was exchanged for a Leyland 'Atlantean'. *(V. Morgan).*

Above: Another former Lothian Leyland PD3/6 acquired from Hewlett & Sutton, Morecambe in May 1983 was **ASC 659B** seen here at the depot on 23rd October 1983. New to Edinburgh (659) in July 1964, it had a Midland Red style front grille fitted to its Alexander E type body, built to H41/29F layout. It was sold after just eleven months use to J. Sykes, Barnsley for scrap in April 1984. *(V. Morgan).*

Above: Another faithful old servant in the Eynon's fleet was **KTJ 205C**, a Leyland 'Titan' PD2/37 with East Lancs H37/28F body purchased off Hewlett & Sutton, Morecambe in May 1983. It passed with Eynon's business to Davies Bros who immediately withdrew it in July 1988, when 23 years old. I took this view on 24th January 1988, capturing the damaged roof dome – a common sight on Eynon's deckers due to their operating terrain through Stradey woods on the B4308 road. *(V. Morgan).*

Above: This former Southdown Motor Services 1965 Leyland 'Leopard' PSU3/1R, **BUF 133C** with a Marshall B53F body was 19 years old when I photographed it here at Old Castle Rd, Llanelli on 20th April 1984. Despite its age, it was still working hard on the tortuous former Western Welsh 401 service between Llanelli and Carmarthen via Pontyberem. *(V. Morgan).*

Above: The 'first' and only DAF in the Eynon's stable was **PBX 280Y** seen here when new. It was a DAF MB200DKFL600 with Belgian built LAG 'Galaxy' C53F coachwork, without a toilet. Eynon's had a penchant for exotic styling and despite their difficulties went ahead and bought this impressive coach in June 1983. *(V. Morgan).*

Above: A rear end view of the LAG 'Galaxy' bodied DAF - **PBX 280Y**, show off its modern styling and the different style of lettering it carried. It was the only vehicle in the fleet to be sign-written with this type of lettering – not very impressive without capital letters. This coach passed to Davies Bros with the Eynon's business in June 1988, but was quickly replaced with a new Leyland 'Tiger' on 1st August 1988. *(V. Morgan).*

Above: Eynon's accepted this Leyland 'Leopard' PSU3A/4R, **DGC 114H** in exchange for Leyland 'Atlantean' EWS 804D and Leyland 'Titan' ASC 654B from West Wales Motors, in a deal struck up by the fleet engineer in June 1983. The Leopard dating from July 1970, with Plaxton 'Panorama Elite I' C53F body was not built to the 'New Bus Grant' specification, and remained in West Wales' livery complete with fleet number throughout its 14 month stay here, as seen on 21/8/1983.
(V. Morgan).

Above: Surprisingly, Eynon's bought two more former Gtr. Glasgow Leyland 'Atlanteans' *after* their bad experience with earlier Mk I's from Glasgow. However, this 1973 Glasgow Mk II 'Atlantean' AN68/1R; **FUS 168L** with Alexander H45/29F body acquired via Strathclyde PTE in July 1983 was a far better vehicle. It's seen here on 11/10/1987 after a repaint into Eynon's 70th anniversary livery, and was finally withdrawn by their successors Davies Bros (Pencader) Ltd in June 1989.

In the meantime, the busy Saturday's only 'London Express' service had been modified to run on Tuesdays and Saturdays throughout the year, and when the company included Thursdays into their London service, National Express challenged them with a *daily* service Llanelli to London running exactly 1 hour in front of Eynon's in both directions. (See advert below).

GOING TO HEATHROW OR LONDON —
GO NATIONAL EXPRESS

RAPIDE COACH TO LONDON

STARTS FROM LLANELLI
ON MONDAY 19th SEPTEMBER 1983

Every Weekday at 5.50 am arriving London 10.00 am
Returning from London at 5.00 pm arriving Llanelli 9.10 pm

In August 1983, the South Wales Transport Co, made further service cuts when they altered their service 102, Swansea – Cross hands – Llanelli route to operate Swansea – Cross Hands – Carmarthen instead. They abandoned a part of the service which ran through the Gwendraeth Valley from Tumble to Pontyates, and onward to Llanelli. The local authority, Dyfed CC quickly re-organised the abandoned service and Eynon's successfully tendered for it. The new service from Tumble Hotel to Pontyates (Station) was incorporated into Eynon's existing service (TGR 311/17) Pontyates (Station) to Burry Port (Station) forming a through service once more from Tumble to Burry Port. The through service which commenced on 30th August-

SAMUEL EYNON & SONS

Public Passenger Operators and Coach Proprietors

Bryn Villa Garage, TRIMSARAN, KIDWELLY, Dyfed.

Telephones:
TRIMSARAN
810244
and
810385

BURRY PORT (Station)......				7.50					5.15	
TRIMSARAN (Bird-in-Hand)..	6.30	7.05	8.15	8.10	10.35	12.35	2.35	4.50	5.35	6.05
CARWAY..................	[illegible]	7.10	8.20	8.15	10.40	12.40	2.40	4.55	5.40	6.10
PONTYATES (Station).......	6.40	7.15		8.20			2.45		5.45	
PONTYBEREM (Square).......	6.45			8.30	S.D.O.		2.55	S.D.O.		
TUMBLE (Hotel)............				8.45			3.10			

TUMBLE (Hotel)............			9.00			3.20				
PONTYBEREM (Square).......			9.15	S.D.O.		3.35	S.D.O.			6.30
PONTYATES (Station).......	7.15		9.20			3.45		4.45		6.35
CARWAY..................	7.20	8.20	9.30	10.50	12.50	3.50	4.55	4.50	6.10	6.40
TRIMSARAN (Bird-in-Hand)..	7.25	8.25	9.35	10.55	12.55	3.50	5.00	4.55	6.15	6.45
BURRY PORT (Station)......	7.45							5.15		

Mondays to Saturdays

S.D.O. = SCHOOLDAYS ONLY.

EFFECTIVE FROM 30 AUGUST 1983

The Proprietors will make every effort to maintain the services detailed herewith but do not hold themselves responsible for delay from any cause whatsoever. Parcels at owner's risk.

-1983 was numbered 195 in the Dyfed CC series of route numbers which had been introduced in 1981. Route numbers were not a mandatory requirement at this period in time so were not displayed by Eynons – not even on their time-tables.

1983 saw the end of the Avon Inflatables workers service, which resulted in the surrender of four licences, and a year later in March 1984, it was the beginning of a year-long miner's strike. The miner's strike affected every business imaginable in the South Wales Coalfield. Eynon's were affected by withdrawal of their colliery contract combined with loss of revenue on local services and tours due to lack of patronage. At the same time the governments 'New Bus Grant' scheme finally came to an end under the Tory Government.

However, in a desperate attempt to keep their image, the company ordered another new coach for delivery at the start of the 1984 tours programme, but were unable to get finance. Alternatively, an arrangement was made between the management and the company's fleet engineer, whereby two AEC 'Reliances' BTH 364/5V were re-financed in his name to raise capital. This money, together with another AEC 'Reliance' XBX 830T as part exchange, paid for the new coach registered A802 XEP, a Leyland 'Tiger' TRCTL11/3R with LAG 'Galaxy' C53F body. It arrived from Yeates the dealer on 29th June 1984, and was sadly the last new Leyland and last new vehicle Eynon's purchased.

At around the same time, West Wales Motors were on the brink of liquidation and a rescue plan was partially arranged by Eynon's fleet engineer to help West Wales overcome their problem. It was stated that West Wales were to sell their premises to Joe Sykes the Barnsley bus dealer in order for him to have a South Wales base, and to re-locate the West Wales fleet at Eynon's depot in Trimsaran. However, in the meantime the West Wales Motors business was purchased by Daryl Davies proprietor of 'D' Coaches, Morriston, (Swansea) on 30th June 1984. He took over the complete business together with the premises and all staff except the transport manager Myrddyn Jones. Mr Jones decided to leave and begin his own coach business in partnership with his son Meirion, trading as: 'Jones International' in August 1984. The partnership purchased their first vehicle in August 1984 and not having their own licences, a spare Eynon's licence disc was borrowed until theirs were granted in October 1984, temporarily declaring their operating centre as Bryn Villa Garage, Trimsaran.

Despite all their difficulties, the fleet engineer then made an arrangement with Joe Sykes the Barnsley bus dealer in 1984 to accept C o F expired buses down from Barnsley, overhaul them using Eynon's facilities, put them through re-certification on Eynon's 'O' licence at the Department of Transport's Ammanford testing station, and return them to Sykes for onward sale. The Department of Transport (VOSA nowadays) wouldn't allow Sykes to submit buses for certifying as he was a registered vehicle breaker and not an operator. The practice of re-certifying Sykes' buses went on for two years until the Eynon's management finally stopped it in April 1986.

Meanwhile, in July 1984 a close association was formed with Emyr W. Phillips, a new travel agent at Burry Port who had taken over an existing travel business known as 'Pembrey Travel'. Pembrey Travel hired Eynon's coaches for most of their travel requirements and consequently became a booking agent for Eynon's advertised tours and London service.

Above: **PBC 108G** was another Leyland 'Atlantean' PDR1A/1 (Mk I) and fitted with a Park Royal H43/31F body. New to Leicester CT (108) in April 1969, it arrived at Eynon's in February 1984, and put directly into service still in Leicester livery as seen here on 15th July 1984. It remained in this livery until sold in August 1985 for further PSV use. *(V. Morgan).*

Above: Former Leicester CT Leyland 'Atlantean' **PBC 115G** was identical to 108 above, but was acquired via West Wales Motors (97) in March 1984 with front end accident damage. Repaired and into service a month later, it was seen here at Carmarthen on 10th October 1984 still unpainted, remaining as such until sold via dealer to S Lynch, Passage East, Ireland in August 1985, for further use – re-registered 9168 KI. *(V. Morgan).*

Above: **EMB 159K** was another Ford R226 owned by Eynon's fleet engineer. Built in 1972 it had a Plaxton 'Panorama Elite II' 53 seat body and operated on Eynon's licence from February 1984 to January 1987. *(V. Morgan).*

Above: Another former Gtr. Glasgow PTE Leyland 'Atlantean' (LA639) **FUS 159L** arrived at Trimsaran in March 1984 having worked for Queencity, Burford, Oxford in the interim period after leaving Strathclyde PTE. Bodied by Alexander (AL type) H45/29F, it was licenced in May 1984 and operated for 3 months only. After being laid up it was sold to J. Sykes, dealer in January 1986 who sold it for further PSV use in December 1988. Alongside is former Strathclyde (LA657). *(V. Morgan)*

Above: This AEC 'Reliance' **OAY 393P** was new to Eynon's in June 1976, and was part exchanged for a new DAF/LAG, PBX 280Y in May 1983. Nine months later in February 1984 it was re-acquired from the dealer; Yeates, Loughborough, but unfortunately came to a sad end on 18th September 1985 when it collided head on with Eynon's XBX 831T (See page 232). *(V. Morgan).*

Above: **DTJ 198J** was another Ford R226 owned by Eynon's fleet engineer. New in March 1971 this also had a Plaxton 'Panorama Elite II' body and operated on Eynon's licence from April 1984 to September 1985. *(V. Morgan).*

Above: Bristol chassis were not a favourite of Eynon's, yet they bought this much travelled Bristol RELH6G, **YHK 729F** off West Wales Motors in March 1984. Bodied by ECW as a 47 seat coach, it was new to Tillings, Chelmsford (T442) in April 1968. West Wales purchased it in December 1983, and fitted it with 53 bus seats before licensing it in February 1984. This view was taken on 24th April 1984, after passing to Eynon's in March 1984. *(V. Morgan).*

Above: This former Southdown Motor Services (1423) Ford R1114, **PUF 263M** with Duple 'Dominant' C49F body, was owned by the fleet engineer at Eynon's. New to Southdown in July 1974, it had latterly operated for Wimpy the National contractor. It operated on Eynon's licence during its short stay at Trimsaran, from April to June 1984; when it passed to Minnard of Aberfan. This view was taken on 23rd May 1984 at Heol Waun-y-clun, Trimsaran. *(V. Morgan).*

Above: **MBX 86H** was built to the order of Eynon's under the 'New Bus Grant' scheme in 1969. Originally registered LBX 547G, delivery of this Leyland 'Leopard' PSU3/3RT with Willowbrook B49F body was not accepted. It eventually passed to West Wales Motors at Tycroes in October 1969, re-painted into their livery and re-registered MBX 86H due to the change of registration year suffix in August 1969. Several owners later it arrived at Trimsaran in May 1984 from James, Llangeitho (Cardiganshire). Withdrawn in February 1988, it was stripped of useful spares and sold for scrap. It is captured here leaving Carmarthen Bus Station on 13th June 1984, (before redevelopment) on a journey to Llanelli.
(V. Morgan).

Above: New to Ribble Motor Services (953) in May 1969, this rather tired looking **HRN 953G** was a Leyland 'Leopard' PSU3A/4R with Plaxton 'Panorama Elite I' C49F body, and was purchased in May 1984 from a St. Albans operator. Licenced in June 1984, it was withdrawn with engine failure in October 1984 and sold for scrap August 1985. *(V. Morgan)*

Above: After purchasing their first LAG 'Galaxy' bodied coach a year earlier, the company bought a second one in 1984. Seen here outside the depot upon delivery on 29th June 1984, still displaying Eynon's garage trade plates is **A802 XEP** a Leyland 'Tiger' TRCTL11/3R with LAG 'Galaxy' C53F coachwork. Sadly, this was the last new Leyland and the last new vehicle purchased by the company. Behind the wheel is Mr. David Eynon, youngest grandson of the company's founder - Samuel Eynon. *(V. Morgan).*

Above: This near side rear view of **A802 XEP**, the company's last new vehicle, show the lines of this Belgian built coach from a different angle. Note the correct gothic style lettering on this coach compared to the lettering on the DAF / Galaxy, PBX 280Y delivered a year earlier (see page150). This Leyland 'Tiger' had the Leyland 245bhp engine coupled to a ZF synchromesh gearbox, and passed to Davies Bros (Pencader) Ltd with the business in June 1988. *(V. Morgan).*

Above: Seen here at Cardiff on 20th February 1988 is AEC 'Reliance' 6U3ZR, **WJF 378S** with Duple 'Dominant Express II' C53F body, which had been new to A.E. & F.R. Brewer, Caerau in May 1978. It was acquired from Brewer in June 1984 and received three styles of livery with Eynon's – this being the final one – the 70th anniversary livery.
WJF 378S was fitted with the AH760 engine coupled to a ZF 6 speed synchromesh gearbox. *(V. Morgan).*

Above: Another vehicle that didn't stay longer than two months was this former Southdown (1220) **EUF 220D** a 1966 Leyland 'Leopard' PSU3/3RT with Plaxton 'Panorama' C49F body. It was acquired from 'D' Coaches, Morriston in June 1984 with front end damage, repaired and briefly operated until August 1984 when it passed to a dealer for onward sale. Its new owners converted it into a racing car transporter. *(V. Morgan).*

Above: This 1970 Leyland 'Leopard' PSU4A/4R with Plaxton 'Panorama Elite I' C40F body looks rather sorry for itself here on 20th July 1984. Registered **KCK 983H** it was new to Ribble Motor Services (983) in March 1970, and arrived here at Trimsaran in June 1984 from Newton, Dingwall, Scotland. It was withdrawn in June 1985 and used for spares before the remains were sold for scrap. *(V. Morgan).*

Left: Former Strathclyde PTE (LA657), **HGD 863L** was one of three Strathclyde Leyland 'Atlantean' AN68/1R's with Alexander AL type H45/31F bodies that were brought down from Joe Sykes the Barnsley dealer in July 1984, in an arrangement with the fleet engineer, to have them overhauled and re-certified through Eynon's 'O' licence at the DoT's test centre, Ammanford. They would then be returned to the dealer for onward sale. The other two Atlanteans (LA663/5) HGD 869/71L were similarly treated, and sold on to 'D' Coaches, Morriston, without going back to Barnsley – sold by the dealer's South Wales agent who also worked at Eynon's. Sykes took one of 'D' Coaches' Leyland PD3/6's ASC 692B in part exchange, and it was actually operated by Eynon's in the interim period before its trip north to the dealer in Barnsley.

The 'Atlantean' HGD 863L (left) was sold to Verwood Transport in Dorset, another company the fleet engineer had become associated with through the purchases of DCD 19C, LSY 140J and MBX 86H. *(V. Morgan).*

Right: Numerically the second Strathclyde PTE Leyland 'Atlantean' received for re-certification in July 1984 was **HGD 869L** seen here at the depot 29th July 1984. After re-certification in September 1984, it was sold to 'D' Coaches, Morriston together with its sister, HGD 871L. *(V. Morgan).*

Below: **FBW 22K** was yet another Ford R226 with Plaxton 'Panorama Elite II' body owned by the fleet engineer. This was purchased in July 1984 from Clements of Nailsea, Bristol and operated on Eynon's licence leased from the engineer until February 1985, when it was sold for conversion into a horsebox with an unidentified owner at Crickhowell. After its conversion into a horsebox, the fleet engineer repossessed it and resold it to J Sykes, Carlton, for scrap in February 1986. *(V. Morgan).*

Above: When Weaver & Best of Tredegar ceased trading in April 1984, J Sykes the dealer bought their remaining vehicles four months later, sending **VBW 821L** this Leyland 'Leopard' PSU3B/4R, with Duple 'Dominant' C51F body to Eynon's along with the AEC 'Reliance' (below) for re-certification. VBW 821L was re-certified in November 1984, but not operated, and was ready for departure to Sykes when I took this view on 11th November 1984. *(V. Morgan).*

Above: **OCU 650J**, an AEC 'Reliance' 6U3ZR with Plaxton 'Panorama Elite II' C53F body, dating from July 1971, was the second vehicle mentioned above as received from Weaver & Best. This was re-certified in March 1985, but not operated, and returned to Joe Sykes the dealer for onward sale – to a non PSV operator in Cheshire in May 1985. *(V. Morgan).*

Above: Jones International of Llandeilo is a company founded by Myrddin Jones, the former transport manager of West Wales Motors, Tycroes in August 1984. This 1977 Leyland 'Leopard' PSU5A/4R, **RGS 92R** with 12 metre Plaxton 'Supreme' C57F body was Jones' first coach, and initially operated on a spare Eynon's licence disc until his own were issued in October 1984. He declared Eynon's as his operating centre, and RGS 92R is seen there in October 1984 after receiving its monthly inspection.

(V. Morgan).

Above: This Leyland 'Leopard' PSU3/3R, **YSC 443K** fitted with Alexander 'Y type' C49F body was new to Scottish Omnibuses (ZH 443) in May 1972. Eynon's acquired this from Kenmargra. Linthwaite, West Yorkshire in September 1984, operated it for two years, then used it for spares and the remains sold for scrap in February 1988. It's seen here at Carmarthen bus station minus destination display, working the 196 Llanelli-Pontyberem-Carmarthen service on 15th December 1984.

(V. Morgan).

Left: This former Lothian Regional Transport Leyland 'Titan' PD3/6 **ASC 692B** was operated briefly on loan in September 1984, during the interim period before its delivery to J Sykes the Barnsley dealer. Sykes had taken it in part exchange from 'D' Coaches of Morriston Swansea, for two Leyland 'Atlanteans' HGD 869/71L that had been re-certified by Eynon's, and garaged there. This 1964 Leyland 'Titan' ASC 692B was one of several former Lothian 'Titans' operated by 'D' Coaches.

Below: **HNT 841N** a 1975 Bedford YRQ with Duple 'Dominant' C45F body, previously owned by Globe Coaches, of Barnsley arrived at Trimsaran in October 1984, and was another vehicle re-certified on behalf of the Barnsley dealer Joe Sykes. It was licenced in February 1985 but not operated. It passed to another dealer in February 1985 for export to Malta in May 1985, where it was re-registered EBY593.

(V. Morgan).

Above: Formerly Alexander Northern (NT 71), **WRS 671L** looked very much like a 'Heavyweight' vehicle but in fact was a 'Lightweight' Ford R1114 with Alexander 'Y type' B53F body new in June 1973. It arrived here in November 1984, and was re-certified on Eynon's 'O' licence in May 1985, returning to J Sykes in June 1985 for onward sale back to Scotland; to Irvine of Law, Strathclyde in July 1985. *(V. Morgan).*

Above: Another Scottish vehicle to migrate south was **RRG 348N,** this Ford R1014 with Duple 'Dominant' C45F body which came to Trimsaran in November 1984 from Alexander Northern (NT 77). Although re-painted in Eynon's livery, it was owned by the fleet engineer who leased it to Eynon's until January 1987. This view was taken on 3rd Nov. 1985. *(V. Morgan).*

Above: Another 'oddball' in the fleet was this 1971 Seddon 'Pennine 4' fitted with a Perkins V8 engine. Registered **URO856J**, it had a Plaxton 'Panorama Elite II' C49F body, and was acquired from Dragon, Stocksbridge, South Yorks in March 1985. It saw three months service and was sold to a local scrap merchant in January 1986. This photograph was taken on 24th March 1985. *(V. Morgan).*

Above: **BAA 884J** was a 1971 Ford R226 with Duple 'Viceroy' C53F body, owned by the fleet engineer. It came from Finchley Coaches, London N12 in April 1985, and was leased to Eynon's until November 1985. It's seen here at the depot alongside the 'Alexander Northern' Ford R1114, WRS 671L on 14th April 1985. *(V. Morgan).*

Above: This pair of 1973 Alexander Y-type 49 seater coaches **YSD 355/3L** were built on Leyland 'Leopard' PSU3/3R chassis, and arrived at Trimsaran in March 1985 from Highland Scottish (L40/L38) via J Sykes (dealer). They were both re-certified in June 1985 but not operated. YSD 353L was sold to 'D' Coaches, Morriston, Swansea, in June 1985 without returning to Sykes, but YSD 355L returned to Sykes for onward sale in June 1985. *(V. Morgan).*

Above: In April 1985 Eynon's acquired **CNY 333V,** a Ford R1114 with Caetano 'Alfa' C53F coachwork, ready for the summer tours programme. It had been new to Thomas, Clydach Vale in November 1979, but had latterly operated for Thorpe, London W10. It was found to be rather slow carrying this heavy coachwork, and throughout its short stay remained in this livery. After its return to the dealer in December 1985, it passed to J Pace (Unscheduled Bus Co.) Bkara, Malta, in February 1986 (re-registered Y-0851, later KCY 851). *(V. Morgan).*

Above: This Leyland 'Tiger' TRCTL11/3R, registered **FNM 861Y**, fitted with Plaxton 'Paramount 3200' C57F coachwork was a dealer loan from May to July 1985, to cover a vehicle shortage due to the failure of a reconditioned engine in one of the company's AEC Reliances. This view was taken on 2nd June 1985. *(V. Morgan).*

Above: **RLJ 89X** was a Leyland 'Leopard' PSU3F/5R with Plaxton 'Supreme IV' C53F coachwork, which had been new to Marchwood Motorways of Totton, Southampton in October 1981. This again only stayed in the fleet from June to December 1985, remaining in the Marchwood livery as seen here on 14th July 1985. *(V. Morgan).*

Above: New in January 1962 to Lancaster CT (102) as 102 UTF, this Leyland 'Leopard' L1 with East Lancs B42D body was re-registered **ACA 297A** by its subsequent owner; Hollis of Queensferry, Clwyd. Eynon's acquired this in June 1985, and it could often be seen working the Dyfed CC tendered service, 195 Tumble to Burry Port. It was withdrawn in February 1986 - when I took this view, and was sold for scrap in February 1988. *(V. Morgan).*

Above: Eynon's fleet engineer acquired **HSF 555N**, this Ford R1014 with Duple 'Dominant Express' C45F body in June 1985 from Alexander Northern (NT 199) for his own fleet but leased it to Eynon's in their livery. New in February 1975, it ran on Eynon's licences from August 1985 to January 1987, when it was returned to the lessor. *(V. Morgan)*

Above: New to Creamline of Tonmawr, West Glamorgan in April 1969 was this Leyland 'Leopard' PSU3A/4R with Plaxton 'Panorama Elite I' C53F body registered **VNY 468G.** It was acquired by Eynon's in August 1985 a short while before Creamline's demise in January 1987. It operated in three different liveries at Trimsaran, and operated the historic last Eynon's journey on the legendary Llanelli - Trimsaran route in June 1988 (see page 193) before transfer to Davies Bros. *(V. Morgan).*

Above: Acquired from Burman, Cradley Heath, Hereford & Worcester, in September 1985 was **RVB 995E**, an ageing 1967 Leyland 'Leopard' PSU3/3R with Plaxton 'Panorama I' C51F body, which saw just nine months service. *(V. Morgan).*

Above: The last 'lightweight' vehicle purchased by the company was **JRB 188N** a Bedford YRT with Duple 'Dominant' C53F body which had been new in June 1975 to Wright of Newark. It had latterly operated with the National Coal Board, where it had been used for staff transport during the famous 'Miner's Strike' 1984/5. Eynon's acquired this well-worn coach in September 1985, and the interior took several days to clean. It operated in three different liveries before passing to Davies Bros, with the business. Dewi Davies sold it within a couple of weeks for scrap. *(V. Morgan).*

Above: Another vehicle to join the motley collection owned by Eynon's fleet engineer was **YUR 995K** a 1971 Ford R226 with Caetano 'Estoril' C53F body. The engineer acquired it from Rhyce-Rees & Clarke, Cliftonville, Bristol, in September 1985, leasing it to Eynon's from October 1985 to January 1987. It was later sold to an unknown Pontyates owner, and converted into a car transporter. Last seen at Blackgang Chine, Isle of Wight - for sale in August 1988. *(V. Morgan).*

Above: KHY 18X this eleven seat non PSV Toyota Hi-ace mini-bus was also operated by Eynon's. It was used mainly as a runabout vehicle, but also operated a workers contract from Carway to the GTS Factory at Pembrey.

On 18th September 1985, two of Eynon's AEC 'Reliances' were badly damaged in a head-on collision with each other at Cwmbach (Stradey Woods) on the main B4308 Trimsaran-Llanelli road. Twenty passengers were injured together with the drivers of both vehicles, one receiving hospitalisation. This notorious road was blocked for several hours that day, and the damage to 'Reliance' OAY 393P was deemed to be beyond economical repair and subsequently written off, the other 'Reliance' XBX 831T was sent to Moseley for extensive repair which took five months and wasn't operated after its return in February 1986. It was sold to a dealer a month later.

A photograph of the damage to OAY 393P can be seen on page 232.

Above: Captured here on 15th December 1985, still in its National Coal Board livery is **OKU 690R** a Willowbrook B49F bodied Bedford YLQ which was new in December 1976 to the National Coal Board, at Barnsley. It had latterly operated for the N C B at Barnsley Main, and was re-certified here in South Wales by Eynon's staff on behalf of J Sykes the Barnsley dealer. It's seen here in this view about to depart to Joe Sykes at Barnsley, and onward sale to a new owner. Behind the bus is my trusty old Morris Minor 1000, 951 ATH. *(V. Morgan).*

Above: Purchased from Thomas Bros, Llangadog, Carmarthenshire in October 1985 was **ACY 119A**, which had previously been registered VWG 383. It was a 1963 Leyland 'Tiger Cub' PSUC1/12 with Alexander 'Y' type C41F body, which was new to Alexander Midland (MPD 244) in May 1963, before passing to Thomas Brothers in January 1979. First licenced by Eynon's in April 1986, it was withdrawn and sold for scrap in February 1988. *(V. Morgan).*

Above: This 1972 Leyland 'Leopard' PSU3/3R with Alexander 'Y' type B53F body, **BWG 838L** also came from Alexander Midland (MPE 138) in October 1985. Although, this one only came to Trimsaran for re-certification on behalf of Joe Sykes the dealer, it wasn't overhauled and re-certified on Eynon's operator's licence until January 1986. *(V. Morgan).*

Above: **TVA 481M** was a 1974 AEC 'Reliance' 6U3ZR with Plaxton 'Panorama Elite III' C51F body, previously operated by Bleanch. Hetton-Le-Hole, Tyne & Wear, which also arrived from Sykes the dealer in October 1985 for re-certification. This was to be the *last* vehicle re-certified on behalf of Sykes in May 1986, as the management finally put an end to the practice!

Above: This ageing AEC 'Reliance' 8U2R with Plaxton 'Panorama I' C53F body, **LVO 93E** arrived from Bannister, Owston Ferry in January 1986, and operated for fourteen months. It had been new to Barton, Chilwell, Notts (1093) in June 1967.

Right: This former Leicester C T Leyland 'Titan' PD3A/1 isn't what it appears to be. Although it carried the registration plate of **78 HBC** it was actually **92 HBC** (chassis no L03019) masquerading as 78 HBC. At some unknown point in its working life the registration plates had been switched.
It had been purchased by Eynon's fleet engineer from the dealer J Sykes, Carlton in March 1986, and had latterly operated with the Swansea R T I T B (NPSV) as a driver trainer. It was not operated at Trimsaran but resold to Sykes in April 1986 for onward sale to a waiting buyer – a film company, where it was used in a film set and completely burned out.
My brother Trevor who was employed as a fitter by Eynon's, was sent to Carlton (Barnsley) by the fleet engineer to collect this vehicle on his behalf. Not having an operational fuel gauge it ran out of fuel on the M4 Motorway near Newport some 70 miles from Trimsaran. After calling for assistance via the Motorway call box, a colleague Noel arrived some considerable time later-after dark, with fuel but forgot to bring an inspection light. They bled the fuel system using the light of a cigarette lighter!
(V. Morgan).

Above: Another 'oddball' in the fleet was this 1976 Gardner 6HLXB powered Seddon 'Pennine 7' with Alexander 'T' type C49F 'Grant Aided' 11 metre body. Registered **MSJ 379P**, it arrived from Thomas of Barry in June 1986, and was new to Western SMT (2573). It's captured here immediately after repaint into Eynon's 70th anniversary livery on 30th August 1987.

Above: This former Ribble Motor Services (1648) **NCK 637**, a 1960 Leyland 'Atlantean' PDR1/1R with Metro-Cammell H44/34F body was owned by Eynon's fleet engineer E J Roberts, and was purchased in August 1986 to work his own school contract. It operated on a borrowed Eynon's licence disc until his own licences were issued in October 1986. *(V. Morgan).*

Above: Pictured here on 23rd April 1988 is **GBX 57N** a Bedford CFS with petrol engine and a 12 seat PSV conversion by Dormobile. Eynon's purchased this in November 1986 from Jones Motors of Login, Carmarthenshire where it was new in October 1974. The unusual style of Eynon's 70th anniversary livery certainly doesn't go amiss on this mini-bus. *(V. Morgan).*

As mentioned earlier, the management finally stopped their engineer re-certifying Joe Sykes' buses on Eynon's 'O' licence in April 1986, and immediately afterwards he applied for his own operator's licence. His licence was granted in June 1986 on PG/6280/SN; E J Roberts T/A Tommy Roberts & Son, Meinciau, Kidwelly. Operating his vehicles from Eynon's premises at Trimsaran he then applied to the local authority Dyfed County Council for his own school contracts. The contracts were awarded to him in August 1986 ready for the new academic year beginning 1st September 1986.

This again didn't bode too well with the Eynon's partnership as it was encroaching on their work, competing directly against them and operating from their premises.

If all this were not enough, Dyfed C C implemented the 1985 Road Traffic Act and brought in deregulation two months early on 31st August 1986 to coincide with the new school year, issuing new school contracts and new tendered local services.

Having said that, the transition into deregulation actually began on 6th January 1986, with various provisions of the Act coming into force on that day, as shown below:

1 The term 'stage carriage service' changed to 'local service'.
2 Road Service Licences were required *only* for 'Local Service'.
3 Requirement to notify 'Express Services' abolished.
4 The term 'Express Carriage' abolished.

From 1st March 1986, the layout of 'Local Service Registration' changed to a different format throughout the country. Basically, the 'South Wales Traffic Area' operator reference number changed from a TGR prefix to a PG prefix as follows:

PG/0809/311	Previously TGR 311/1 Registered 27/3/1986	Llanelli (Town Hall) to Carmarthen (Bus station) via: Trimsaran. D/Deck operation.
PG/0810/311	Previously TGR 311/15 Registered 27/3/1986	Llanelli (Town Hall) to Carmarthen (Bus station) via: Pontyberem. S/Deck operation.
PG/0811/311	Previously TGR 311/17 Registered 27/3/1986	Burry Port (Station) to Tumble (Hotel) via: Pontyates. D/Deck operation.

Deregulation unfortunately brought about additional problems for the company. Competitor South Wales Transport registered a 'new' service 130, Llanelli to Carmarthen via Trimsaran, Carway and Pontyates, directly challenging Eynon's on their Trimsaran route with cheaper fares and running five minutes in front of them. That service commenced on 1st September 1986, using brand new Mercedes-Benz L608D mini-buses with the branding 'Sosban Link'. SWT had 'legally' diverted their commercially operated 130 service (Llanelli - Five Roads - Pontyates to Carmarthen) via Trimsaran and Carway, abandoning the communities of Maengwynne, Five Roads, Cynheidre and the Llanelli side of Pontyates. At the same time, the 184 Llanelli – Maengwynne service was abandoned, and the 173/174 Llanelli – Burry Port – Kidwelly service was curtailed at Pembrey (Trenel), completely abandoning a section of service from Pembrey to Kidwelly, together with two early morning 173/174 journeys from Llanelli to Trenel. Fortunately, Kidwelly residents were still reliably served by **Eynon's** buses for journeys to Llanelli (via Trimsaran B4308) and to Carmarthen (via A484). The Carmarthen service twenty year's earlier had been jointly operated between Eynon's and SWT.

After SWT had given the obligatory notice of withdrawal of services 173, 174, 184 and deviation of service 130, the local authority invited operators to tender for the withdrawn SWT services. Eynon's successfully tendered for the former 130 route which had to be renumbered 131 not to clash with SWT's service. It operated Llanelli – Five Roads – Pontyates – Ponthenry to Meinciau, with just one journey daily extending to Carmarthen, and was registered as:

PG/5112/311 Llanelli (Town Hall) to Carmarthen (Bus station) via Pontyates. No. 131
D/Deck operation, Monday – Saturday.

The subsidy on the 131 service which commenced on 1st September 1986 worked out at £90.00 per day, and at the time Eynon's stated that the subsidy was sufficient to run an empty bus all day, any passengers they carried would be their bonus. They also successfully tendered for the two early morning journeys on service 173/4 Llanelli – Pembrey (Trenel), which commenced on 1st September 1986, registered as:

PG/5113/311 Llanelli (Bus Station) to Pembrey (Trenel). No. 173/174
D/Deck operation, Monday – Saturday.

The third County Council supported service which Eynon's began operating on 1st September 1986 was a schools 'local service' starting from Felinfoel (Panteg) via Llanelli (Town Hall) to Graig Comprehensive School in Pwll. This service was registered as:

PG/5114/311 Llanelli (Panteg) to Graig Comprehensive School. No. 273
D/Deck operation, schooldays only.

After just six weeks of operation, that route was extended to start at Swansea Castle Roundabout (Swansea Road) Llanelli, and operated via Andrew Street Corporation Avenue, Felinfoel Road, Town Hall Square and West End.

The abandoned part of South Wales Transport's 173/174 Kidwelly to Trenel service was also taken over after a three month absence - with local authority funding on 1st December 1986. This service was given a new route number – 269 not to clash with the SWT 173/4 service, as the new Eynon's 269 service was modified to extend beyond Trenel to terminate at Burry Port (Railway Station), incorporating part of Eynon's 195 service, Burry Port to Tumble. The section of 195 service incorporated into the new 269 service was Burry Port (Railway Station) to Pembrey (Butchers Arms). Furthermore, the 269 service was timed to make connections at Kidwelly (Borough Offices) with Eynon's 199 service northward to Carmarthen and/or eastward to Trimsaran – an alternative means of travelling from Burry Port to Trimsaran. This particular local service registration read:

PG/5643/0311 Kidwelly (Castle) to Burry Port (Railway Station). No. 269
D/Deck operation, starting 1/12/86, Mondays to Saturdays, five journeys per day except bank holidays.

POACHING CLAIM

A family-owned bus company which has run the Llanelli-Trimsaran route since 1920 has hit out at South Wales Transport for poaching customers with their new Sosban Link mini-buses.

The S.W.T. buses are picking up passengers five minutes before the Eynon's service arrives, both to and from Llanelli.

Now Eynon's, a business of 69 years' standing, are having to count the cost of lost customers and are waiting until the end of the month before deciding their next move.

"But we are definitely not going to stop our service," stressed trustee, Mr. David Lodwick. "It is costing us money though, we are losing passengers. When our buses arrive most people have been picked up."

LUCRATIVE

S.W.T., however, said that under last year's Transport Act, they have been left with no choice but to provide an efficient and commercial organisation, so their new plans have included the lucrative Trimsaran run.

It is the first time since the 1930s that Eynon's, which employ 35 full-time workers, have had any competition on the route. Both companies are charging passengers 50p. each way.

Under the new Act, bus companies had to register the routes they intended covering and Mr. Lodwick said it came as a complete shock to discover S.W.T. planned the Trimsaran service.

They have also started a seven-bus-a-day Carway service, a route which Eynon's have also run for years, although with fewer buses.

Eynon's with a fleet of 30 buses, have now bowed out completely from that, concemtrating instead on a Carmarthen run through Five Roads which S.W.T. have given up.

'DISAPPOINTING'

It is the Trimsaran service, however, which is causing sparks to fly.

"They are poaching our customers by being five minutes ahead of us," said Mr. Lodwick. "It is very disappointing, we have always had a good relationship with S.W.T. but they are refusing to even change their time-table. We are very shocked by it all."

He admitted, however, that his old Carway customers were getting a better service with the new mini-buses.

Area Manager for S.W.T. Dyfed, Mr. Geraint Humphries, explained the Trimsaran time-table had not been made to poach passengers but was merely following the same times as the Carmarthen route through Five Roads that they recently stopped.

COMMERCIAL

"We have had to become a fully commercial organisation. I'm aware that Eynon's have been operating the Trimsaran route for many years.

"However, one criticism of the Transport Act was that some routes would be without a service and others have two or more. I am responsible for trying to safeguard the jobs of my 60 to 70 employees."

There had been teething troubles with Sosban Link generally, he went on, with congestion problems in Market-street as buses arrived in the town centre. But passengers were enthusiastic about the service, especially those living in Carway.

During all this 'deregulation' controversy, senior business partner James Maurice Eynon (Jim) became very ill and sadly passed away in November 1986, leaving his share of the business to his son David Eynon, who also worked in the business. Jim, the youngest son of the founder had been an active partner in the business until his passing at the age of 79, and had driven the company's first charabanc at the age of 17 when he received his first driving licence.

However, in an effort to save the floundering company, just days after celebrating New Year 1987, partner Thomas-John Eynon (grandson of the founder) made a visit to Hills Coaches at Tredegar and bought four second-hand Leyland 'Leopards' which were delivered to Trimsaran by Hills' staff on 7th January 1987. After the arrival of these Leylands UCK 500, PUF 173H, PUF 174H and FWO 153L, the fleet engineer's four 'hired' vehicles were returned to him, and in a rage he immediately left the premises taking *all* his buses with him including Eynon's two AEC 'Reliances' BTH 364/5V which as mentioned earlier were re-financed using his name. Shortly afterwards he sold both AEC's without even using them. Losing these AEC's left Eynon's two vehicles short to fulfil their peak vehicle requirements, resulting in another visit to Hills in March 1987 to purchase two more 'Leopards' PUF 163H and GAX 355L.

Soon after the fleet engineer's hasty departure from the establishment, there was an unexpected visit from the Department of Transport's vehicle examiners, who carried out a full fleet check issuing several prohibition notices. This highlighted the poor maintenance carried out by the former engineer, resulting in vehicles put off the road until they were re-certified, and a public inquiry. The company's loyal garage staff worked all through the night in order to get the vehicles concerned re-certified the following day at the D o T's Ammanford testing station.

Immediately after this issue management had to engage a new garage foreman, and my younger brother Trevor Morgan, a company employee was given the position, directly responsible for all maintenance and repair issues at Eynon's garage together with all clerical issues involving engineering. Trevor then set about a new image for the fleet, and as it was the company's seventieth anniversary, repainted the buses into a smart revised style of livery - using the same fleet colours.

Furthermore, a company associate Mr. David Gravell had fifty vinyl seventieth anniversary transfers manufactured as a good-will gesture, to apply onto the buses in order to commemorate the historic occasion. The vinyl's read: **1917–1987 Eynon's** as shown below.

Returning to Mr E J Roberts the company's former fleet engineer, he continued to operate his fleet of eight vehicles from a temporary base at a transport yard in Pontyates from 7th January 1987, before moving to Sarn Garage, Pontyates in July 1987. Sarn Garage (next door to Pontyates fire station) which was at one time used by John Evans & Sons of Bancffosfelen to house one of their buses, then became his new operating centre.

However, by the end of January 1987 barely four weeks after leaving Eynon's employ, he became involved with a 'new' passenger vehicle operator to the area; Gower & Martin of Burry Port. The partnership R M Gower & J D Martin trading as 'Celtic Coaches (Wales)' bought two of Roberts' contracts together with three of his vehicles, and immediately commenced operating on 2nd February 1987, using Roberts' licence discs until their own six licence discs; PG/6341/SN were granted on 30th June 1987.

R M Gower concurrently operated his own separate taxi and mini-bus business at Burry Port which operated on a restricted operator licence PG/6238/R.

The Gower & Martin partnership however split up after a very short time (February 1988) with J D Martin continuing to operate Celtic Coaches alone, applying for a new operator licence in March 1988; PG/6407/SN, but still in the name of Celtic Coaches (Wales). R M Gower on the other hand continued with his taxi and mini-bus business and took on the responsibility of operating E J Roberts' remaining school contracts, using Roberts' vehicles and licences until his own licences were eventually granted in September 1989 on PG/6512/SN. Surrendering his restricted licence, Gower then purchased the remaining part of Roberts' business, together with his three vehicles and school contracts, and traded as Gower Coaches, Burry Port.

Mr Roberts surrendered his operator licence; PG/6280/SN in October 1989 – taking up the position of a South Wales agent for the bus & coach dealer Joe Sykes of Carlton, near Barnsley. The association with Joe Sykes had commenced during his vocation at Eynon's!

Above: Another former Ribble Motor Services vehicle arrived at Trimsaran in January 1987, via Hills of Tredegar. **UCK 500** was a 1964 Leyland 'Leopard' PSU3/1R with Marshall B53F body. It passed to Davies Bros (Pencader) Ltd with the business in June 1988, where it was re-registered BDE 67B. The reg. no UCK 500 was transferred to a Willowbrook 'Warrior' bodied 'Leopard'.

Above: Pictured here on 17th January 1988 is former Southdown Motor Services (473) **PUF 173H** a 1969 Leyland 'Leopard' PSU3/1R with Northern Counties DP49F body, which was acquired from Hills Tredegar in January 1987. It passed to Davies Bros (Pencader) Ltd, (181) with the business, where I had the privilege of driving it on its last ever journey, Stradey School Llanelli to Trimsaran on 27th February 1990. Withdrawn that day, it was later cannibalised and cut up on site in Nov 1990. *(V. Morgan).*

Above: **PUF 174H** was another former Southdown Leyland 'Leopard' PSU3/1R with unusual looking Northern Counties dual purpose 49 seat body acquired from Hills Tredegar in January 1987. This also passed to Davies Bros (182) with the business, but never operated on Davies Bros' licence discs as it was withdrawn (surplus to requirement) in July 1988, before the Eynon's licence discs were exchanged for Davies Bros (Pencader) Ltd, discs. It was then used for spare parts before being scrapped on site 15th March 1990. This view was also taken at the depot yard on 17th January 1988, alongside PUF 163H. *(V. Morgan).*

Above: Captured here being refuelled at the end of its shift on 3rd June 1988 is **FWO 153L** a Leyland 'Leopard' PSU4B/4R with Willowbrook B47F body, which had been new to Hills of Tredegar in September 1972. Hills bought it new with the aid of the 'Bus Grant' scheme of that period, and Eynon's acquired it from Hills in January 1987. Note the extremely high steering wheel – almost in the drivers face – it had been fitted with an incorrect steering column by Hills and was really awful to steer!
(V. Morgan).

Above: A vehicle shortage created by the former fleet engineer claiming possession of two AEC 'Reliances', led management back to Hills, Tredegar to buy two more vehicles in March 1987. One was **PUF 163H** above, another former Southdown 'Leopard' / NCME and is seen here in the sunshine of 10th January 1988, repainted into Eynon's 70th anniversary livery. After passing to Davies Bros (180) in June 1988, it was withdrawn 3 months later and broken up on 19th March 1990.

Above: New to Hills in October 1972 was **GAX 355L** a 'Grant Aided' Leyland 'Leopard' PSU3B/4R with Plaxton 'Panorama Elite Express III' C53F coachwork. It had been refurbished by Plaxton in Sept 1982 and fitted with this Supreme IV front end. Eynon's bought it in March 1987 and I photographed it here outside the former Cardiff C T tram depot on 19th March 1988 still in Hills livery. It passed to Davies Bros (176) in June 1988, where I converted it to bus seating using seats from a redundant ECW bodied Daimler Fleetline in February 1992. It was a peach to drive and I used this vehicle on schools daily thereafter for over three years until the rear end of the bodywork literally fell apart in March 1995. It was then cannibalised.

(V. Morgan).

Above: Pictured here at Carmarthen bus station on 23rd April 1987 is **SGF 483L** a very tidy Bristol RELH6L (Leyland engine) fitted with an uncommon combination of Plaxton 'Panorama Elite II' coachwork. It was new in May 1971 to Isle of Man Road Services (40) registered 40 WMN, and re-registered with this 1973 registration number on return to the mainland. Eynon's acquired this coach from Riddler, Dulverton in March 1987, and it passed to Davies Bros (178) with the business in June 1988, but remained on Eynons licence disc until sold a month later. *(V. Morgan).*

In April 1987, Eynon's purchased their last double decker bus which is seen below; a Mk II Leyland 'Atlantean' with a 76 seat Alexander AL high-bridge type body and 'Panoramic' windows from Rees & Williams of Tycroes, Carmarthenshire. This 'Atlantean' OVK 144M was a well maintained and well-kept vehicle but had a slightly bent roof! The headroom in the upper deck had been reduced by 25mm after passing under a low bridge near Tenby with only 13ft 9ins clearance, whilst working an excursion to Tenby under Rees & Williams ownership.

Above: A splendid view of an excellent vehicle. **OVK 144M**, this Leyland 'Atlantean' AN68/1R with Alexander AL type H42/34F body fitted with panoramic windows, was new to Tyneside PTE (145) in August 1973. Eynon's acquired it locally from Rees & Williams of Tycroes in April 1987. It's seen here on 1st October 1987, freshly repainted into Eynon's 70th anniversary livery. This decker passed to Davies Bros (188) with the business in June 1988 and was a nice bus to drive. I was the last Davies Bros employee to drive it before its sale to Wooley, Llanedwen, Anglesey (Gwynedd) in April 1991. The vehicle in the background is 'Leopard' HTJ 131F before it's repaint into the 70th anniversary livery. *(V. Morgan).*

However, going back to the earlier issue of January 1987 regarding the company's fleet inspection and history of bad maintenance, a public inquiry was eventually held on 17th July 1987. The Traffic Commissioner apparently took a very dim view of the company's maintenance record under the leadership of the former fleet engineer but eventually decided to grant renewal of Eynon's operator licence for a period of *one year only*, with a vehicle allocation of 2 mb, 24 sd, and 6 dd. A 'National' licence replaced the 'International' licence previously held, and a new operator number PG/6343/SN was issued in the name of - Trustees' of the estate of the late Samuel Eynon (T/A: Samuel Eynon & Sons), Bryn Villa Garage, Trimsaran. A strange title considering Samuel Eynon had died 34 years earlier. Thirty-two vehicle licence discs were still held at this point in time yet the fleet consisted of only twenty vehicles, considerably lower than in 1976-7 when there were 35 vehicles owned. The original 'International' licence PG/311/SI was surrendered on 1st August 1987, upon receipt of the new 'National' licence PG/6343/SN.

Consequently, all the 'local service' licences were renumbered as follows:

PG/809/6343	Llanelli – Trimsaran – Kidwelly – Carmarthen.
PG/810/6343	Llanelli – Felinfoel – Pontyberem – Carmarthen.
PG/811/6343	Burry Port – Tumble (Hotel).
PG/5112/6343	Llanelli – Five Roads – Pontyates – Carmarthen.
PG/5113/6343	Pembrey (Trenel) – Llanelli.
PG/5114/6343	Llanelli (Swansea Castle R/about) – Graig School.
PG/5643/6343	Kidwelly (Castle) – Burry Port (Station).

Left: This tours advertisement appeared in the Llanelli St newspaper dated 26th December 1987, promoting the Lond Express service as a London shopping trip. The price by now h slowly crept up from its original £3.00 seven years earlier b was still far cheaper than National Express' Rapide Service.

Opposite page, top left: The front cover of Eynon's ultima 'Tours & Mini-Breaks' brochure which commenced from April 1988, and included tours and mini-breaks throughout t season until October 1988. In the meantime Davies Br absorbed the business and honoured all the tours and mini-brea as per brochure. The mini-breaks were London 3 days for £ Blackpool Illuminations 5 days £75, and Paris 4 days £117.

Opposite page, top right: Is a rear cover view of the sa 'Tours & Mini-Breaks' brochure which is over stamped by t booking agent – Pembrey Travel, Burry Port.

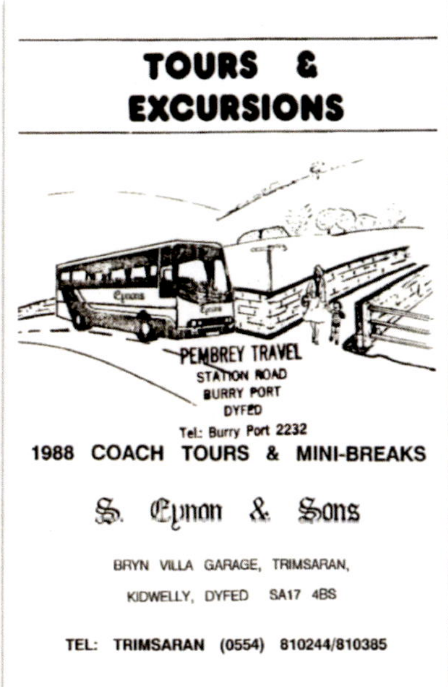

Above: This 1978 Ford Transit, **VLK 662S**, pictured here on 25th April 1988 had a 16 seat body built by Dormobile. Fitted with a petrol engine, it was purchased in November 1987 from Barrett, Great Mongham, Kent, and was used for a multitude of duties ranging from local service to private hire. It passed briefly to Davies Bros (193) in June 1988. *(V. Morgan).*

Above: **HCS 793N** this Leyland 'Leopard' PSU3/3R with Alexander 'Y type' B53F body was purchased from Scottish Bus Group Engineering in January 1988. It's captured here on 21st February 1988 operating in the livery it carried upon arrival. The repaint into Eynon's livery had commenced as Davies Bros took over, but was stopped and changed into Davies Bros' style of livery, receiving fleet number 183. It gave 10 years' service before finally being sold for a caravan conversion. *(V. Morgan).*

Above: Freshly repainted into Eynon's 70th anniversary livery and about to leave Trimsaran for recertification on 14th April 1988 is **SCS 328M,** a Leyland 'Leopard' PSU3/3R with Alexander 'Y type' B53F body, fitted with 'panoramic' windows. It was acquired in February 1988 from Northern Scottish (NPE139) and had been new to Western SMT (2459) in June 1974. I captured my brother, Trevor – the garage foreman in this view, admiring his handy-work. He never forgave me for that. Trevor sadly passed away in November 2004, at the young age of 57. We had worked together for 31 years.

Above: It was intended to re-certify and operate this Leyland 'Leopard' PSU3/3R, **SCS 327M** when purchased off Geoff Ripley the dealer in March 1988 but circumstances changed. Immediately after SCS 328M had its repaint and re-certification its engine 'blew up' so the engine of 327 was fitted to 328. In the meantime the business was sold to Davies Bros who didn't want 327 so Eynon's returned it to the dealer minus engine and gearbox. SCS 327M also came from Northern Scottish. *(V. Morgan).*

The first two vehicles acquired by the establishment in their last year of operation were their preferred heavyweights – Leyland. Arriving in January and February respectively, they were Leyland 'Leopard' PSU3/3R's with Alexander 'Y type' B53F bodies, registered HCS 793N and SCS 328M. A third one, SCS 327M arrived a month later but was not operated – its engine was used in SCS 328M due to an engine failure, and SCS 327M was later returned to G Ripley the Carlton dealer in June 1988.

The Leyland 'Leopards' were quickly followed by the very last vehicle acquired by the Eynon's concern. It was an AEC 'Reliance' with Duple 'Dominant II' C53F coachwork registered NMJ 289V, which had been new to NAT Holidays, of London W8 in June 1980. It was acquired in February 1988 from Gravell's (dealer) Pinged Hill Garage, Kidwelly, who had re-possessed it from Gower & Martin (T/A: Celtic Coaches) Burry Port when the partnership dissolved in February 1988, as mentioned on page 182.

Celtic Coaches (Wales) nevertheless continued to operate with J D Martin at the helm, who successfully applied for a local authority funded Sundays only circular service, Llanelli – Trimsaran – Kidwelly – Burry Port – Pwll – Llanelli. Part of this service, Llanelli – Trimsaran – Kidwelly had previously been operated by Eynon's as their 199 service, but was now incorporated into the South Wales Transport's Llanelli – Burry Port – Pembrey, 174 service, to form a circular route. The new Sunday 'circular' service granted to Celtic Coaches (Wales), commenced on 3rd April 1988, using the existing route numbers – 199 and 174 respectively. The service however was short lived, Celtic Coaches wound up in May 1989.

Above: One of the last few AEC 'Reliances' built in 1980 was this particular coach **NMJ 289V**. New to NAT Holidays, London W8 in J 1980, it had a few owners before arriving at Eynon's in February 1988, through the Kidwelly dealer, Pinged Hill Garage. Eynon's bought coach at a knock down price after re-possession from the previous owners, Gower & Martin. Eynon's were about to re-paint it into fleet liv when other engineering work took preference. I must point out however, that this particular photograph has already appeared on the inter posted by a person who claims it to be his view! I took this photograph on 21st February 1988 at Eynon's yard after the paintwork had b rubbed down in anticipation of a repaint. The repaint into Eynon's livery never took place as Davies Bros were by then about to absorb business. Consequently it became the first Eynon's vehicle to receive Davies Bros livery in June 1988, and carried fleet number 174. **NMJ 289V** was an AEC 'Reliance' 6U2R model with pneumo-cyclic transmission, and a Duple 'Dominant II' C53F body fitted with a Bri dome and manually operated entrance door. *(Vernon Morgan).*

On 19th March 1988, I became redundant from my job as a Mobile Plant Fitter, with the closure of the National Coal Board's Plant Workshops at Ammanford. In my search for another job I visited the Eynon's establishment and spoke to the partners who kindly employed me in my profession; a motor mechanic – joining my younger brother Trevor the garage foreman once again.

I had the honour of being the last person employed by the Eynon's partnership, commencing my employment there on 28th March 1988, and one of my first jobs was to overhaul the engine of LAG bodied DAF MB200, PBX 280Y which had been 'cooked' – two cracked cylinder heads.

Having settled down at my new workplace by May 1988, management announced that they were making the last two conductors Elias Davies and Dawn Roberts redundant because the establishment had been sold and the new proprietor didn't want conductors, every local service would be one person operated. The management also stated that Mr D J R Bending of South Wales Transport had been trying to purchase the business, but a more favourable deal had been made with Davies Bros (Pencader) Ltd, who bought the complete undertaking for £220,000.

Sadly, after 71 years of loyal service to the community, Eynon's ran their last buses on Saturday 4th June 1988. The last vehicle to operate Samuel Eynon's pioneering Llanelli – Trimsaran – Kidwelly route 199 (with extension to Llansaint) at 10.15 pm from Llanelli (Town Hall) bus station that evening was a nine-teen year old Leyland 'Leopard' PSU3A/4R registered VNY 468G, with Plaxton 'Panorama Elite' C53F coachwork, driven by David Thomas (Dai Bach), one of my colleagues from the garage. It returned from Llansaint at 11.00 pm in service to Trimsaran (depot) by 11.20 pm. However, the *last* vehicle to leave Llanelli bus station was SCS 328M a Leyland 'Leopard' with Alexander 'Y type' body working service 131 to Meinciau via Five Roads and Pontyates at 10.35 pm. That bus was driven by John Hazel, and also arrived back at the depot at 11.20 pm.

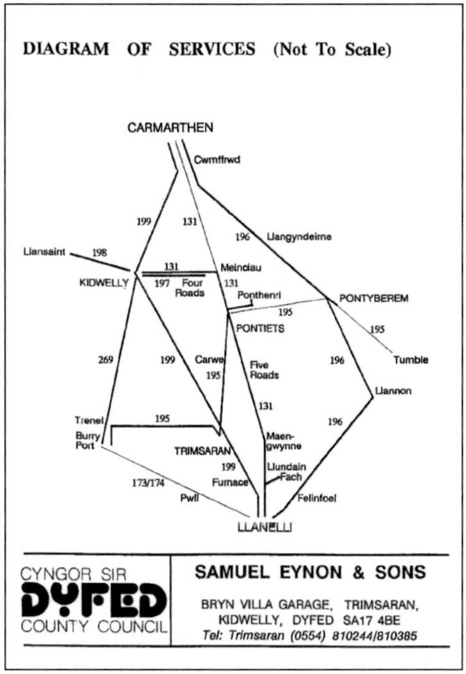

Above: The very last time table issued for Eynon's bus services, by Dyfed County Council and dated 1st February 1988.

Above & Left:
Every picture tells a story – Farewell to Eynon's - the very last Eynon's bus to leave Llanelli Town Hall bus station for Trimsaran and Kidwelly on Saturday 4th June 1988. Davies Bros (Pencader) Ltd, absorbed Eynon's 71 year old business on 5th June 1988. A sad end to a much loved reliable family business.

The coach was driven on this historic trip by my colleague David Thomas (Dai Bach) posing for the camera in both views of the 19 year old coach, VNY 468G, a Leyland 'Leopard' with Plaxton 'Panorama Elite' coachwork.

These views were hurriedly taken that evening as Dai kept telling me – hurry up, I want to catch a pint in the club!
(Vernon Morgan).

EPILOGUE

On Sunday 5th June 1988, Davies Bros (Pencader) Ltd, officially took over the old established family business of Samuel Eynon & Sons at Trimsaran. All members of staff excluding the General Manager, David Ieuan Lodwick (JP) who retired, transferred to Davies Brothers under the Transfer of Undertakings (Protection of Employment) regulations.

The family controlled Davies Brothers business was under the ownership of J D Davies; E O Davies and S O Davies. The Managing Director, John Dewi Davies was the only son of the late William John Davies, founder of the Davies Bros empire.

Twenty-three vehicles passed into the fleet of Davies Bros (Pencader) Ltd, with the Eynon's business together with all their licences, local services, express services, works contracts and school contracts. Included in the deal was the former residence of Samuel Eynon, 'Bryn Villa', latterly used as an office, both garages and the depot yard at Heol Waun-y-clun, Trimsaran. Thirty-two vehicle licences were held by Eynon's at the point of take-over, which Davies Bros, temporarily used until 31st July 1988. Davies Bros, had applied for 28 extra licences on their licence application number PG/4742/SI, Davies Bros (Pencader) Ltd, which were issued to commence on 1st August 1988. The thirty-two Eynon's licence discs were all cancelled on 11th August 1988 after receipt of Davies Bros' 28 additional discs on 31st July.

From this date, vehicles based at the Trimsaran operating centre were licensed to Davies Bros (Pencader) Ltd, nevertheless Trimsaran depot operated financially as a separate entity - Davies Bros (Trimsaran) Ltd, Eynon's Garage, Heol Waun-y-clun, Trimsaran, SA17 4BS.

Davies Bros (Carmarthen) Ltd, was another separate entity for their Carmarthen operations.

The local services, workers contracts, school contracts and express services transferred to Davies Bros, were:

131 Llanelli (Town Hall) to Meinciau, Kidwelly, and Carmarthen,
via: Five Roads, Pontyates and Ponthenry.

173/174 Llanelli (Town Hall) to Trenel (Pembrey) (early morning service),
via: Pwll and Burry Port.

195 Burry Port (Station) to Tumble (Hotel),
via: Pembrey, Pinged, Trimsaran, Pontyates, Pontyberem and Cwmmawr.

196 Llanelli (Town Hall) to Carmarthen (Bus Station),
via: Felinfoel, Llannon, Pontyberem, Bancffosfelen and Llangyndeirne.

197 Kidwelly (Borough Offices) to Four Roads.
via: Mynydd-y-garreg with connections to Carmarthen and Llanelli.

198 Kidwelly (Borough Offices) to Llansaint,
with connections to Carmarthen and Llanelli.

199 Llanelli (Town Hall) to Carmarthen (Blue Street),
via: Trimsaran, Kidwelly, Llandyfeilog and Cwmffrwd.

269 Burry Port (Station) to Kidwelly (Borough Offices),
via: Ashburnham Road, Pembrey Square and Butchers Arms,
with connections to Carmarthen and Trimsaran.

273 Llanelli (Andrew Street) to Pwll (Graig & Stradey Comprehensive Schools),
via: Corporation Avenue, Panteg, Felinfoel Road, and Llanelli (Town Hall).
Operated on Schooldays only.

SCHOOL CONTRACTS:

Kidwelly (Boot & Shoe) to St John Lloyd Comprehensive School, including St Marys Infants School, Havard Road, Llanelli.

Kidwelly (Boot & Shoe) to Glan-y-mor Comprehensive School, Burry Port.

Trimsaran (Argoed Cres.) to Graig Comprehensive School, Pwll.

Trimsaran (Argoed Cres.) to Stradey Comprehensive School, Llanelli.

Pembrey & Burry Port to Stradey Comprehensive School, Llanelli.

Burry Port to Maridunum, Cambria and Bro-Myrddin Comprehensive Schools, Carmarthen.

Kidwelly & Croesyceiliog to Maridunum, Cambria and Bro-Myrddin Comprehensive Schools, Carmarthen.

Four Roads & Kidwelly to Maridunum, Cambria and Bro-Myrddin Comprehensive Schools, Carmarthen.

WORKERS CONTRACTS:

British American Optical Factory, Mynydd-y-Garreg: Two shifts per day M-F.
B A O F to Llanelli (Rail Station) via: Kidwelly and Burry Port.

B A O F to Penygroes via: Pontyates, Pontyberem, Tumble, and Cross Hands.

B A O F to Trimsaran and Carway.

B A O F to Kidwelly and Llansaint.

National Coal Board:
Cynheidre Colliery (Shaft 1 & 2) to Pwll (Sandy Road).
via: Pontyates, Meinciau, Four Roads, Mynydd-y-Garreg, Kidwelly, Pembrey and Burry Port. Three shifts per day M – F and Saturday (AM), Return of night shift.

GTS Components Factory (Pembrey) to Burry Port, Trimsaran and Carway.

EXPRESS SERVICES:

> London (Marble Arch). Tuesday, Thursday and Saturdays, throughout the year.
> Picking up at Trimsaran, Pontyates, Kidwelly, Burry Port, Pwll,
> Llanelli (Town Hall), Llangennech, Hendy and Swansea (Castle Street).
>
> Cardiff (Greyfriars Road). Tuesdays and Saturdays throughout the year.
> Picking up at Trimsaran, Pontyates, Kidwelly, Burry Port, Pwll,
> Llanelli (Town Hall), Llangennech and Hendy.

'Private Hire' included all the work for the famous Llanelli RFC; 'The Scarlets' for all their away games, team coach and supporters coaches. This often necessitated 'hiring in' or cross-hiring coaches from other operators. There was also a comprehensive day tours programme and extended tours with destinations of Paris, Blackpool and London.

Managing Director Dewi Davies immediately set about replacing some of the Eynon's stock with new and second-hand vehicles and within days of the take-over went to a well-known London 'bus' dealer and bought two ECW dual-purpose bodied Leyland 'Tigers' TPC 105X / WPH 136Y together with two Daimler 'Fleetline' double decker's WHL 279J / LHD 307K where the sales person making out the 'Bill of Sale' asked – how would you like to pay for them Mr Davies, to which he replied – I'm afraid you'll have to take a cheque as I don't carry that much cash around with me - £52,000.

A month later, a very tidy Leyland 'Leopard' registered OUT 11W arrived from Stuart Johnson the dealer, and a 'Leopard' with Duple 'Dominant' 55 seat bus body from Cleveland Transit (359) HEF 359N. These were followed by three brand new Leyland 'Tiger' coaches, F612-4 RBX which entered service on 1st August 1988, with dual fleet-names Eynon's / Davies Bros. Dual fleet-names were also applied to some second-hand purchases acquired in later months, along with most of the former Eynon's stock.

The Eynon's fleet-name however was gradually phased out, the last vehicle carrying the name was Daimler 'Fleetline' UMS 97J, which was withdrawn in December 1994.

Returning to TPC 105X, WPH 136Y, WHL 279J, HEF 359N and OUT 11W mentioned above, they all ran on Eynon's licence discs until Davies Bros received their additional 28 discs in the name of Davies Bros (Pencader) Ltd, on 31st July 1988. From that date, those vehicles together with the remaining former Eynon's stock, all carried the Davies Bros (Pencader) Ltd, operator licence discs PG 4742, and Davies Bros (Pencader) Ltd, legal lettering.

A few months later in 1989, the double fronted house 'Bryn Villa', former residence of the late Samuel Eynon, latterly used as the company's office, together with the adjoining garage known as 'Bryn Villa Garage' were put on the market. It was sold for £60,000 with Davies Bros recovering a large part of their outlay to purchase the Eynon's business. Trimsaran depot was afterwards controlled from a 'Portakabin' office on the yard alongside the 'double-decker' garage, which was then re-named 'Eynon's Garage'.

Left: A view of 'Bryn Villa' the former residence of Samuel Eynon which had latterly been used as the company's office. This double fronted eight roomed house was included in the sale of Eynon's business to Davies Bros. The house/office together with the large garage to its rear (Bryn Villa Garage) was sold by Davies Brothers after a short while, recovering a large part of their outlay purchasing the business. This view was taken in 1961/2 long before the roadway 'Heol Waun-y-clun' was widened. It's hard to believe that 11 metre coaches were making the turn through the gateway between the lamp post and office wall into the garage – but they were!

Above: **TPC 105X** was one of a pair of ECW dual-purpose bodied Leyland 'Tiger' TRCTL11/2R's purchased by Davies Bros in June 1988 to modernise the Trimsaran fleet. Due to a vehicle shortage, they were both pressed into service in the livery they carried upon arrival, and operated on Eynon's licence discs until they were transferred to Davies Bros (Pencader) Ltd, on 1st August 1988.

Above: **WPH 136Y** was the other Leyland 'Tiger' TRCTL11/2R with ECW bodywork (DP53F in this case) that Davies Bros, bought in June 1988 to replace the ageing Eynon's fleet. Simultaneously, it operated on Eynon's licence until 1st August 1988.

Above: Two Daimler 'Fleetlines' were purchased in the same deal as the 'Tiger's above. **WHL 279J** pictured here was one of them, an Alexander N type, H43/33F bodied 'Fleetline' CRG6LX, that also ran on Eynon's licence discs until 1st August 1988. It operated in the livery of its previous owner; Hedingham & District O C until sold in April 1991.

Above: Built to the 'New Bus Grant' specification, **OUT 11W** was a Leyland 'Leopard' PSU3E/4R with Plaxton 'Supreme Express IV' C53F body, which had been new to Leicester C T (11) in March 1981. Davies Bros acquired this immaculate coach from Cottrell, Mitcheldean (Glos) in July 1988 and operated it on Eynon's licence until 31st July. It was a wonderful vehicle to drive, and I photographed it here outside 'Bryn Villa' freshly lettered on 21st July 1988, 14 days after its arrival.

Above: This Duple 'Dominant' B55F bodied Leyland 'Leopard' PSU3C/4R, **HEF 359N** also operated on the Eynon's licence discs until 1st August 1988, but never carried Eynon's branding. It was new in July 1975 to Cleveland Transit (359) and was purchased from dealer Wacton Bus with a view of re-bodying it in due course with a Willowbrook 'Warrier' body. That never took place.

Above: Three replacement 'front line coaches' arrived simultaneously with the change of registration year prefix to 'F' and transfer of licences on 1st August 1988. They arrived complete with **Eynon's** branding as shown here on **F612 RBX** a Leyland 'Tiger' TRCTL11/3RZ with Duple 340, C55F coachwork. *(Vernon Morgan).*

Above: Davies Bros even included the **Eynon's** name and telephone number to the rear panels of Trimsaran based vehicles as shown here on **F612 RBX**, but I really can't understand the logic behind the branding – 'WE LEAD OTHERS FOLLOW' -- bearing in mind *their* demise eleven years later. *(Vernon Morgan).*

SUMMARY OF ROAD SERVICE LICENCES

TGR 311/1	Llanelly (Town Hall)	– Carmarthen (Lammas Street).
TGR 311/2	Excursions & Tours starting from Llanelly (Town Hall).	
TGR 311/3	Trimsaran	– Llanelli (Stradey).
TGR 311/4	Carmarthen (Lammas St.)	– Croes-y-ceiliog.
TGR 311/5	Excursions & Tours starting from Trimsaran.	
TGR 311/6	Mynydd-y-garreg	– Llanelly (Town Hall).
TGR 311/7	Excursions & Tours starting from Pontyates (Square).	
TGR 311/8	Nothing Recorded	
TGR 311/9	Llanelly	– Trimsaran.
TGR 311/10	Trimsaran	– Llanelly (Als Square).
TGR 311/11	Carway	– Llanelli (Town Hall).
TGR 311/Sp/1	Trimsaran	– Burry Port.
TGR 311/12	Pembrey (RAF Camp)	– Llansaint (Manor Farm Camp).
TGR 311/13	Trimsaran (Bird-in-hand)	– Felinfoel (Morris Motors, Nuffield Works).
TGR 311/Sp/2	Llanelli (Town Hall)	– Carmarthen (Lammas Street).
TGR 311/Sp/3	Carmarthen (Lammas St.)	– Croes-y-ceiliog.
TGR 311/Sp/4	Carway	– Llanelli (Town Hall).
TGR 311/Sp/5	Trimsaran (Bird-in-hand)	– Felinfoel (Morris Motors Nuffield Works).
TGR 311/14	Trimsaran (Bird-in-hand)	– Felinfoel (Fisher & Ludlow Factory).
TGR 311/Sp/6	Llanelli (Town Hall)	– Carmarthen (Lammas Street).
TGR 311/15	Llanelli (Town Hall)	– Carmarthen (Lammas Street).
TGR 311/16	Drefach (Square)	– Cynheidre Colliery (Shaft No. 3).

TGR 311/17 Pontyates (Railway Station) – Burry Port (Railway Station).

TGR 311/Sp/7 Pontyates (Railway Station) – Burry Port (Railway Station).

TGR 311/Sp/8 Trimsaran – Dafen (Avon Inflatables Ltd).

TGR 311/Sp/9 Penyfan – Dafen (Avon Inflatables Ltd).

TGR 311/Sp/10 Llanelli – Machynys (Avon Inflatables Ltd).

TGR 311/Sp/11 Pontarddulais – Llanelli (Avon Inflatables Ltd).

TGR 311/18 Llanelli – Machynys (Avon Inflatables Ltd).

TGR 311/19 Trimsaran – Dafen (Avon Inflatables Ltd).

TGR 311/20 Penyfan – Dafen (Avon Inflatables Ltd).

TGR 311/21 Pontarddulais – Llanelli (Avon Inflatables Ltd).

TGR 311/22 Kidwelly – Cynheidre Colliery (Shaft No. 3).

TGR 311/23 Excursions & Tours starting from Kidwelly (Borough Offices).

Change of licensing format from 1st March 1986.

PG/0809/311 Llanelli (Town Hall) – Carmarthen (Bus Stn). Previously TGR 311/1

PG/0810/311 Llanelli (Town Hall) – Carmarthen (Bus Stn). Previously TGR 311/15

PG/0811/311 Burry Port (Rly Stn.) – Tumble (Hotel). Previously TGR 311/17

PG/5112/311 Llanelli (Town Hall) – Carmarthen (Bus Stn). No. 131

PG/5113/311 Llanelli (Town Hall) – Pembrey (Trenel). No. 173/174

PG/5114/311 Llanelli (Swansea Rd) – Graig Comprehensive School. No. 273

PG/5613/311 Kidwelly (Castle) – Burry Port (Railway Station). No. 269

Change of Operator licence on 1st August 1987.

PG/809/6343 Llanelli – Trimsaran – Kidwelly – Carmarthen. No. 199

PG/810/6343 Llanelli – Felinfoel – Pontyberem – Carmarthen. No. 196

PG/811/6343 Burry Port (Railway Station) – Tumble (Hotel). No. 195

PG/5112/6343 Llanelli – Five Roads – Pontyates – Meinciau – Carmarthen. No. 131

PG/5113/6343 Llanelli – Burry Port – Trenel (Pembrey). No. 173/4

PG/5114/6343 Llanelli (Swansea Rd) – Graig Comprehensive School. No. 273

PG/5643/6343 Kidwelly (Castle) – Burry Port (Railway Station). No. 269

ROUTE MAP

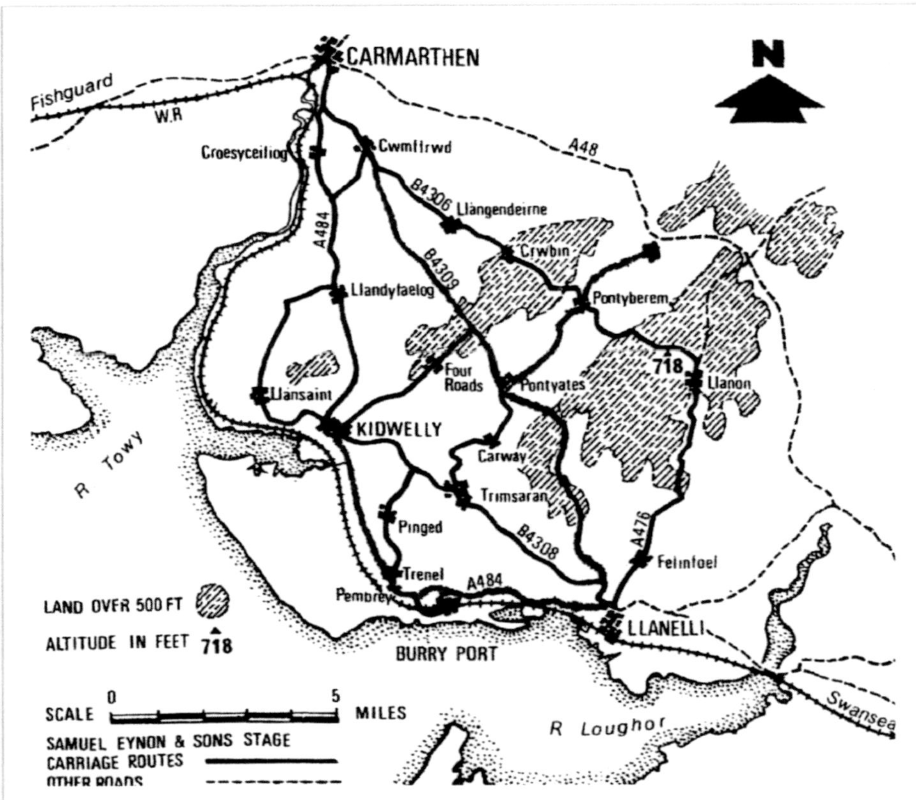

TICKETS USED

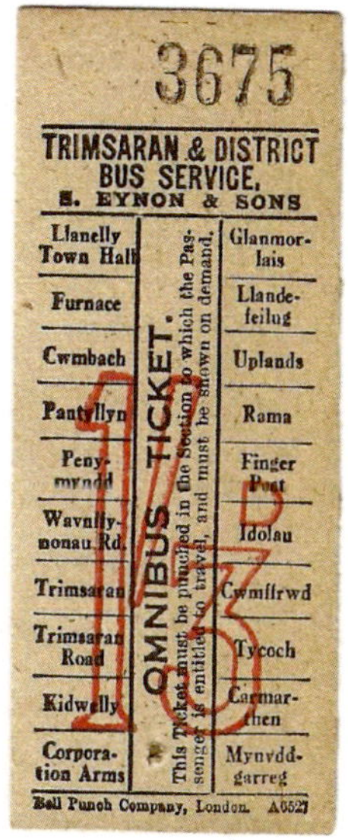

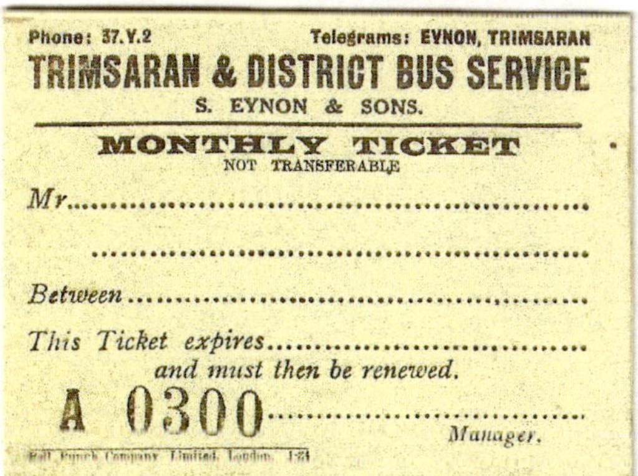

Phone: 37.Y.2 Telegrams: EYNON, TRIMSARAN

TRIMSARAN & DISTRICT BUS SERVICE

S. EYNON & SONS.

MONTHLY TICKET

NOT TRANSFERABLE

Mr..

....

Between..

This Ticket expires....................................

and must then be renewed.

A 0300....................................

Manager.

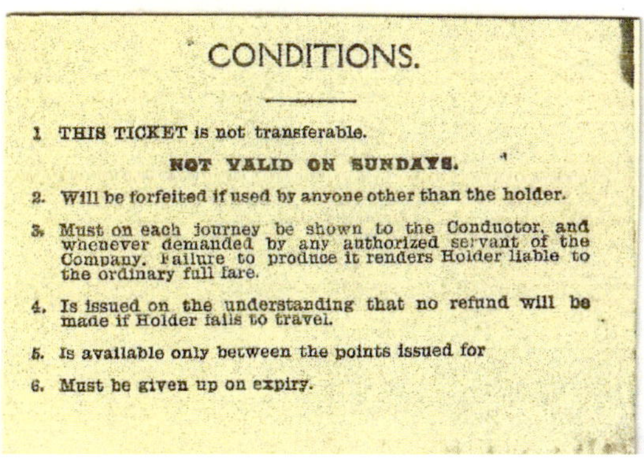

CONDITIONS.

1 THIS TICKET is not transferable.

NOT VALID ON SUNDAYS.

2. Will be forfeited if used by anyone other than the holder.

3. Must on each journey be shown to the Conductor, and whenever demanded by any authorized servant of the Company. Failure to produce it renders Holder liable to the ordinary full fare.

4. Is issued on the understanding that no refund will be made if Holder fails to travel.

5. Is available only between the points issued for

6. Must be given up on expiry.

A 4436
TRIMSARAN & DISTRICT
MOTOR SERVICE.
PROPS.: SAMUEL EYNON & SONS
Carway
Trimsaran Road Station
This Ticket is available for one journey in each direction, and is AVAILABLE ON DAY OF ISSUE ONLY.
LLANELLY
Bell Punch Co., Ltd. London.
S. EYNON & SONS No. 4877
CONTRACT TRAVEL TICKET
(SCHOLARS)
Available only between
and
IS NOT VALID FOR INTERMEDIATE TRAVEL
Commencing
EXPIRING
Bell Punch Company, Ltd., London.
B 3106
TRIMSARAN & DISTRICT
MOTOR SERVICE
PROPS.: SAMUEL EYNON & SONS
STAR SQUARE
OMNIBUS TICKET.
This ticket must be issued in the presence of the Passenger and must be shown on demand.
LLANELLY
Bell Punch Company, London.
I 4901
OUT
WEEKLY TICKET
IN
NOT TRANSFERABLE
PRICE
MON.
TUES.
WED.
THUR.
FRI.
SAT.
From To
BETWEEN
AND
Name
Address
This contract is issued on the understanding that it is only used by the person named, & between the points stated above.
Bell Punch Company Limited, London. 12-55
EYNON'S
OVER 1/-
UNDER 1/-
STAGE
SINGLE
FROM
TO
RETURN
X 36488
Bell Punch Company, Ltd., London.
NOT TRANSFERABLE
ISSUED SUBJECT TO COY'S REGULATIONS
EYNONS
PENCE
EYNONS
PENCE
SINGLE

No	Reg. No.	Chassis make & Type	Chassis Number	Body make & Type	Seats	Date New	Remarks / Additional information Previous owner	Date Acq.	Date w/drawn
	BO 227	Studebaker		Car				1917	?
	BX1669	Fiat 18BL (3.5 ton)		Charabanc	Ch25	12/1920	New	12/1920	7/1926
	BX 2404	Leyland G7 n/c		Leyland 'Edinburgh style'	B32R	2/1922	New	2/1922	?
	BX 4035	Leyland A9 n/c	19654	Leyland 'Chester style'	B20R	12/1923	New	12/1923	?
3	BX 5872	Leyland C7 36hp n/c	35618	Leyland 'Edinburgh style'	B26R	7/1925	New	7/1925	?
2	BX 6996	Leyland C9 30hp n/c	36308	Buckingham 'All-weather Coach'	C26F	7/1926	New	7/1926	1/1936
	BX 7794			Car		5/1927	New	5/1927	?
	BX 6130	Ford 'T' 20hp		Ford saloon car		8/1925	Ex. R. Thomas. Newchurch, Carmarthen.	1927	?
4	BX 8048	Leyland Lion PLSC1	45943	Leyland	B31R	7/1927	New	7/1927	1/1945
5	TH 804	Leyland Tiger TS1	61046	Leyland	B31R	5/1930	New	5/1930 lic: 6/30	12/1951
7	TH 2970	Leyland Tiger TS4	1874	Leyland	B32R	12/1932	New	12/1932	8/1955
6	OF 5483	Leyland Titan TD1	70743	Leyland (1933)	B32R	9/1929	Ex. Dunlop Rubber Co. Birmingham. (See note A)	4/1933	7/1950
8	TJ 599	Leyland Tiger TS4	2402	Leyland (see note B)	B32F	-/1933	Ex. Leyland Motors demonstrator. (See note B)	5/1934	1/1955
	BX8368	Dennis F	80035	Hall Lewis?	B31R	12/1927	Acquired with the business of J. Hughes. Trimsaran, Carms.	10/1935	not operated
	TH 838	Dennis EV	17880		B32R	6/1930	Acquired with the business of J. Hughes. Trimsaran, Carms.	10/1935	not operated
9	TH 8834	Leyland Tiger TS8	14372	Leyland	B32R	6/1937	New (Later re-numbered 12)	6/1937	4/1959

	GJ 2397	Leyland Titan TD1	71030	Leyland (see note C)	B32R	6/1930	Ex. Premier Omnibus Co. London W2. via: Lewis & Jacob. Maesteg, Glam.	4/1944	2/1950
	CBX 435 (UP 5095)	Leyland Tiger TS3	61578	(see note D)	B32R	-/1930	Ex. Stockton-Upon-Tees Corpn. (see note D)	9/1944	2/1950
12	CK 4731	Leyland Tiger TS6(oil)	2673	Leyland (see note E)	C33F	-/1933	Ex. Ribble M S (1377) via: Corvedale. Ludlow, Salop. (11)	2/1947	5/1959
9	DTH 103	Leyland Tiger PS1	462004	Duple	DP35F	9/1947	New	9/1947 lic: 10/47	5/1960
10	EK 8878	Leyland Titan TD2(oil)	1741	Northern Counties (see note F)	L24/24R	9/1932	Ex. Wigan C T (83) via: Red & White M S (846)	5/1948 lic: 7/48	12/1955
11	JY 5026	Leyland Titan TD4c	5675	Weymann	L24/24R	5/1935	Ex. Plymouth C T (98) via: Williams (Pioneer) Laugharne.	7/1949	7/1951
	TF 7310	Leyland Titan TD2(oil)	130	Leyland (see note G)	L24/26R	12/1931	Ex. Williams (Pioneer) Laugharne, Carmarthenshire. (see note G)	9/1949	9/1956
14	FTH 831	Leyland Titan PD2/1	501386	Leyland	L27/26R	8/1950	New	8/1950	8/1963
	WN 9474	Leyland Titan TD4	10065	Leyland	H28/26R	3/1936	Ex. Swan Motors. Bishopston, Swansea via: Daniel Jones. Abergwili, Carms (7)	2/1951	12/1955
15	GBX 987	Leyland Titan PD2/3	505677	Leyland	L27/26RD	7/1951	New	7/1951	1/1964
16	GTH 737	Leyland Royal Tiger PSU1/15	515349	Leyland	C41C	4/1952	New	4/1952	6/1966
	BV 4454	Leyland Tiger TS7	6169	Eastern Coach Works (Rebodied)	C35F	5/1935	Ex. Cronshaw. London NW4. via: D. Jones. Abergwili, Carms (1)	7/1954	by 1958
17	EVT 382	Leyland Tiger TS7	13193	Willowbrook	B37F	6/1937	Ex. Baxter. Hanley, Staffs. (10)	11/1954	9/1958
18	LBX 811	Leyland Tiger Cub PSUC1/2T	552950	Willowbrook	DP41F	5/1955	New	5/1955	3/1972
20	BSM 170	Leyland Tiger TS7	7335	Eastern Coach Works (1943)	B35R	1935	Ex. Western S M T. Kilmarnock. (862)	8/1955	6/1957
21	BSM 171	Leyland Tiger TS7	7336	Eastern Coach Works (1943)	B35R	1935	Ex. Western S M T. Kilmarnock. (863)	7/1955	by 2/1958
19	BTH 175	Leyland Titan TD7	307106	Leyland	L27/26R	10/1941	Ex. J. James. Ammanford, Carms. (165) (see note H)	9/1955	10/1958

21	CS 7034	Leyland Titan TD5	17386	Leyland (1950)	H30/26R	1938	Ex. Western S M T. Kilmarnock.	11/1955	10/1958
23	CS 8046	Leyland Titan TD5	300753	Leyland (1950)	H30/26R	1939	Ex. Western S M T. (147) Kilmarnock.	11/1955	11/1957
	LKH 351	Leyland Tiger PS1	500181	Plaxton	FC35F	7/1950	Ex. Bluebird. Hull.	7/1957	3/1961
	RBX 394	Leyland Tiger Cub PSUC1/2	584036	Duple 'Donnington'	C41F	5/1958	New	5/1958	3/1962
	FOR 639	Leyland Titan PD1A	462947	Leyland	H30/26R	5/1947	Ex. Hants & Sussex. Emsworth, Hants. (LO51)	10/1958	10/1962
	JXN 320	Leyland Titan 7RT	484905	Park Royal	H30/26R	12/1948	Ex. London Transport (RTL 8)	9/1958 lic.10/58	10/1962
	JXN 358	Leyland Titan 7RT	485224	Park Royal	H30/26R	12/1948	Ex. London Transport (RTL35)	7/1958 lic.10/58	8/1962
28	GUE 250	Leyland Tiger PS1	473445	Northern Coach Builders	B34F	1948	Ex. Stratford Blue, Stratford-upon-Avon, Warwickshire. (44)	4/1959	9/1964
	TAB 577	Leyland Tiger Cub PSUC1/2T	565428	Duple 'Britannia'	C41C	7/1957	Ex. Johnson. Stourbridge. West Midlands.	5/1959	by 8/1974
	KAW 677	Leyland Royal Tiger PSU1/17	531884	Leyland	B44F	1954	Ex. Whittle. Highley. Shropshire.	1/1960	10/1962
	DBX 260	Leyland Tiger PS1	462767	Burlingham (1945)	B34F	5/1947	Ex. J. James & Sons. Ammanford, Carms. (200)	12/1959 lic.1/60	4/1962
	LTG 269	Leyland Royal Tiger PSU1/15	520909	Leyland	C41C	4/1952	Ex. Rhondda Transport. Porth, Mid-Glamorgan. (329)	3/1960	5/1964
	XTH 300	Leyland Leopard L2	610336	Burlingham 'Seagull' 70	C41F	5/1961	New	5/1961	5/1963
	JTH 791	Leyland Tiger Cub PSUC1/1T	534848	Duple Midland	B44F	5/1954	Ex. Davies Bros. Pencader, Carms. (46)	3/1962 lic.4/62	6/1966
	818 ATH	Leyland Leopard L2	621244	Plaxton 'Panorama'	C41F	6/1962	New	6/1962	5/1965
	LYF 150	Leyland Titan 7RT	510925	Park Royal	H30/26R	4/1951	Ex. London Transport (RTL 1209)	8/1962	5/1968
	EUH 959	Leyland Titan PD2/3	502568	Leyland	L27/26R	8/1950	Ex. Western Welsh O C (959)	10/1962	9/1963

EUH 964	Leyland Titan PD2/3	502770	Leyland	L27/26R	9/1950	Ex. Western Welsh O C (964)	10/1962	10/1965
EUH 966	Leyland Titan PD2/3	502948	Leyland	L27/26R	9/1950	Ex. Western Welsh O C (966)	3/1963	10/1965
EUH 953	Leyland Titan PD2/3	502570	Leyland	L27/26R	8/1950	Ex. Western Welsh O C (953)	3/1963	9/1963
405 CTH	Bedford SB5	92133	Duple 'Bella Vega'	C41F	5/1963	New	5/1963	5/1965
LYF 35	Leyland Titan 7RT	504847	Park Royal	H30/26R	1/1951	Ex. London Transport (RTL1111)	9/1963	8/1971
LYF 38	Leyland Titan 7RT	510151	Park Royal	H30/26R	2/1951	Ex. London Transport (RTL1114)	9/1963	8/1971
LYF 40	Leyland Titan 7RT	510148	Park Royal	H30/26R	2/1951	Ex. London Transport (RTL1116)	9/1963	8/1971
LYR 808	Leyland Titan 7RT	515031	Park Royal	H30/26R	1/1952	Ex. London Transport (RTL1276)	9/1963	8/1971
LYR 959	Leyland Titan 7RT	515360	Park Royal	H30/26R	2/1952	Ex. London Transport (RTL1311)	9/1963	8/1971
695 ETH	Bedford VAL14	1254	Plaxton 'VAL'	C52F	5/1964	New	5/1964	6/1966
FBX 489	Commer Avenger I	23A0132	Plaxton 'Q2'	C32F	9/1949	Ex. O. Rowlands. Carway, Carms. (See note I)	7/1964	9/1964
BTH 987C	Bedford VAL14	1683	Duple 'Vega Major'	C52F	5/1965	New	5/1965	1/1967
CBX 9C	Bedford SB13	95782	Harrington 'Crusader IV'	C41F	5/1965	New	5/1965	9/1967
CBX 238C	Bedford SB13	97295	Duple 'Firefly'	C41F	5/1965	New	5/1965	1/1968
HUH 25	Leyland Tiger Cub PSUC1/1	534373	Weymann 'Hermes'	B44F	12/1953	Ex. Western Welsh O C (1025)	10/1965	7/1966
HUH 27	Leyland Tiger Cub PSUC1/1	534414	Weymann 'Hermes'	B44F	1/1954	Ex. Western Welsh O C (1027)	10/1965	2/1968
KXW 58	Leyland Titan 7RT	497088	Metro-Cammell	H30/26R	3/1950	Ex. London Transport (RTL708)	10/1965	5/1969

LLU 866	Leyland Titan 7RT	502410	Metro-Cammell	H30/26R	8/1950	Ex. London Transport (RTL876)	10/1965	9/1967
ETH 210D	Bedford VAM14	6816997	Plaxton 'Panorama'	C45F	6/1966	New (See note J)	6/1966	2/1968
ETH 260D	Bedford VAL14	6824783	Duple 'Vega Major'	C52F	6/1966	New	6/1966 lic.8/66	1/1968
ETH 320D	Bedford VAM14	6843680	Plaxton 'Panorama'	C45F	6/1966	New	6/1966	1/1967
FTH 989E	Bedford VAL14	6862280	Duple 'Viceroy'	C52F	1/1967	New	1/1967 lic.5/67	10/1968
GBX 542E	Bedford VAM14	6864468	Plaxton 'Panorama'	C45F	5/1967	New	5/1967 lic.6/67	10/1968
YXD 14	AEC Reliance	2MU3RA 2944	Duple 'Britannia'	C40F	1960	Ex. K. W. Daventry, Northants.	8/1967	5/1970
933 DVA	AEC Reliance	2MU3RA 3983	Burlingham 'Seagull' 70	C41F	1962	Ex. Woburn. London WC1.	8/1967	4/1968
JBO 107	Leyland Tiger Cub PSUC1/1	543475	Weymann 'Hermes'	B44F	10/1954	Ex. Western Welsh O C (1107)	2/1968	1/1970
JBO 127	Leyland Tiger Cub PSUC1/1	543590	Weymann 'Hermes'	B44F	10/1954	Ex. Western Welsh O C (1127) (See note K)	2/1968	-/1972
799 OCV	AEC Reliance	2U3RA 4298	Harrington 'Cavalier'	C51F	6/1962	Ex. Blue Saloon (ABC) Guildford.	3/1968	5/1970
JTH 92F	AEC Reliance	6MU3R 7038	Duple 'Commander IV'	C45F	5/1968	New	5/1968	11/1973
JTH 424F	AEC Reliance 691	6U3ZR 7119	Plaxton 'Panorama I'	C51F	5/1968	New	5/1968 lic:7/68	by 9/1973
JTH 425F	AEC Reliance 505	6MU3R 7036	Plaxton 'Panorama I'	C43F	5/1968	New	5/1968 lic.6/68	10/1973
LBX 547G	Leyland Leopard PSU3/3R	900561	Willowbrook	DP49F	5/1969	New (See note L)	not delivered	
LBX 548G	Leyland Leopard PSU3/3RT	900562	Willowbrook	DP49F	7/1969	New	7/1969	12/1981
HLW 177	AEC Regent III 3RT	0961071	Park Royal (1949)	H30/26R	9/1947	Ex. London Transport (RT190) (See note M)	1/1970	10/1972
KGU 414	AEC Regent III 3RT	09613123	Weymann	H30/26R	8/1949	Ex. London Transport (RT1545)	1/1970	10/1972

SJJ 317	Leyland Tiger Cub PSUC1/2	554951	Harrington 'Wayfarer IV'	C37C	2/1955	Ex. George Ewer Group, London N16 via: Fussell. Swansea. For spares.	10/1969	not operated
HOD 691E	Bedford VAL14	7807952	Duple 'Viceroy'	C52F	2/1967	Ex. Trathen. Yelverton, Devon.	5/1970	by 7/1971
FCH 28	Leyland Tiger Cub PSUC1/1	534840	Weymann 'Hermes'	B44F	6/1954	Ex. Trent M T (378) via: R. I. Davies. Tredegar.	5/1970 lic: 7/70	by 5/1971
NLE 849	AEC Regent III 3RT	09616921	Weymann	H30/26R	6/1953	Ex. London Transport (RT3742)	8/1970	10/1972
KXW 215	AEC Regent III 3RT	09613617	Saunders	H30/26R	3/1950	Ex. London Transport (RT3106)	9/1970	10/1972
OBX 1 J	Leyland Leopard PSU3A/4R	7000647	Caetano 'Lisboa'	C51F	11/1970	New (See note N)	11/1970	5/1974
LKG 225	Leyland Olympian LW2	564430	Weymann	B44F	8/1956	Ex. Western Welsh O C (1225)	2/1971	by 8/1973
MUH 131	Leyland Tiger Cub PSUC1/1	565412	Weymann 'Hermes'	B44F	9/1956	Ex. Western Welsh O C (1131)	2/1971	by 7/1974
9747 NA	Leyland Tiger Cub PSUC1/2	606799	Park Royal	DP40F	3/1961	Ex. Manchester C T (47) via: S E L N E C PTE, Lancs.(2)	4/1971	9/1975
9750 NA	Leyland Tiger Cub PSUC1/2	606821	Park Royal	DP40F	3/1961	Ex. Manchester C T (50) via: S E L N E C PTE, Lancs.(5)	4/1971	12/1975
UWU521F	Leyland Leopard PSU4/3R	800408	Willowbrook	DP41F	4/1968	Ex. Tetley. Leeds. Yorks.	6/1971	10/1980
6911 HA	Leyland Leopard PSU3/3R	629546	Harrington 'Crusader'	C49F	4/1963	Ex. Bowen. Birmingham.	6/1971	12/1973
PBX 700J	AEC Reliance	6MU4R 7778	Plaxton 'Panorama Elite Express II'	C45F	7/1971	New	7/1971	8/1979
LCO 839	Leyland Titan PD2/12	551465	Metro-Cammell 'Orion'	H30/26R	1956	Ex. Plymouth C T (39)	9/1971	7/1974
LCO 841	Leyland Titan PD2/12	551491	Metro-Cammell 'Orion'	H30/26R	1956	Ex. Plymouth C T (41)	9/1971	7/1974
LCO 846	Leyland Titan PD2/12	551802	Metro-Cammell 'Orion'	H30/26R	1956	Ex. Plymouth C T (46)	9/1971	7/1974
LCO 847	Leyland Titan PD2/12	551809	Metro-Cammell 'Orion'	H30/26R	1956	Ex. Plymouth C T (47)	9/1971	7/1974
LCO 854	Leyland Titan PD2/12	551827	Metro-Cammell 'Orion'	H30/26R	1956	Ex. Plymouth C T (54)	8/1971	7/1974

VKH 672	Leyland Tiger Cub PSUC1/1	576106	Park Royal	B39F	9/1957	Ex. East Yorkshire M S (672)	9/1971 lic.11/71	by 8/1974
RBX 760K	Leyland Leopard PSU3/1R	7102667	Willowbrook	DP49F	12/1971	New	12/1971 lic.1/72	5/1983
NNY 58	Leyland Tiger Cub PSUC1/1	534075	Weymann 'Hermes'	B44F	2/1954	Ex. Thomas Bros. Port Talbot. via: South Wales Transport (301)	4/1972	by 8/1973
XRR 539	Leyland Tiger Cub PSUC1/2	576869	Willowbrook	DP41F	1/1958	Ex. Nunn & McAndrew. Leamington, Warks.	5/1972	by 7/1974
STH 555K	Leyland Leopard PSU3B/4R	7201364	Plaxton 'Panorama Elite Express II'	C51F	6/1972	New	6/1972	9/1983
RCY 343	AEC Regent V	LD3RA 518	Weymann	H39/32F	5/1958	Ex. South Wales Transport (701)	10/1972	11/1974
RCY 344	AEC Regent V	LD3RA 519	Weymann	H39/32F	5/1958	Ex. South Wales Transport (702) (See note O)	10/1972	by 8/1975
RCY 346	AEC Regent V	LD3RA 521	Weymann	H39/32F	5/1958	Ex. South Wales Transport (704) (See note P)	10/1972	2/1977
RCY 365	AEC Regent V	LD3RA 540	Weymann	H39/32F	5/1958	Ex. South Wales Transport (723)	10/1972	10/1974
TTH 500L	Leyland Leopard PSU3B/4R	7202387	Caetano 'Lisboa' II	C51F	10/1972	New (See note Q)	10/1972	7/1977
MAX 133	Bristol LS6G	101.057	Eastern Coach Works	C39F	2/1954	Ex. Red & White (UC354) via: Irvine. Law, S. Lanarkshire.	10/1972	by 5/1973
UBX 55L	Leyland Leopard PSU3B/4R	7200757	Plaxton 'Panorama Elite Express III'	C51F	12/1972	New	12/1972	5/1983
WWV 564	Leyland Leopard L1	601835	Harrington 'Cavalier'	DP39F bus seats	12/1960	Ex Silver Star. Porton Down, Wilts (39) via: Wilts & Dorset (909)	4/1973	by 9/1978
VTH 5L	Leyland Leopard PSU3B/4R	7300425	Plaxton 'Panorama Elite Express III'	C53F	5/1973	New	5/1973	11/1979
VTH 655L	Leyland Leopard PSU3B/4R	7300781	Duple 'Dominant Express'	C51F	6/1973	New (lic to D. I. Lodwick when new)	6/1973	10/1982
WTH 255M	Leyland Leopard PSU5/4R	7301533	Caetano 'Lisboa' II	C57F	10/1973	New	10/1973	2/1977
KNK 350G	Bedford VAS5	9T467484	Duple 'Vista 25'	C29F	6/1969	Ex. Raff. Gravesend, Kent.	10/1973	1/1976
DHN 300H	Bedford VAS5	0T480672	Plaxton 'Panorama'	C29F	7/1970	Ex. Kinch. Mountsorrel, Leics.	10/1973	11/1979

RNN 266	Leyland Tiger Cub PSUC1/2	543484	Alexander (Scottish Bus Group style)	DP45F	1954	Ex. Barton. Chilwell, Notts. (678)	1/1974	2/1975
RNN 617	Leyland Tiger Cub PSUC1/2	543473	Alexander (Scottish Bus Group style)	DP43F	1954	Ex. Barton. Chilwell, Notts. (679)	1/1974	2/1975
946 MRR	AEC Reliance	2U3RA 4147	Yeates 'Europa'	C51F	8/1962	Ex. Barton. Chilwell, Notts. (946)	1/1974	2/1975
947 MRR	AEC Reliance	2U3RA 4148	Yeates 'Europa'	C53F	6/1962	Ex. Barton. Chilwell, Notts. (947)	1/1974	2/1975
945 MRR	AEC Reliance	4MU3RA 3861	Yeates 'Europa'	C51F	6/1962	Ex. Barton. Chilwell, Notts. (945)	2/1974	3/1975
864 HAL	AEC Reliance	2MU3RV 3044	Plaxton 'Panorama'	C41F	2/1961	Ex. Barton. Chilwell, Notts. (864)	2/1974	3/1975
XTH944M	AEC Reliance	6U3ZR 24350	Caetano 'Lisboa' II	C53F	5/1974	New	5/1974 lic.6/74	8/1978
CKP 441K	Bedford VAS5	2T473600	Duple 'Vista 25'	C29F	3/1972	Ex. Horlock. Northfleet, London. (94)	6/1974 lic.10/74	9/1977
OCO 511	Leyland Titan PD2/40	580417	Metro-Cammell 'Orion'	H30/26R	5/1958	Ex. Plymouth C T (111)	7/1974	10/1974
OCO 512	Leyland Titan PD2/40	580898	Metro-Cammell 'Orion'	H30/26R	5/1958	Ex. Plymouth C T (112)	7/1974	9/1975
OCO 514	Leyland Titan PD2/40	580900	Metro-Cammell 'Orion'	H30/26R	5/1958	Ex. Plymouth C T (114)	7/1974	7/1976
OCO 516	Leyland Titan PD2/40	580909	Metro-Cammell 'Orion'	H30/26R	5/1958	Ex. Plymouth C T (116)	7/1974	9/1975
OCO 519	Leyland Titan PD2/40	580921	Metro-Cammell 'Orion'	H30/26R	5/1958	Ex. Plymouth C T (119) (see note R)	7/1974	7/1976
JCH 265	Leyland Titan PD2/12	551737	Metro-Cammell 'Orion'	H33/26RD	1956	Ex. Trent M T (755) via: Whippet. Hilton, Cambs.	7/1974	3/1976
UKG 273	Leyland Tiger Cub PSUC1/2	605833	Metro-Cammell	DP41F	1/1961	Ex. Western Welsh (1273) via: Wylie. Thorne, N.Yorks.	8/1974	9/1975
PBN 657	Leyland Titan PD2/27	600915	Metro-Cammell 'Orion'	FH35/27F	1/1961	Ex. Bolton C T (139) via: Rennie. Dunfermline, Fife.	11/1974	1/1978
GCY 74N	Leyland Leopard PSU3B/4R	7400391	Plaxton 'Panorama Elite Express III'	C53F	10/1974	New (See note S)	not delivered	
GNY431N	Leyland Leopard PSU3B/4R	7400390	Plaxton 'Panorama Elite Express III'	C53F	11/1974	New (See note S)	11/1974	8/1978

HFP 118N	Bedford YRQ	EW451609	Plaxton 'Panorama Elite III'	C45F	2/1975	New	2/1975	2/1978
HFP 119N	Bedford YRQ	EW451616	Plaxton 'Panorama Elite III'	C45F	2/1975	New	2/1975	2/1978
JXD 548D	Bedford VAL14	6831579	Plaxton 'Panorama I'	C52F	4/1966	Ex. Fulton. Sacriston, Durham.	4/1975 lic: 5/75	by 10/1976
XUP 457F	Bedford VAL70	7855237	Plaxton 'Panorama II'	C52F	5/1968	Ex. Martindale. Ferryhill, Durham (5)	5/1975	by 10/1976
SCG 856	Leyland Tiger Cub PSUC1/2	576011	Weymann	DP41F	11/1957	Ex. King Alfred M S. Winchester. via: Hants & Dorset (2702)	5/1975	2/1978
TRN 733	Leyland Leopard PSU3/3RT	L02492	Plaxton 'Panorama'	C49F	10/1963	Ex. Ribble M S (733)	5/1975 lic: 6/75	8/1976
TRN 735	Leyland Leopard PSU3/3RT	L02308	Plaxton 'Panorama'	C49F	10/1963	Ex. Ribble M S (735)	5/1975	5/1976
TRN 739	Leyland Leopard PSU3/3RT	L02886	Plaxton 'Panorama'	C49F	11/1963	Ex. Ribble M S (739)	5/1975 lic: 7/75	7/1981
TRN 759	Leyland Leopard PSU3/3RT	L03594	Plaxton 'Panorama'	C49F	2/1964	Ex. Ribble M S (759)	by6/1975 lic: 7/75	7/1976
UBN 904	Leyland Titan PD3A/2	611980	East Lancs. (fitted St Helens type front)	FH41/32F	3/1962	Ex. Bolton C T (171) via: Shennan. Drongan, Ayrshire.	8/1975 lic: 9/75	7/1980
UBN 907	Leyland Titan PD3A/2	612030	East Lancs. (fitted St Helens type front)	FH41/32F	2/1962	Ex. Bolton C T (174) via: Shennan. Drongan, Ayrshire.	8/1975 lic: 9/75	9/1978
KCK 854	Leyland Titan PD3/4	570834	Burlingham 'Sabrina' (see note T)	FH41/31F	10/1957	Ex. Ribble M S (1508)	8/1975 lic: 2/76	2/1978
KCK 866	Leyland Titan PD3/4	571498	Burlingham 'Sabrina' (see note T)	FH41/31F	1/1958	Ex. Ribble M S (1520)	8/1975 lic: 2/76	2/1978
TRN 743	Leyland Leopard PSU3/3RT	L02446	Plaxton 'Panorama'	C49F	11/1963	Ex. Ribble M S (743) via: Edmunds. Rassau.	7/1975 lic: 9/75	8/1981
WCG 104	Leyland Tiger Cub PSUC1/1	595155	Weymann	B45F	10/1959	Ex. King Alfred M S. Winchester. via: Hants & Dorset (2704)	9/1975 lic: 10/75	7/1981
NAY 438P	AEC Reliance	6U3ZR 32770	Plaxton 'Supreme Express'	C53F	3/1976	New	3/1976	5/1983
BUX 236L	Bedford YRQ	CW454206	Duple 'Dominant'	C45F	5/1973	Ex. Pinged Hill Garage, (Gravells) Kidwelly.	4/1976	7/1977
OAY 393P	AEC Reliance	6U3ZR 33182	Plaxton 'Supreme Express'	C53F	6/1976	New	6/1976	5/1983

RFF 118L	AEC Reliance	6U3ZR 7879	Van-Hool 'Vistadome'	C53F	7/1973	Ex. Parry. Blaenau Ffestiniog, Gwynedd.	6/1976	7/1977
BGV 238L	Bedford YRQ	2T474511	Caetano 'Cascais II' Express	C45F	2/1973	Ex. Beeston. Hadleigh, Suffolk.	6/1976	7/1977
RUH656M	Ford R1014	BCO4MA 46713	Willowbrook 'Expressway'	C45F	3/1974	Ex. Tri-Afon Motors. (Peter Smith) Garnswllt, West Glam.	6/1976 lic.1/77	9/1977
HGE 469L	Bedford YRQ	CW451813	Willowbrook 'Expressway'	C45F	4/1973	Ex. Bellairs & Dootson. Leigh, Lancashire.	9/1976 lic.10/76	11/1982
DBC 263K	Ford R192	BCO4KR 57328	Caetano 'Cascais'	C45F	5/1972	Ex. Grahams. Kettering, Northants. On loan from Moseley, (Dealer)	5/1977	6/1977
PTH 647R	Bedford YMT	GW451280	Duple 'Dominant II'	C53F	7/1977	New	7/1977	8/1978
RTH 130S	Bedford YMT	GW451411	Duple 'Dominant II'	C53F	7/1977	New	8/1977	8/1978
SGD 610	Leyland Atlantean PDR1/1	622038	Alexander 'A type'	H44/34F	10/1962	Ex. Greater Glasgow PTE (LA32)	9/1977 lic.7/78	12/1979
SGD 621	Leyland Atlantean PDR1/1	621451	Alexander 'A type'	H44/34F	11/1962	Ex. Greater Glasgow PTE (LA43)	9/1977 lic.7/78	9/1979
SGD 635	Leyland Atlantean PDR1/1	621223	Alexander 'A type'	H44/34F	11/1962	Ex. Greater Glasgow PTE (LA57)	9/1977 lic.7/78	by 10/1979
TCK 459	Leyland Leopard PSU3/1R	629164	Marshall	B53F	1963	Ex. Ribble M S (459)	9/1977 lic.2/78	12/1980
TCK 462	Leyland Leopard PSU3/1R	629228	Marshall	B53F	1963	Ex. Ribble M S (462)	9/1977 lic.2/78	3/1981
JHF 821	Leyland Atlantean PDR1/1	610395	Metro-Cammell	H44/33F	7/1961	Ex. Wallasey C T (21) via: Godfrey Abbott. Sale, Cheshire.	11/1977 lic.7/78	4/1980
FKY 250E	Leyland Titan PD3A/2	L63139	Neepsend (Fitted St. Helens type front)	H40/30F	1/1967	Ex. Bradford C T (250) via: W. Yorkshire PTE (2250)	2/1978 lic.7/78	11/1979
TRN 753	Leyland Leopard PSU3/3RT	L03373	Plaxton 'Panorama'	C49F	1/1964	Ex. Ribble M S (753) via: John Lewis. Morriston, Glam.	8/1978	7/1979
527 VRB	Bristol Lodekka FLF6B	199.095	Eastern Coach Works	H38/32F	8/1962	Ex. Trent M. T. (688) (see note U)	9/1978	10/1978
528 VRB	Bristol Lodekka FLF6B	199.096	Eastern Coach Works	H38/32F	8/1962	Ex. Trent M. T. (689) (see note U)	9/1978	10/1978
VCS 431	Albion Lowlander LR1	62120D	Alexander 'C type'	H40/31F	1963	Ex. Western SMT (N1877) (see note U)	9/1978	10/1978

217 HUM	Leyland Leopard PSU3/3R	L04091	Plaxton 'Panorama'	C49F	3/1964	Ex. West Wales Motors. Tycroes, Carms (67). (see note V)	10/1978	by 10/1979
EVL 550E	Leyland Panther PSUR1/1R	701346	Roe	B49F	6/1967	Ex. Lincoln C T (42)	10/1978	7/1980
EVL 552E	Leyland Panther PSUR1/1R	701410	Roe	B49F	7/1967	Ex. Lincoln C T (44)	10/1978 lic.11/78	7/1980
EVL 553E	Leyland Panther PSUR1/1R	701411	Roe	B49F	7/1967	Ex. Lincoln C T (45)	10/1978	7/1980
NCR268M	Ford Transit	BCO5NB 54045	Bristol Street Motors	B12F	9/1973	Ex. E. J. James. Burry Port, Carms.	2/1979	12/1983
XBX 830T	AEC Reliance	6U3ZR 37970	Plaxton 'Supreme Exp. IV'	C53F	6/1979	New	6/1979	6/1984
XBX 831T	AEC Reliance	6U3ZR 37974	Plaxton 'Supreme Exp. IV'	C53F	6/1979	New	6/1979	9/1985
4991 VT	AEC Reliance	2U3RA 4994	Duple 'Commander I'	C49F	1964	Ex. Potteries M T (C991) via: G. Davies. Ebbw Vale.	8/1979	2/1980
BOF 857C	AEC Reliance	2MU4RA 5836	Harrington 'Grenadier'	C43F	3/1965	Ex. G. Davies. Ebbw Vale.	8/1979	not operated
MLL 934	AEC Regal IV RF	9821LT 668	Metro-Cammell	B39F	9/1952	Ex. London Transport (RF516)	9/1979	11/1979
MLL 938	AEC Regal IV RF	9821LT 647	Metro-Cammell	B39F	9/1952	Ex. London Transport (RF520) Returned with mechanical fault.	9/1979	not operated
MXX 489	AEC Regal IV RF	9821LT 915	Metro-Cammell	B39F	3/1953	Ex. London Transport (RF512)	9/1979	2/1981
HEO 278	Leyland Titan PD2A/27	611309	Massey	H37/27F	10/1961	Ex. Barrow-in-Furness C T (108)	9/1979	3/1985
BTH 364V	AEC Reliance	6U3ZR 37261	Duple 'Dominant Exp. II'	C53F	10/1979	New	10/1979	1/1987
BTH 365V	AEC Reliance	6U3ZR 37886	Duple 'Dominant Exp. II'	C53F	11/1979	New	11/1979	1/1987
BUF 528C	Leyland Titan PD2/37	L20884	Weymann	H37/27F	1/1965	Ex. Brighton C T (28) via: Warrington B T (98)	1/1980 lic.2/80	10/1987
BUF 529C	Leyland Titan PD2/37	L20885	Weymann	H37/27F	1/1965	Ex. Brighton C T (30) via: Warrington B T (99)	1/1980 lic.2/80	3/1986
JRJ 272E	Leyland Titan PD2/40	L64821	Metro-Cammell 'Orion'	H36/28F	4/1967	Ex. Salford C T (272) via: Gtr. Manchester PTE (3118)	4/1980 lic.5/80	3/1984

JRJ 277E	Leyland Titan PD2/40	L65096	Metro-Cammell 'Orion'	H36/28F	4/1967	Ex. Salford C T (277) via: Gtr. Manchester PTE (3123)	4/1980 lic.5/80	12/1983
TRN 387	Leyland Titan PD3A/1	623806	Metro-Cammell 'Orion'	H39/31F	11/1963	Ex. Preston C T (85)	5/1980 lic.6/80	3/1981
JRJ 261E	Leyland Titan PD2/40	L64304	Metro-Cammell 'Orion'	H36/28F	4/1967	Ex. Salford C T (261) via: Gtr. Manchester PTE (3107)	7/1980 lic.10/80	2/1984
HRO 659C	Bedford SB5	95555	Duple 'Bella Vega'	C41F	5/1965	Ex. Brown & Simmonds. Kingswood, Bristol. (see note W)	9/1980	11/1981
RBO 119G	Bedford J2SZ10	9T124426	Plaxton 'Embassy'	C20F	7/1969	Ex. Williams. Llansamlet. West Glam.	10/1980 lic.12/80	4/1982
BVJ 160B	Bedford VAS1	1701	Plaxton 'Embassy'	C29F	7/1964	Ex. A. A. Thomas. Gorseinon, Swansea.	11/1980	4/1982
PFH 886F	Ford R192	BCO4FL 24858	Duple 'Viceroy'	C45F	4/1968	Ex. Brown & Simmonds (4). Kingswood, Bristol. (see note W)	2/1981	3/1984
KDB 405F	Leyland Leopard PSU4/1R	703983	East Lancs.	B43D	3/1968	Ex. Stockport C T (405) via: Gtr. Manchester PTE (5085)	3/1981	5/1984
HTJ 131F	Leyland Leopard PSU4/2R	800347	East Lancs.	B43F	4/1968	Ex. Leigh C T (20) via: Gtr. Manchester PTE (6060)	3/1981	31/7/88
FTF 703F	Leyland Titan PD3/4	702351	East Lancs.	H41/32F	11/1967	Ex. Ramsbottom UDC (9) via: Gtr. Manchester PTE (6409)	3/1981 lic.12/82	4/1983
OTJ 334G	Leyland Titan PD3/4	804987	East Lancs.	H41/32F	2/1969	Ex. Ramsbottom UDC (10) via: Gtr. Manchester PTE (6410)	3/1981	2/1984
ABV 357B	Bedford J2SZ10	187981	Plaxton 'Embassy'	C20F	3/1964	Ex. Smith. Cymmer, West Glam. Accident damaged – for spares.	4/1981	not operated
ELU 504C	Bedford SB5	95467	Duple 'Bella Vega'	C41F	6/1965	Ex. Travelways. Barry, S.Glam. Acquired for spares. (see note W)	6/1981	not operated
HTJ 134F	Leyland Leopard PSU4/2R	800434	East Lancs.	B43F	4/1968	Ex. Leigh C T (23) (for spares) via: Gtr. Manchester PTE (6063)	6/1981	not operated
TRK 5F	Leyland Leopard PSU3A/2RT	802605	Plaxton 'Panorama I'	C51F	7/1968	Ex. Llynfi. Maesteg, Glam. (127)	7/1981	10/1982
TRK 6F	Leyland Leopard PSU3A/2RT	802710	Plaxton 'Panorama I'	C51F	7/1968	Ex. Llynfi. Maesteg, Glam. (128)	7/1981	6/1983
SDD 334G	Ford R192	BCO4FL 19985	Duple 'Viceroy'	C45F	7/1969	Ex. Brown & Simmonds (3). Kingswood, Bristol. (see note W)	8/1981	3/1984
VWG 407	Bedford VAS1	1340	Duple 'Bella Vista' (7ft 6ins wide body)	C29F	c5/1963	Ex. Alexander Midland (MW269) via: James. Llangeitho, Cards.	8/1981	3/1982

369 FGB	Bedford VAS1	1012	Duple 'Bella Vista' (7ft 6ins wide body)	C29F	1962	Ex. David MacBrayne Ltd. (17) via: James. Llangeitho, Cards.	8/1981	8/1982
KHU 308L	Ford Transit	BCO5LJ 57158	Ford	12	11/1972	Ex. Avon AHA (Non PSV) Bristol.	9/1981	operated as NPSV
KTH 530X	Volvo B58-56	16344	Plaxton 'Supreme IV'	C53F	8/1981	New	8/1981	4/1982
JBX 693X	Volvo B58-56	16765	Plaxton 'Supreme IV'	C53F	11/1981	New (see note X)	11/1981	5/1982
JBX 694X	Volvo B58-56	16532	Duple 'Dominant II'	C53F	11/1981	New (see note X)	11/1981	5/1982
KDB 406F	Leyland Leopard PSU4/1R	703996	East Lancs.	B43D	3/1968	Ex. Stockport C T (406) via: Gtr. Manchester PTE (5086)	11/1981 lic.12/81	6/1984
FEK 1 F	Leyland Titan PD2/37	702676	Massey	H37/27F	4/1968	Ex. Wigan C T (25) via: Gtr. Manchester PTE (3290)	11/1981 lic.1/82	31/7/88
PTH 100K	Bedford SB5	1T490212	Duple 'Vega 31'	C41F	9/1971	Ex Gwyn Williams, Lower Tumble, Carms (29). (see note W)	11/1981	6/1983
JRC 254D	Leyland Leopard PSU3/3R	L43547	Metro-Cammell (on Weymann shell)	DP51F	4/1966	Ex. Trent M T (254) via: Dean Forest. Joys Green, Glos.	6/1982	3/1984
WYB741H	AEC Reliance 691	6U3ZR 7282	Duple 'Commander IV'	C51F	8/1969	Ex. Dean Forest. Joys Green, Glos. (see note W)	6/1982	4/1984
JWA 966J	Ford R226	BCO4KG 51987	Plaxton 'Panorama Elite II'	C53F	4/1971	Ex. Williams & Lewis. Blaina, Gwent.	10/1982	not operated
HEL 203D	Leyland Atlantean PDR1/1	L61314	Metro-Cammell	H43/31F	9/1966	Ex. Bournemouth C T (203) via: Waddon. Caerphilly, Glam.	11/1982 lic.6/83	31/7/88
ARN 599C	Leyland Leopard PSU3/1R	L24485	Weymann	B53F	5/1965	Ex. Ribble M S (599) via: Waddon. Caerphilly, Glam.	11/1982 lic.12/82	3/1985
ARN 605C	Leyland Leopard PSU3/1R	L24679	Weymann	B53F	5/1965	Ex. Ribble M S (605) via: Waddon. Caerphilly (for spares)	11/1982	not operated
DCD 19C	Leyland Titan PD2/37	L41166	Weymann	H37/27F	10/1965	Ex. Brighton C T (19) via: Wood. Verwood, Dorset.	12/1982	4/1983
LSY 140J	Ford R192	BCO4KU 57358	Plaxton 'Panorama Elite II'	C45F	11/1970	Ex. Wood. Verwood, Dorset.	2/1983	3/1985
YTE 952D	Leyland Tiger Cub PSUC1/12	L70320	Massey	B45F	1/1967	Ex. Fishwick. Leyland, Lancs. (3) via: West Wales. Tycroes, Carms.(80)	4/1983	8/1985
LBX 550G	Leyland Tiger Cub PSUC1/12T	854696	Willowbrook	DP45F	4/1969	Ex. West Wales. Tycroes, Carms. (59)	4/1983	3/1986

EPT 615G	Leyland Leopard PSU3/3R	900446	Plaxton 'Derwent' II	B55F	7/1969	Ex. Summerson. West Auckland. via: West Wales. Tycroes, Carms (81)	4/1983	11/1986
ASC 654B	Leyland Titan PD3/6	L20904	Alexander 'E type'	H41/29F	6/1964	Ex. Lothian R T (654) via: Hewlett & Sutton. Morecambe, Lancs.	5/1983	6/1983
ASC 659B	Leyland Titan PD3/6	L21051	Alexander 'E type'	H41/29F	7/1964	Ex. Lothian R T (659) via: Hewlett & Sutton. Morecambe, Lancs.	5/1983	4/1984
KTJ 205C	Leyland Titan PD2/37	L25040	East Lancs.	H37/28F	4/1965	Ex. Lancaster C T (205) via: Hewlett & Sutton. Morecambe.	5/1983	31/7/88
EWS 804D	Leyland Atlantean PDR1/1	L62453	Alexander 'A type'	H43/31F	10/1966	Ex. Lothian R T (804)	5/1983	not operated
PBX 280Y	DAF MB200DKFL600	231395	LAG 'Galaxy'	C53F	5/1983	New	5/1983	31/7/88
DGC 114H	Leyland Leopard PSU3A/4R	7001487	Plaxton 'Panorama Elite'	C53F	7/1970	Ex. West Wales. Tycroes, Carms. (73)	6/1983	6/1984
BUF 133C	Leyland Leopard PSU3/1R	L25180	Marshall	B53F	10/1965	Ex. Southdown M S (133) via: Dean Forest. Joys Green. Glos.	6/1983 lic.2/84	2/1987
FUS 168L	Leyland Atlantean AN68/1R	7203683	Alexander 'AL type'	H45/29F	2/1973	Ex. Strathclyde (LA648)	7/1983 lic.10/83	31/7/88
PBC 108G	Leyland Atlantean PDR1A/1	803374	Park Royal	H43/31F	4/1969	Ex. Leicester C T (108)	2/1984	8/1985
EMB159K	Ford R226	BCO4LU 57525	Plaxton 'Panorama Elite II'	C53F	4/1972	Ex. Stevens. Tividale, W-Midlands. (see note W)	2/1984	2/1987
OAY 393P	AEC Reliance	6U3ZR 33182	Plaxton 'Supreme Express'	C53F	6/1976	Re-acquired from dealer.	2/1984	9/1985
YHK 729F	Bristol RELH6G	RELH-4-129	Eastern Coach Works (coach shell / bus seats)	DP53F Bus seats	4/1968	Ex. Tillings. Chelmsford (T442) via: West Wales. Tycroes, Carms.	3/1984	1/1986
PBC 115G	Leyland Atlantean PDR1A/1	803392	Park Royal	H43/31F	4/1969	Ex. Leicester C T (115) via: West Wales. Tycroes (97)	3/1984 lic.4/84	8/1985
FUS 159L	Leyland Atlantean AN68/1R	7203682	Alexander 'AL type'	H45/29F	1/1973	Ex. Strathclyde (LA639) via: Queencity. Burford, Oxford.	3/1984 lic.5/84	1/1986
DTJ 198J	Ford R226	BCO4KR 44435	Plaxton 'Panorama Elite II'	C53F	3/1971	Ex. Costelloe. Barnoldswick, Lancs. (see note W)	3/1984 lic.4/84	9/1985
DDF 300L	AEC Reliance	6U3ZR 8009	Plaxton 'Panorama Elite Express II'	C53F	8/1972	Ex. Dean Forest. Joys Green, Glos. (see note Z)	4/1984	not operated
PUF 263M	Ford R1114	BCO4PJ 55522	Duple 'Dominant'	C49F	7/1974	Ex. Southdown (1423) via: Wimpy, National Contractor. (see note W)	4/1984	6/1984

HRN 953G	Leyland Leopard PSU3A/4R	803782	Plaxton 'Panorama Elite I'	C49F	5/1969	Ex. Ribble M S (953) via: Teahan. St. Albans, Hertford.	5/1984 lic.6/84	10/1984
MBX 86H	Leyland Leopard PSU3/3RT	900561	Willowbrook	B49F	7/1969	Ex. James. Llangeitho, Cardigan. (see note Y)	5/1984	2/1988
EUF 220D	Leyland Leopard PSU3/3RT	L61730	Plaxton 'Panorama'	C49F	7/1966	Ex. Southdown M S (1220) via: West Wales. Tycroes, Carms.	6/1984	8/1984
KCK 983H	Leyland Leopard PSU4A/4R	903545	Plaxton 'Panorama Elite I'	C40F	3/1970	Ex. Ribble M S (983) via: Newton. Dingwall, Highland.	6/1984	6/1985
A802 XEP	Leyland Tiger TRCTL11/3R	8201459	LAG 'Galaxy'	C53F	6/1984	New	6/1984	7/1988
WJF 378S	AEC Reliance	6U3ZR 36686	Duple 'Dominant II' Exp.	C53F	5/1978	Ex. Brewer. Caerau, Bridgend.	6/1984	31/7/88
HGD 863L	Leyland Atlantean AN68/1R	7204353	Alexander 'AL type'	H45/29F	4/1973	Ex. Strathclyde (LA657) (see note Z)	7/1984 lic.7/84	not operated
HGD 869L	Leyland Atlantean AN68/1R	7300106	Alexander 'AL type'	H45/29F	5/1973	Ex. Strathclyde (LA663) (see note Z)	7/1984 lic.9/84	not operated
HGD 871L	Leyland Atlantean AN68/1R	7300108	Alexander 'AL type'	H45/29F	4/1973	Ex. Strathclyde (LA665)(see note Z) via: Richardson. Helston, Cornwall.	7/1984 lic.9/84	not operated
FBW 22K	Ford R226	BCO4LE 46187	Plaxton 'Panorama Elite II'	C53F	4/1972	Ex. Clements. Nailsea, N-Somerset. (see note W)	7/1984	2/1985
VBW821L	Leyland Leopard PSU3B/4R	7204442	Duple 'Dominant' Express	C51F	7/1973	Ex. Weaver & Best. Tredegar, Gwent. (see note Z)	8/1984 lic.11/84	not operated
RGS 92R	Leyland Leopard PSU5A/4R	7604781	Plaxton 'Supreme'	C57F	3/1977	(see note A1)	8/1984	10/1984
OCU 650J	AEC Reliance	6U3ZR 7799	Plaxton 'Panorama Elite II'	C53F	7/1971	Ex. Weaver & Best. Tredegar, Gwent. (12) (see note Z)	8/1984 lic.3/85	not operated
ASC 692B	Leyland Titan PD3/6	L22020	Alexander 'E type'	H41/29F	9/1964	Ex. 'D' Coaches. Morriston, Swansea. Loan from J. Sykes (dealer) Barnsley.	9/1984	9/1984
YSC 443K	Leyland Leopard PSU3/3R	7200489	Alexander 'Y type'	C49F	5/1972	Ex. Scottish Omnibuses (ZH443) via: Kenmargra. Linthwaite, W-Yorks.	9/1984 lic.10/84	9/1986
HNT 841N	Bedford YRQ	EW452670	Duple 'Dominant'	C45F	3/1975	Ex. Globe. Barnsley, S-Yorks. (see note Z)	10/1984 lic.2/85	not operated
LDH 139J	Ford R226	BCO4KG 53754	Duple 'Viceroy'	C53F	6/1971	Ex. Brown. Horley, Surrey. For spares (see note W)	10/1984	not operated
KHY 18X	Toyota Hiace		Toyota	11	by 7/82	Ex. Private Owner, Llanelli.	NPSV -/1984	6/1988

WRS 671L	Ford R1114	BCO4ML 63958	Alexander 'Y type'	B53F	6/1973	Ex. Alexander Northern (NT71) (see note Z)	11/1984 lic.5/85	not operated
RRG 348N	Ford R1014	BCO4PT 62871	Duple 'Dominant'	C45F	8/1974	Ex. Alexander Northern (NT77) (see note W)	11/1984	1/1987
URO 856J	Seddon Pennine 4	48516	Plaxton 'Panorama Elite II'	C49F	1971	Ex. Dragon. Stocksbridge, S-Yorks.	3/1985	6/1985
YSD 353L	Leyland Leopard PSU3/3R	7202939	Alexander 'Y type'	C49F	1/1973	Ex. Western SMT (2393) via: Highland Scottish (L38) (see note Z)	3/1985 lic.6/85	not operated
YSD 355L	Leyland Leopard PSU3/3R	7203049	Alexander 'Y type'	C49F	1/1973	Ex. Western SMT (2395) via: Highland Scottish(L40) (see note Z)	3/1985 lic.6/85	not operated
BAA 884J	Ford R226	BCO4KA 48563	Duple 'Viceroy'	C53F	6/1971	Ex. Finchley Coaches. London N12. (see note W)	4/1985	11/1985
CNY 333V	Ford R1114	BCRSUR 278480	Caetano 'Alfa'	C53F	11/1979	Ex. Thomas. Clydach Vale, Glam. via: Thorpe. London, W10.	4/1985	12/1985
FNM 861Y	Leyland Tiger TRCTL11/3R	8200541	Plaxton 'Paramount 3200'	C57F	1/1983	Ex. Goldenport. London, SW16. Dealer loan.	5/1985	7/1985
ACA 297A (102 UTF)	Leyland Leopard L1	603603	East Lancs.	B42D	1/1962	Ex Lancaster CT (102) Reg:102UTF via: Hollis. Queensferry, Flintshire.	6/1985	2/1986
HSF 555N	Ford R1014	BCO4PJ 54206	Duple 'Dominant' Express	C45F	2/1975	Ex. Alexander Northern (NT199) (see note W)	6/1985 lic.8/85	1/1987
RLJ 89X	Leyland Leopard PSU3F/5R	8030127	Plaxton 'Supreme IV'	C53F	10/1981	Ex. Marchwood. Totton, Hants.	6/1985	12/1985
VNY 468G	Leyland Leopard PSU3A/4R	901368	Plaxton 'Panorama Elite I'	C53F	4/1969	Ex. Creamline. Tonmawr, W-Glam.	8/1985	31/7/88
RVB 995E	Leyland Leopard PSU3/3R	L65211	Plaxton 'Panorama I'	C51F	1967	Ex. Burman. Cradley Heath, West Midlands.	9/1985	6/1986
JRB 188N	Bedford YRT	EW451061	Duple 'Dominant'	C53F	6/1975	Ex National Coal Board. Derby area.	9/1985 lic.11/85	7/1988
YUR 995K	Ford R226	BCO4LC 59203	Caetano 'Estoril'	C53F	9/1971	Ex. Rhyce-Rees & Clarke. Cliftonville, Kent. (see note W)	9/1985 lic:10/85	1/1987
OKU 690R	Bedford YLQ	FW454030	Willowbrook	B49F	12/1976	Ex. National Coal Board. Barnsley Main. South Yorks. (see note Z)	10/1985 lic:12/85	not operated
ACY 119A (VWG383)	Leyland Tiger Cub PSUC1/12	626910	Alexander 'Y type'	C41F	5/1963	Ex. Alexander Midland (MPD244) via; Thomas Bros. Llangadog, (VWG383)	10/1985 lic:4/86	2/1988
BWG838L	Leyland Leopard PSU3/3R	7203934	Alexander 'Y type'	B53F	10/1972	Ex. Alexander Midland (MPE138) (see note Z)	10/1985 lic:1/86	not operated

TVA481M	AEC Reliance	6U3ZR 28507	Plaxton 'Panorama Elite III'	C51F	6/1974	Ex. Bleanch. Hetton-le-hole, Tyne & Wear. (see note Z)	10/1985 lic:5/86	not operated
FUS 169L	Leyland Atlantean AN68/1R	7203558	Alexander 'AL type'	H45/29F	2/1973	Loan from 'D' Coaches. Morriston, Swansea.	10/1985	10/1985
LVO 93E	AEC Reliance	6U2R6835	Plaxton 'Panorama I'	C53F	6/1967	Ex. Barton. Chilwell, Notts. (1093) via: Bannister. Owston Ferry, Lincs.	1/1986	3/1987
78 HBC	Leyland Titan PD3A/1	L03019	East Lancs.	H41/33R	1964	Ex. Swansea R T I T B (Non PSV) (see note W, and note A2)	3/1986	4/1986
MSJ 379P	Seddon Pennine 7	59898	Alexander 'T type'	C49F	7/1976	Ex. Western SMT (2573) via: Thomas. Barry, South Glam.	6/1986	2/1988
NCK 637	Leyland Atlantean PDR1/1R	591354	Metro-Cammell	H44/34F	3/1960	Ex. Ribble M. S. (637) via: Evans. Chew Stoke, Somerset. (see note W)	8/1986	10/1986
GBX 57N	Bedford CFS	DY625043	Dormobile	12	10/1974	Ex. Jones Motors. Login, Whitland, Carmarthenshire.	11/1986	31/7/88
UCK 500	Leyland Leopard PSU3/1R	L03363	Marshall	B53F	3/1964	Ex. Ribble M S (500) via: Hills. Tredegar, Gwent.	1/1987	31/7/88
PUF 173H	Leyland Leopard PSU3/1RT	804829	Northern Counties	DP49F	9/1969	Ex. Southdown M S (473) via: Hills. Tredegar, Gwent.	1/1987	31/7/88
PUF 174H	Leyland Leopard PSU3/1RT	804831	Northern Counties	DP49F	10/1969	Ex. Southdown M S (474) via: Hills. Tredegar, Gwent.	1/1987	31/7/88
FWO 153L	Leyland Leopard PSU4B/4R	7201340	Willowbrook	B47F	9/1972	Ex. Hills. Tredegar, Gwent.	1/1987	31/7/88
PUF 163H	Leyland Leopard PSU3/1RT	804483	Northern Counties	DP49F	10/1969	Ex. Southdown M S (463) via: Hills. Tredegar, Gwent.	3/1987	31/7/88
GAX 355L	Leyland Leopard PSU3B/4R	7202571	Plaxton 'Panorama Elite E III' (Fitted 'Supreme IV' front)	C53F	10/1972	Ex. Hills. Tredegar, Gwent.	3/1987	31/7/88
SGF 483L (40 WMN)	Bristol RELH6L	RELH-4-327	Plaxton 'Panorama Elite II'	C51F	5/1971	Ex. I o M Road Services 40 (40 WMN) via: Riddler. Dulverton, Somerset.	3/1987	7/1988
OVK144M	Leyland Atlantean AN68/1R	7301847	Alexander 'AL type'	H42/34F	8/1973	Ex. Tyneside P T E (145) via:- Rees & Williams. Tycroes, Carms.	4/1987	31/7/88
VLK 662S	Ford Transit	BDO5TR 54799	Dormobile	B16F	1978	Ex. Barrett. Great Mongham, Kent.	11/1987	2/7/88
HCS 793N	Leyland Leopard PSU3/3R	7405880	Alexander 'Y type'	B53F	3/1975	Ex. Western S M T (2508) via: Scottish Bus Group Engineering.	1/1988	31/7/88
SCS 328M	Leyland Leopard PSU3/3R	7401296	Alexander 'Y type'	B53F	6/1974	Ex. Western S M T (2459) via: Northern Scottish (NPE139)	2/1988	31/7/88

SCS 327M	Leyland Leopard PSU3/3R	7401594	Alexander 'Y type'	B53F	6/1974	Ex. Western S M T (2458) via: Northern Scottish (NPE138)	3/1988	not operated
NMJ 289V	AEC Reliance	6U2R 38576	Duple 'Dominant II'	C53F	6/1980	Ex. Gower & Martin (T/A: Celtic Coaches) Burry Port, Carms (7)	2/1988	31/7/88

The vehicles listed below were owned by E. J. Roberts, T/A: Tommy Roberts & Son, Meinciau. Carmarthenshire. They operated on E. J. Roberts' licence discs; **PG 6280** from Eynon's premises until 7th January 1987.

HAD 289L	Seddon Pennine 6	53035	Plaxton 'Panorama Elite III'	C57F	1973	Ex. Hopkins. Ogmore Vale, Mid-Glam.	6/1986	1/1987
NCK 637	Leyland Atlantean PDR1/1R	591354	Metro-Cammell	H44/34F	3/1960	Ex. Ribble M S (1648) via: Evans. Chew Stoke, Avon (8/1996)	10/1986	1/1987
LJH 245L	Bedford YRT	CW452170	Plaxton 'Panorama Elite III'	C53F	3/1973	Ex. Limebourne. London, SW8. (6) via: Briggs. Carr Vale, Derby.	7/1986	1/1987
JUG 555L	Ford R226	BC04LY 56184	Plaxton 'Panorama Elite II'	C53F	8/1972	Ex. Gwyn Williams & Sons. Lower Tumble, Carmarthenshire (48).	8/1986	1/1987
BCP 592R	Ford R1114	BC04SY 69040	Plaxton 'Supreme'	C53F	7/1977	Ex. Miller. Calder Bank, Strathclyde.	11/1986	1/1987

The following vehicles were actually owned by **Davies Bros (Pencader) Ltd,** but operated on Eynon's licences from the time of their arrival at Trimsaran in June /July 1988 until 31st July, 1988 when Eynon's 32 licences were finally surrendered in exchange for 28 Davies Bros. (Pencader) Ltd, licence discs.

TPC 105X	Leyland Tiger TRCTL11/2R	8103203	Eastern Coach Works	DP49F	7/1982	Ex. London Country (TL5) via: Kentish Bus. Northfleet, London.	6/1988	31/7/88
WPH 136Y	Leyland Tiger TRCTL11/2R	8200387	Eastern Coach Works	DP49F	9/1982	Ex. London Country (TL36) via: Kentish Bus. Northfleet, London.	6/1988	31/7/88
WHL 279J	Daimler Fleetline CRG6LX	63760	Alexander 'N type'	H43/33F	5/1971	Ex. West Riding. (279) via: Hedingham & District (L120)	6/1988	31/7/88
OUT 11W	Leyland Leopard PSU3E/4R	8030608	Plaxton 'Supreme Express IV'	C53F	3/1981	Ex. Leicester C T (11) via: Cotterell. Mitcheldean, Glos.	7/1988	31/7/88
HEF 359N	Leyland Leopard PSU3C/4R	7501211	Duple 'Dominant'	B55F	7/1975	Ex. Cleveland Transit. Stockton-on-tees (359)	7/1988	31/7/88

ADDITIONAL VEHICLE NOTES

Note A	**OF 5483** (Bus No. 6) was new in September 1929 as a box van with the Dunlop Rubber Co, Birmingham. It was purchased by Eynon's in 1933 direct from Leyland Motors Ltd, re-bodied with a brand new Leyland B32R body in 1933.
Note B	**TJ 599** (Bus No. 8) was originally a demonstrator with Leyland Motors Ltd, fitted with a Leyland C32R body. Its body was extensively rebuilt by Jeffreys Commercial Motors, Swansea immediately after WW II, when it was converted to front entrance layout and fitted with bus seating.
Note C	**GJ 2397** had been re-bodied with a second-hand 1932 style Leyland body at some point during WW II, before Eynon's ownership. The body was extensively rebuilt by Jeffreys Commercial Motors, Swansea, whilst with Eynon's.
Note D	**CBX 435** was acquired via the Ministry of War Transport after military service in September 1944. It was previously registered UP 5095 and had lost its original registration number whilst working for the M O D during WW II.
Note E	**CK 4731** (Bus No. 12) had its Leyland C31R body converted to C33F layout by Jeffreys Commercial Motors, Swansea, and was retro-fitted with an 'oil' engine (diesel).
Note F	**EK 8878** (Bus No. 10) had its 'Leyland style' Northern Counties piano fronted body rebuilt by Jeffreys Commercial Motors, Swansea in May 1948. It had been acquired in 1948 from Red & White Services, where it was allocated F/N 846 but not operated. This was the first double decker operated by Eynon's. EK 8877 was also acquired from Red & White as a source of spares.
Note G	**TF 7310** was new to Leyland Motors as a demonstrator fitted with 'gearless' transmission (an early form of 'automatic' transmission). Leyland Motors later converted it to manual gearbox and sold it to James of Ammanford, passing to Williams (Pioneer) Laugharne before arriving at Eynon's in September 1949. Its 'piano fronted' Leyland body was also rebuilt by Jeffreys, Swansea in 1949.
Note H	**BTH 175** (Bus No. 19) later renumbered 24, was a wartime 'unfrozen' Leyland TD7 built to the order of W Alexander & Sons Ltd, Falkirk, Scotland, and stored (frozen). It was released from storage (unfrozen) by the Ministry of War Transport in 1941, and diverted to J James & Sons Ltd, Ammanford, Carmarthenshire. It was acquired by Eynon's in September 1955.
Note I	**FBX 489** a Commer 'Avenger I' was operated and maintained by Eynon's from July to September 1964 after acquiring Oliver Rowlands of Carway's licence (T/A: Oliver's Coaches). The coach was returned to Rowlands 'off hire' in September 1964 and laid up at his garage until sold in 1969.
Note J	**ETH 210D** a Bedford VAM14 carried an incorrect registration number plate ETH120D from new in June 1966, to February 1967 when it was corrected. (See photo on page 60).
Note K	**JBO 127** was converted to PSUC1/1T specification by fitting a two speed rear axle in 1968.
Note L	**LBX 547G** This Leyland 'Leopard' PSU3/3RT was ordered by Eynon's but not delivered by the dealer Arlington Motors, Cardiff. It remained at Arlington's from 5/1969 to 10/1969 when it eventually passed to West Wales Motors of Tycroes, repainted in their livery and re-registered MBX86H due to the change of year suffix in August, voiding the 'G' suffix. After many owners, Eynon's purchased this vehicle in May 1984 (15 years later) from James Bros, Llangeitho, Cardigan.

Note M	**HLW 177** was formerly London Transport (RT 190). During overhaul at London Transport in May 1957, its original Park Royal body was interchanged with the Park Royal body off (RT 1173) JXC 481. Sometime after Eynon's disposed of HLW 177 (RT 190), Cobham Bus Museum purchased the registration number from DVLA, to re-patronise the registration number to its original Park Royal body which is now in preservation still fitted to the chassis of (RT 1173) JXC 481. However, the now preserved HLW 177 (RT190) is **not** the original Eynon's vehicle. It's **JXC 481** masquerading as **HLW 177,** and featured in the 1998 film 'Good night Mr. Tom' staring actor John Thaw.
Note N	**OBX 1J** was the pride of Eynon's fleet, a Leyland 'Leopard' with Caetano 'Lisboa' coachwork which was exhibited at the Commercial Motor Show, Earls Court, London in September 1970. It was purchased by the company after the event closed, and carried a non-standard livery of two-tone 'metallic' blue with blue moquette seating and blue tinted interior fluorescent lighting.
Note O	**RCY 344** This AEC 'Regent V' received an overall advertisement livery of yellow and white for the 'Renault' dealership of Pinged Hill Garage Ltd, Kidwelly in October 1974.
Note P	**RCY 346** This AEC 'Regent V' received an all-over advertising livery in March 1974, for the **'Eisteddfod Genedlaethol yr Urdd 1975'** which was basically red, white and green. It reverted back to fleet livery in May 1975, when the event finished.
Note Q	**TTH 500L** the Caetano 'Lisboa II' bodied Leyland 'Leopard' was exhibited at the Commercial Motor Show, Earls Court, London in September 1972. It was not a 'grant aided' vehicle.
Note R	**OCO 519** a former Plymouth City Transport, Leyland 'Titan' was converted into a towing vehicle after withdrawal from passenger service in July 1976. Fitted with a tow-bar for recovery work, and weighted down with concrete building blocks, it ran on garage trade plates by December 1976. In February 1977 its roof and upper deck windows were removed to use as a tree lopper.

The former Plymouth C T, Leyland 'Titan' OCO 519 converted to tree lopper and recovery vehicle.

Note S	**GNY 431N** a Leyland PSU3B/4R 'Leopard' with Plaxton Panorama Elite Express III was originally ordered by Dorothy June Vowles (T/A: W G Vowles), Merthyr Tydfil but diverted to Eynon's in November 1974, in a white livery with blue waist band, to which they added a red waist band. Alternatively, Eynons had ordered an identical 'Leopard' with Plaxton body registered GCY74N, which was diverted to West Wales Motor Services, Tycroes in full Eynon's livery in October 1974. Both coaches were built to full bus grant specification and had consecutive chassis numbers 7400390 & 7400391.
Note T	**KCK 854/866** Leyland PD3/4 'Titans' were fitted with Burlingham fully fronted bodies that were nick-named 'Sabrinas' by the staff of their original owners Ribble Motor Services. KCK 854 received an all over advertisement, basically blue and orange for a local travel agent; Richards Travel, Llanelli in January 1976.
Note U	**527/8 VRB** Bristol 'Lodekka' FLF6B/ECW and **VCS 431** an Albion 'Lowlander'/Alexander were hired from Lister (dealer) Bolton, from September to October 1978, to cover vehicle shortages after engine failures on the three Greater Glasgow PTE 'Atlanteans'.
Note V	**217 HUM** The former West Wales Motor Services, Leyland 'Leopard'/Plaxton Panorama coach, was donated to Eynon's during their troubled times by competitors Maldwyn and Derrick Williams directors of Gwyn Williams & Sons Ltd, Lower Tumble, delivered in full Eynon's livery.
Note W	**HRO 659C, PFH 886F, ELU 504C, SDD 334G, PTH 100K, WYB 741H, EMB 159K, DTJ 198J, PUF 263M, FBW 22K, LDH 139J, RRG 348N, BAA 884J, HSF 555N, YUR 995K, 78 HBC, NCK 637** were all owned by E J Roberts the depot engineer at Eynon's, and were leased to Eynon's to operate their contracts. They all operated on Eynon's licences with the exception of ELU 504C/LDH 139J which were acquired for spares, and 78 HBC which was not operated at all (see Note A2 below).
Note X	**JBX 693/4X** Were delivered as JBX 293/2X respectively. They were both owned by Gravell's (Pinged Hill Garage) Kidwelly, who leased them to Eynon's. They carried Eynon's livery with the branding: 'Eynons **G** Executive'. The **G** was for Gravells.
Note Y	**MBX 86H** This Leyland 'Leopard' was originally registered **LBX 547G (see Note L opposite)**. It had been ordered by Eynon's in 1969, but not delivered to them, eventually passing to West Wales Motor Services, Tycroes in their livery, October 1969. It was re-registered MBX 86H due to the change of registration year suffix from G to H on 1st August 1969.
Note Z	**DDF 300L, HGD 863/869/871L, VBW 821L, OCU 650J, HNT 841N, WRS 671L, YSD 353L, YSD 355L, OKU 690R, BWG 838L, TVA 481M** were vehicles recertified by Eynon's on their 'O' licence and returned to Joe Sykes the Barnsley dealer for onward sale. Sykes was unable to submit vehicles for re-certification.
Note A1	**RGS 92R** a Leyland 'Leopard' was the first vehicle owned by M & M Jones (Jones International) Llandeilo when he began his own coach business. He operated RGS 92R on a borrowed Eynon's operator disc from 8-10/1984, until the granting of his own licence, and declared Eynon's garage as his operating centre.
Note A2	**78 HBC** This vehicle was actually **92 HBC** (chassis No. L03019) carrying the number plate off **78 HBC**. Previously a driver trainer with the Swansea R T I T B, it was sold to E J Roberts (Eynon's fleet engineer) in 3/1986, not operated and resold to J Sykes (dealer) 4/1986 for onward sale to a film company. It was used in a film set where it was set on fire and completely burnt out.

VEHICLE DISPOSALS

BO 227	No trace.
BX 1669	Replaced by BX 6996 in 7/1926 with no further trace.
BX 2404	No trace.
BX 4035	No trace.
BX 5872	Sold to Showman 3/1934. Last licenced 1937.
BX 6996	Sold at unknown date & converted into a lorry. Last licenced 1/1936.
BX 7794	No trace.
BX 6130	No trace.
BX 8048	Sold to Showman 1/1945. Last licenced 1950.
TH 804	No trace.
TH 2970	Sold to Showman in Scotland 1955.
OF 5483	No trace.
TJ 599	Sold to: Sir John Jackson Ltd, (Contractors) Carway open-cast site 1955-used as mobile office.
BX 8368	Sold to: D J Davies, Merthyr. 1936. Later re-bodied with a coach body built by D J Davies.
TH 838	Sold to: Showman 1936.
TH 8834	Sold to: Bird (dealer) Stratford-upon-Avon by 1/1960. Scrapped by Bird.
GJ 2397	No trace.
CBX 435	No trace.
CK 4731	Sold to: Bird (dealer) Stratford-upon-Avon by 1/1960. Scrapped by Bird.
DTH 103	No trace.
EK 8878	Sold for scrap.
JY 5026	Sold for scrap by 7/1951.
TF 7310	Sold for scrap 1956.
FTH 831	Sold to: Super Coaches (dealer) Upminster, Essex 9/1963. To: Dover. Brentwood, Essex, 10/1963 for spares.
WN9474	Sold to Showman 1955.
GBX 987	Out of use at garage 12/1963 – 3/1964. Sold to: Bird (dealer) Stratford-on-Avon by 6/64, still there 3/1965. Scrapped later.
GTH 737	Sold to: Arlington (dealer) Cardiff 6/1966. To: Way (Scrap dealer) Cardiff Docks by 7/1968.
BV 4454	Sold – noted as immobile caravan at Keepers Lodge, Trimsaran by 1958.
EVT 382	No trace.
LBX 811	Sold to: Sykes (dealer) Blackerhill by 8/1972.
BSM 170	Sold to: R G Peters, Pembrey, Carms. 6/1957.
BSM 171	Scrapped by 7/1958.
BTH 175	Exchanged for RTL's at Bird (dealer) Stratford-on-Avon 10/1958. Scrapped by Birds.
CS 7034	Exchanged for RTL's at Bird (dealer) Stratford-on-Avon 10/1958. Scrapped by Birds.
CS 8046	Written off after colliding with arched bridge at Kidwelly 11/1957. Sold for scrap.
LKH 351	Sold to: J Howell. Burry Port 3/1961. To: O'Connor & Davies (Contractors) Llanelli 8/1965.
RBX 394	Sold to: Arlington (dealer) Cardiff 3/1962. To: Morlais. Merthyr Tydfil (2) 4/1962
FOR 639	Sold to: Jones (Scrap dealer) Cardiff by 4/1963.
JXN 320	Sold to: Arlington Motors (dealer) Cardiff 10/62. To: Jones (Scrap dealer) Cardiff by4/1963.
JXN 358	Sold to: Bird (dealer) Stratford-on-Avon, in exchange for LYF150 by 7/1962. To: Refreshment stall at Bacons End, Castle Bromwich 5/1964.
GUE 250	Sold to: David North (Scrap dealer) Sandy Bridge Yard, Llanelli 1/1965. Scrapped 12/1965.
TAB 577	Sold by 8/1974. No trace.
KAW677	Sold to: Arlington Motors (dealer) Cardiff 10/1962. To: Morlais. Merthyr Tydfil 10/1962.
DBX 260	No trace.
LTG 269	Sold to: Arlington Motors (dealer) Cardiff 5/1964. To: Maberly Parker (NPSV) Tongwynlais, South Glamorgan 5/1964.

XTH 300	Sold to: Lees. Beeston, Nottingham 6/1963.
JTH 791	Sold to: Arlington Motors (dealer) Cardiff 6/1966. To: Jenkins. Pontardulais W-Glam. 8/1966.
818 ATH	Sold to: Arlington Motors (dealer) Cardiff 5/1965. To: West Wales, Tycroes (48) 6/1965.
LYF 150	Sold to: Arlington Motors (dealer) Cardiff, 5/1968. To: Way (Scrap dealer) Cardiff Docks, 6/1968. Still there derelict 1/1977.
EUH 959	Sold to: Super Coaches (PVS dealer) Upminster, Essex 11/1963. To: Ledgard. Leeds 12/1963.
EUH 964	Sold to: PVS (dealer) Essex, 11/1965. To: Cooke (scrap dealer) London E14, 11/1965.
EUH 966	Sold to: PVS (dealer) Essex, 11/1965. To: Cooke (scrap dealer) London E14, 11/1965.
EUH 953	Sold to: PVS (dealer) Essex, 9/1963. To: Samuel Ledgard. Leeds 12/1963.
405 CTH	Sold to: Arlington (dealer) Cardiff 5/1965. To: M. David. Pontycymmer, Mid-Glam. 7/1965.
LYF 35	Sold to: P Sykes (scrap dealer) Barnsley, S-Yorkshire. 8/1971.
LYF 38	Sold to: P Sykes (scrap dealer) Barnsley, S-Yorkshire. 8/1971.
LYF 40	Sold to: P Sykes (scrap dealer) Barnsley, S-Yorkshire. 8/1971.
LYR 808	Sold to: P Sykes (scrap dealer) Barnsley, S-Yorkshire. 8/1971.
LYR 959	Sold to: P Sykes (scrap dealer) Barnsley, S-Yorkshire. 8/1971.
695 ETH	Sold to: Arlington (dealer) Cardiff, 6/1966. To: Llynfi Motors. Maesteg, Mid-Glam. (100) 7/66.
FBX 489	Hired from July – September 1964. Returned to owner off hire 9/1964 (See photo page 239).
BTH987C	Sold to: Arlington (dealer) Cardiff, 1/1967. To: Porthcawl Omnibus Co, Mid-Glam. 6/1967.
CBX 9C	Sold to: Arlington (dealer) Cardiff, 9/1967. To: Bryn Demery. Morriston, W-Glam. 9/1967.
CBX238C	Sold to: Arlington (dealer) Cardiff, 1/1968. To: Richards Bros. Moylegrove, Pembs. 2/1968.
HUH 25	Sold to: Arlington (dealer) Cardiff, 7/1966. To: Silcox. Pembroke Dock, Pembs. (76) 9/1966.
HUH 27	Sold to: North (dealer) Sherburn-in-Elmet, N-Yorkshire. 2/1968. To: Johnson. Goldthorpe, S.Yorks for scrap 6/1969.
KXW 58	Broken up at depot for spares by 12/1969.
LLU 866	Sold to: Arlington (dealer) Cardiff, 9/1967. To: Way (scrap dealer) Cardiff Docks 11/1967. Still there derelict 1/1977.
ETH210D	Sold to: Arlington (dealer) Cardiff, 2/1968. To: Blagdon Lioness. Blagdon, Bristol. 5/1968.
ETH260D	Sold to: Arlington (dealer) Cardiff, 1/1968. To: Edwards Bros, Beddau, Mid-Glam. 1/1968.
ETH320D	Sold to: Arlington (dealer) Cardiff, 2/1967. To: Thomas Motor Service. Barry, S-Glam 4/67.
FTH989E	Sold to: Arlington (dealer) Cardiff, 10/1968. To: P S Davey. Swansea, W-Glam. 12/1968.
GBX542E	Sold to: Arlington (dealer) Cardiff, 9/1968. To: Edwards Bros, Beddau, Mid-Glam. 10/1968.
YXD 14	Sold to: Hood. Wold Newton, Humberside, 5/1970.
933 DVA	Sold to: Llynfi Motors. Maesteg, Mid Glam. (105) 5/1968.
JDO 107	No trace.
JBO 127	No trace.
799 OCV	Sold to: unknown dealer, 5/1970. To: Hambridge. Kidlington, Oxford 12/1970
JTH 92F	Sold to: Arlington (dealer) Cardiff 11/1973. To: G & H Tours. Pentyrch, Mid-Glam. 11/1974.
JTH 424F	Sold to: unknown dealer by 9/1973. To: Robertson. Harthill, Strathclyde 5/1974.
JTH 425F	Sold to: Moseley (dealer) 10/1973. To: Lane. Llanvetherine, Gwent. 2/1974.
LBX547G	Was a cancelled order. Delivered to West Wales. Tycroes, Carms, as MBX 86H in 10/1969.
LBX548G	Sold to: unknown scrap dealer at Barnsley, S-Yorks. 6/1982.
HLW 177	Sold to: P Sykes (dealer) Barnsley, S-Yorks. 10/1972. (See also 'Additional Vehicle Notes')
KGU 414	Sold to: P Sykes (dealer) Barnsley, S-Yorks. 10/1972.
SJJ 317	Acquired for spares only. Remains cut up at depot by 3/1972.
HOD691E	Sold to: Thomas. Usk, Gwent, by 7/1971.
FCH 28	No trace.
NLE849	Sold to: P Sykes (dealer) Barnsley, S-Yorks. 10/1972.
KXW215	Sold to: P Sykes (dealer) Barnsley, S-Yorks. 10/1972.
OBX 1J	Sold to: Whitelaw. Bearsden, Glasgow 7/1974. To Smith, Wilmcote. To Shennan, Drongan, 7/1974.
LKG 225	No trace.
MUH 131	Sold to: Terry Davies (scrap dealer) Bynea, Carmarthenshire. 7/1974 for scrap.

9747 NA	Sold to: P Sykes (dealer) Barnsley, S-Yorks. 9/1975.
9750 NA	Withdrawn at garage, 7/1976. No further trace.
UWU521F	Sold to: J Sykes (scrap dealer) Carlton, 2/1983.
6911 HA	Sold to: Mann. Coleshill, West Midlands, 12/1973.
PBX 700J	Sold to: G Davies. Ebbw Vale, Gwent, 8/1979.
LCO 839	Sold to: R Hitchcock (scrap dealer) Sandy Rd, Llanelli, 7/1974.
LCO 841	Sold to: R Hitchcock (scrap dealer) Sandy Rd, Llanelli, 7/1974.
LCO 846	Sold to: R Hitchcock (scrap dealer) Sandy Rd, Llanelli, 7/1974.
LCO 847	No trace.
LCO 854	No trace.
VKH 672	Sold to: Lister (dealer) Bolton, by 9/1974.
RBX 760K	Sold to: J Sykes (dealer) Carlton, 7/1983. To: G Jones (breaker) Carlton, body scrapped and chassis returned to Sykes (11/1983). Chassis exported to Australia via: PSO Exports Ltd.
NNY 58	Sold to: Terry Davies (scrap dealer) Bynea, Llanelli by 1/1974.
XRR 539	No trace.
STH 555K	Written off in accident 9/1983. Used for spares by 6/1984. Remains cut up for scrap 5/1988.
RCY 343	No trace.
RCY 344	Sold to: Pinged Hill Garage, Kidwelly (NPSV) as a mobile advertisement, 1975.
RCY 346	Sold to: Paul Sykes (dealer) Barnsley, 11/1977 in exchange for JHF 821. To: A Barraclough (scrap dealer) Carlton, by 12/1977.
RCY 365	Used for spares by 1/1975. Remains cut up for scrap at depot 1/1977.
TTH 500L	Sold to: Morris Bros. Swansea 7/1977.
MAX 133	Sold to: P Sykes (dealer) Blackerhill, Barnsley by 5/1973. To: Asquith (NPSV), Firkhamgate, Yorkshire, 7/1973.
UBX 55L	Sold to: Hewlett & Sutton. Morecambe, Lancs. 5/1983.
WWV 564	Derelict at depot 1/1980. Sold to: F Wells (scrap dealer) Rotherham, 3/1982.
VTH 5L	Destroyed by fire at depot, 29/11/1979. Remains cut up for scrap 1980.
VTH 655L	Withdrawn 10/1982 after TRK 5F collided into its rear end. Being used for spares 7/1983. Remains sold to J Sykes (dealer) Carlton, for scrap 5/1984.
WTH255M	Sold to unknown dealer, 2/1977. To: Thorpe. Edgeware, London, 5/1977.
KNK 350G	Sold to: Merlyns Coaches. Skewen, West Glam. 1/1976.
DHN 300H	Destroyed by fire at depot yard 29/11/79. Remains cut up for scrap 1980.
RNN 266	Sold to: P Sykes (dealer) Barnsley for scrap by 5/1975.
RNN 617	Sold to: P Sykes (dealer) Barnsley for scrap 5/1975.
946 MRR	Sold to: Moseley (dealer) Cinderford 3/1975. To: Claireaux. Hadleigh, Suffolk 5/1976.
947 MRR	Sold to: Moseley (dealer) Cinderford 3/1975. To: Claireaux. Hadleigh, Suffolk 5/1976.
945 MRR	Sold to: Moseley (dealer) Cinderford 3/1975. To: Runnalls. Townshend, Cornwall 10/1975.
864 HAL	Sold to: R Williams. Splott, Cardiff 6/1975.
XTH944M	Sold to: unknown dealer, 8/1978. To: Ribblesdale, Blackburn, Lancs. 7/1979.
CKP 441K	Sold to: P Sykes (dealer) Barnsley 9/1977. To: O'Donnell. Lumb, W.Yorks. 8/1978.
OCO 511	No trace.
OCO 512	No trace.
OCO 514	Being used for spares by 12/1976. Scrapped 2/1977.
OCO 516	Sold 9/1975. No further trace.
OCO 519	(See notes on page 225) Sold to: J Sykes (scrap dealer) Barnsley, for scrap 2/1983.
JCH 265	Used for spares, remains cut up at depot for scrap by 1977.
UKG 273	Sold to: P Sykes (dealer) Barnsley, for scrap 9/1975.
PBN 657	Sold to: Lister (dealer) Bolton, 2/1978. To: A Barraclough. Carlton, for scrap by 6/1978.
GCY 74N	Was a cancelled order - delivered to West Wales Motors, Tycroes in 10/1974. (See additional vehicle notes - Note S).
GNY431N	Sold to: Kirkby (dealer) Sheffield 8/1978. To: Rennie. Dunfermline, Fife 7/1981.
HFP 118N	Sold to: T S Lewis. Rhydlewis, Cardigan 2/1978.

HFP 119N	Sold to: T S Lewis. Rhydlewis, Cardigan 2/1978.
JXD 548D	Sold to: Moseley (dealer) Cinderford by 10/1976. To: Brown & Preddy. Gloucester 6/1977.
XUP 457F	Sold to: Moseley (dealer) Cinderford by 10/1976. To: John. Llanharry, Mid-Glam, by 6/77.
SCG 856	Sold to: Lister (dealer) Bolton 9/1978. Immediately scrapped.
TRN 733	Used for spares by 7/1977. Derelict 1/1980. Later scrapped on site.
TRN 735	Used for spares by 7/1977. Derelict 1/1980. Used as store-shed by 2/1980. Sold to: J Sykes (dealer) Barnsley 9/1984 and scrapped.
TRN 739	Sold to: Lister (dealer) Bolton, 11/1981.
TRN 759	Sold to: P Sykes (dealer) Barnsley 3-7/1977.
UBN 904	Sold to: C F Booth (dealer) Rotherham, S-Yorks. 7/1980.
UBN 907	Sold to: Lister (dealer) Bolton, 9/1978.
KCK 854	Sold to: Lister (dealer) Bolton, 2/1978. To: A. Barraclough (scrap dealer) Carlton, Yorkshire, by 18/3/1978.
KCK 866	Sold to: Lister (dealer) Bolton, 2/1978.
TRN 743	Sold to: F Wells (dealer) Rotherham, S-Yorks, 10/1981. To: Holmeswood, Rufford, Lancashire, for spares by 7/1982.
WCG 104	Sold for preservation to: Friends of King Alfred Preservation Group, Winchester, Hampshire, 7/1981. Now restored to its former glory.
NAY 438P	Sold to: M David. Pontycymmer, Mid- Glam. 5/1983.
BUX 236L	Sold to: Moseley (dealer) 7/1977. To: Maiden. Worcester, 9/1977.
OAY 393P	Sold to: Yeates (dealer) Loughborough 5/1983, and re-acquired 2/1984. (See page 232).
RFF 118L	Sold to: Morris Bros. Swansea, West Glam. 7/1977.
BGV 238L	Sold to: Moseley (dealer) Cinderford, Glos. 7/1977.
RUH 656M	Sold to: P Sykes (dealer) Barnsley, 9/1977. To: Boot. Dronfield, Derby (NPSV) 1/1978.
HGE 469L	Sold to: Waddon. Caerphilly, Mid-Glam. 11/1982.
DBC 263K	Returned to Moseley (dealer) off hire 6/1977.
PTH 647R	Sold to: Moseley (dealer) 8/1978. To: Foster. Glastonbury, Somerset 8/1978.
RTH 130S	Sold to: Moseley (dealer) 8/1978. To: Bowers. Bridgend, Mid-Glam. 12/1978.
SGD 610	Used for spares, 1/1980. Remains sold to Bowen Metals, Pontarddulais, W.Glam. 6/1980.
SGD 621	Sold to: Lister (dealer) Bolton, 9/1979. To: Booth (scrap dealer) Rotherham, 10/1979.
SGD 635	Used for spares, 1/1980. Remains sold to Bowen Metals, Pontarddulais, W.Glam. 6/1980.
TCK 459	Sold to: Lister (dealer) Bolton, 3/1981.
TCK 462	Sold to: Lister (dealer) Bolton, 3/1981.
JHF 821	Sold to: Lister (dealer) Bolton, 4/1980.
FKY 250E	Destroyed by fire at depot yard along with DHN 300H & VTH 5L on 29/11/1979. Remains cut up for scrap 1980. The fire had broken out in Bedford VAS: DHN 300H.
TRN 753	Derelict 1/1980. Remains sold to Bowen Metals, Pontarddulais, W.Glam, for scrap 6/1980.
527 VRB	Returned to Lister (dealer) Bolton, off hire 10/1978.
528 VRB	Returned to Lister (dealer) Bolton, off hire 10/1978.
VCS 431	Returned to Lister (dealer) Bolton, off hire 10/1978. Sold to: Clackmannan District Council (NPSV) 3/1979.
217 HUM	Derelict 1/1980. Sold to: F Wells (scrap dealer) Rotherham, S-Yorks. 2/1982.
EVL 550E	Sold to: Lister (dealer) Bolton, 7/1980.
EVL 552E	Sold to: Lister (dealer) Bolton, 7/1980.
EVL 553E	Sold to: Lister (dealer) Bolton, 7/1980.
NCR268M	Derelict at depot yard 6/1984 &10/1985. Sold for scrap.
XBX 830T	Sold to: Yeates (dealer) Loughborough, Leicester 6/1984. To: Nesbit. Somerby, Lincs. 12/1984.
XBX 831T	Involved in a head on collision with Eynon's OAY 393P on 18/9/85. Returned from repair 2/1986 but not operated. Sold to: Stuart Johnson (dealer) Harthill, South Yorks, 3/1986. To: Boydon. Winkhill, Staffs, by 10/1986.

4991 VT	Derelict by 6/1980. Scrapped at depot by O'Neal (scrap dealer) Halfway, Llanelli. 4/1986.
BOF 857C	Not operated. Sold to: F Wells (scrap dealer) Rotherham, S-Yorks. 11/1981.
MLL 934	Used for spares in 2/1980. Remains sold for scrap, 3/1983.
MLL 938	Not operated. Returned to London Transport in exchange for MXX 489 (RF 512).
MXX 489	Disused from 2/1981. Sold for preservation to Llanelli Railway Preservation Society 5/1987.
HEO 278	Sold to: J Sykes (scrap dealer) Carlton, Barnsley, 3/1985.
BTH 364V	To: E J Roberts. Meinciau, Carms. 1/1987 (not operated). To: Stuart Johnson (dealer) Harthill, 3/1987. To: Whaites. Settle, N-Yorks. 8/1987.
BTH 365V	To: E J Roberts. Meinciau, Carms. 1/1987 (not operated). To: Stuart Johnson (dealer) Harthill, 3/1987. To: Whaites. Settle, N-Yorks. 8/1987.
BUF 528C	Disused from 10/1987. Passed to Davies Bros (Pencader) Ltd, with the business in 6/1988, but not operated. To: Gwernllwyn Country Club, Cross Hands, as immobile advert 7/1988.
BUF 529C	Used for spares. Remains cut up for scrap at depot, 5/1986.
JRJ 272E	Sold to: J Sykes (scrap dealer) Carlton, 3/1984.
JRJ 277E	Sold to: J Sykes (scrap dealer) Carlton, 3/1984. To: G Jones (scrap dealer) Carlton, 3/1984. Scrapped 3/1984.
TRN 387	Sold to: Lister (dealer) Bolton, 3/1981. Used on contract hire to Knowsley Safari Park, Merseyside by 4/1981.
JRJ 261E	Sold to: J Sykes (scrap dealer) Carlton, 2/1984. To: A Barraclough (scrap dealer) Carlton, 3/1984.
HRO 659C	Sold to: F Wells (dealer) Rotherham, S-Yorks, 11/1981. Body removed, chassis exported. To: Nur Bros. Chittagong, Bangladesh. 3/1982.
RBO 119G	Sold 10/1982. Noted in the yard of a company making caravan conversions at Morriston, Swansea, 10/1982.
BVJ 160B	Sold for scrap 2/1983.
PFH 886F	Sold to: J Sykes (dealer) Carlton, 3/1984. To: Woodmansey Beaver Jazz Band, Beverley, Humberside (Non PSV) 4/1984.
KDB 405F	Sold to: J Sykes (dealer) Carlton for scrap 5/1984.
HTJ 131F	Sold to: Davies Bros (Pencader) Ltd, (186) with the business 6/1988. Ran on Eynon's licence until 31/7/88. Transferred to Davies Bros licence disc; 1/8/88. Withdrawn 7/1990. Sold for preservation 8/1996 to: Paul Williams. Fazeley, Staffs, minus gearbox.
FTF 703F	Sold to: West Wales Motors (95) Tycroes, Carmarthenshire 4/1983.
OTJ 334G	Sold to: J Sykes (dealer) Carlton, 2/1984. To: Collingwood. Wheatley Hill, Durham, as a PSV licenced driver trainer 4/1984.
ABV 357B	Not operated. Acquired accident damaged for spares, remains cut up for scrap 10/1982.
ELU 504C	Not operated. Acquired for spares only. Remains towed away to F Wells (scrap dealer) Rotherham, 12/1981.
HTJ 134F	Not operated. Acquired for spares only. Remains scrapped on site by O'Neil (scrap dealer) Halfway, Llanelli 12/1983.
TRK 5F	Written off 10/1982 after it collided into the rear of Eynon's VTH 655L. Sold to: J Sykes (dealer) Carlton for scrap 7/1983.
TRK 6F	Sold to: J Sykes (dealer) Carlton, 9/1983. Noted at Alton Towers 8/86 converted to caravan.
SDD 334G	Sold to: J Sykes (dealer) Carlton, 3/1984. To: Little Hulton Legionaires Morris Troupe, Gtr. Manchester (Non PSV) 7/1984.
VWG 407	Sold to: Private owner at Burry Port for caravan conversion 3/1982. To: Private owner at Carway 1983. To: Small-holding at Five Roads & derelict 1992. Presumed scrapped c1999.
369 FGB	Sold 8/1982. To: D Smith. Glyn Neath, West Glam (caravan) by 6/1983. Re-registered: ACY58A by 7/1985. To: Smith. Penydarren, W-Glam (caravan) 11/1986 - same person?
KHU 308L	Sold to: Private owner 5/1984.
KTH 530X	Sold to: Moseley (dealer) Cinderford, 4/1982. To: Stone. Bath, Somerset 5/1982.
JBX 693X	Returned to lessor 4/1982. Sold to: Thomas. Clydach Vale, Mid-Glam 5/1982.
JBX 694X	Returned to lessor 4/1982. Sold to: Thomas. Clydach Vale, Mid-Glam 5/1982.

KDB 406F	Sold to: J Sykes (dealer) Carlton for scrap 6/1984.
FEK 1F	Sold to: Davies Bros. (Pencader) Ltd, (190) with the business 6/1988. Ran on Eynon's licence until 31/7/88. Transferred to Davies Bros licence; 1/8/88. W/drawn 7/90, re-reg: ODE47F in 9/91. To: Lattimore. Ampthill, Beds (P) to provide parts for a similar preserved bus 2/1992.
PTH 100K	Sold to: Dean Forest. Joys Green, Gloucester 6/1983. To: J Sykes. Carlton, for scrap 1984.
JRC 254C	Withdrawn after accident 3/1984. Used for spares. Derelict at depot, passed as such to Davies Bros (Pencader) Ltd, 6/1988. Remains broken up for scrap on site 11/1990.
WYB741H	Sold to: J Sykes (dealer) Carlton for scrap 4/1984.
JWA 966J	Sold to: J Sykes (dealer) Carlton for scrap 7/1983.
HEL 203D	Sold to: Davies Bros (Pencader) Ltd, (191) with the business 6/88. Transferred to Davies Bros licence disc, 1/8/1988.
ARN 599C	Sold to: J Sykes (dealer) Carlton for scrap 9/1985.
ARN 605C	Not operated. Used for spares, remains sold to J Sykes (dealer) Carlton for scrap 7/1984.
DCD 19C	Sold to: West Wales Motors (92) Tycroes, Carmarthenshire 4/1983.
LSY 140J	Sold to: Lane. Tredegar, Gwent 3/1985.
YTE 952D	Sold to: G Ripley (dealer) Carlton for scrap 3/1987.
LBX 550G	Used for spares. Remains sold to G Ripley (dealer) Carlton for scrap 3/1987.
EPT 615G	Sold to: G Ripley (dealer) Carlton for scrap 2/1988.
ASC 654C	Sold to: West Wales Motors (97) Tycroes, Carmarthenshire 6/1983.
ASC 659C	Sold to: J Sykes (dealer) Carlton for scrap 4/1984.
KTJ 205C	Sold to: Davies Bros (Pencader) Ltd. (192) with the business 6/1988. Ran on Eynon's licence until sold 7/1988. To: Gwernllwyn Country Club, Cross Hands, Carmarthenshire, as a static all over advertisement for the Country Club 7/1988, together with BUF 528C.
EWS 804D	Not operated. Sold to West Wales Motors (96) Tycroes, Carmarthenshire 5/1983.
PBX 280Y	Sold to: Davies Bros (Pencader) Ltd (173) with the business 6/1988. Ran on Eynon's licence until sold 31/7/88. To: Arlington (dealer) London 7/1988. To: Clayton. Leicester 11/1989.
DGC 114H	Sold to: Moseley (dealer) 6/1984. To: J Sykes (dealer) Carlton 6/1984. To: Groves. Sheffield 6/1984.
BUF 133C	Sold to: A J S (scrap dealer) Carlton 2/1987.
FUS 168L	Sold to: Davies Bros (Pencader) Ltd (189) with the business 6/1988. Transferred to Davies Bros licence disc 1/8/1988.
PBC 108G	Sold to: J Sykes (dealer) Carlton 8/1985. To: Anelay. Scunthorpe, North Lincs. 9/1985.
EMB 159K	Sold to: J Sykes (dealer) Carlton 2/1987. To: Hill. Wolverhampton, West Midlands by 10/1987, and re-registered EAA559 by 2/1988.
OAY 393P	Written off after head on collision with Eynon's XBX 831T on 18/9/1985. Used for spares, stripped to bare shell by 1/1986. Remains cut up for scrap on site 4/1986.

AEC 'Reliance' OAY 393P pictured after its head on crash with XBX 831T on the B4308 road, 18/9/1985.

YHK 729F	Sold to: J Sykes (dealer) Carlton 1/1986. No further trace.
PBC 115G	Sold to: J Sykes (dealer) Carlton 8/1985. To: S Lynch. Passage East, Waterford. S. Ireland (8/1985) re-registered: 9168KI.
FUS 159L	Sold to: J Sykes (dealer) Carlton 1/1986. To: Relph. Welwyn Garden City, Herts. 12/1988.
DTJ 198L	Sold to: J Sykes (dealer) Carlton 9/1985. No further trace.
DDF 300L	Returned to J Sykes (dealer) Carlton, after re-certification 5/1984.
PUF 263M	Sold to: Minnard. Aberfan, Mid-Glam. 6/1984.
HRN 953G	Sold to: J Sykes (dealer) Carlton 8/1985.
MBX 86H	Stripped of all useful parts. Remains to: G Ripley (scrap dealer) Carlton 2/1988.
EUF 220D	Sold to: J Sykes (dealer) Carlton 8/1984. To: Terry Crossland. Horbury, West Yorks. (Racing car Transporter) by 7/1987.
KCK 983H	Derelict by 1/1986. Sold to: J Sykes (dealer) Carlton 3/1986. To: A J S (scrap dealer) 3/86.
A802 XEP	Sold to: Davies Bros (Pencader) Ltd, (172) with the business 6/1988. Ran on Eynon's licence disc until sold to Arlington (dealer) London, 31/7/1988. Sold to: Finchley Coaches. London, N12. 6/1989.
WJF 378S	Sold to: Davies Bros (Pencader) Ltd, (175) with the business 6/1988. Ran on Eynon's licence until 31/7/1988. Transferred to Davies Bros licence disc; 1/8/1988. Withdrawn 12/1996. Sold to: Conrad Thomas. Llanelli, 2/1997 for preservation but later scrapped.
HGD 863L	Returned to: J Sykes (dealer) Carlton, after re-certification 7/1984. Sold to: Wood. (Verwood Transport) Verwood, Dorset by 8/1984.
HGD 869L	Returned to: J Sykes (dealer) Carlton, after re-certification 9/1984. Sold to: 'D' Coaches. Morriston, Swansea 9/1984.
HGD 871L	Returned to: J Sykes (dealer) Carlton, after re-certification 9/1984. Sold to: 'D' Coaches. Morriston, Swansea 9/1984.
FBW 22K	Sold to: G Warren. Crickhowell, Powys, for conversion to horsebox, 2/1985. Re-possessed by owner - E J Roberts 4/1985. Sold to: J Sykes (dealer) Carlton for scrap 2/1986.
VBW 821L	Returned to: J Sykes (dealer) Carlton 11/1984. To: N C B North East area (NPSV) 12/84.
RGS 92R	This vehicle, owned by M & M Jones, Llandeilo ran on a borrowed Eynons licence disc from 8-10/1984, until Jones, T/A: Jones International, Llandeilo received their own licences.
OCU 650J	Returned to: J Sykes (dealer) Carlton, after re-certification 3/1985. Sold to: Pied Pipers & Ladybird Dancing Troup. Partington, Cheshire. (NPSV) 5/1985.
ASC 692B	Operated on loan in the interim period before its return to J Sykes (dealer) from 'D' Coaches Morriston, in exchange for Leyland 'Atlanteans' HGD869/71L above in 9/1984. Sold to: Patterson's School of Motoring. Wishaw, North Lanarkshire (NPSV) by 11/1986.
YSC 443K	Sold to: G Ripley (dealer) Carlton for scrap 2/1988.
HNT 841N	Sold to: Robson (dealer) Wolsingham 2/1985 for export to Malta - 5/1985, re-registered: EBY593.
LDH 139J	Not operated. Used for spares by 2/1985. Remains broken up on site 2/1986.
KHY 18X	Sold to Davies Bros (Pencader) Ltd, with the business 6/1988.
WRS 671L	Returned to: J Sykes (dealer) Carlton, after re-certification 6/1985. Sold to: W Irvine. Law, Strathclyde 7/1985.
RRG 348N	Returned to: E J Roberts. Meinciau, off loan 1/1987.
URO 856J	Sold to: O'Neil (scrap dealer) Halfway, Llanelli 1/1986 & subsequently broken up.
YSD 353L	Returned to: J Sykes (dealer) Carlton, after re-certification 6/1985. Sold to: 'D' Coaches. Morriston, Swansea, 6/1985.
YSD 355L	Returned to: J Sykes (dealer) Carlton after re-certification 6/1985.
BAA 884J	Sold to: J Sykes (dealer) Carlton 11/1985. No further trace.
CNY 333V	Returned to dealer 12/1985. Sold to: J. Pace, Bkara (Unscheduled Bus Co. Malta) 2/1986. Re-registered: Y-0851 later KCY851.
FNM 861Y	Returned to dealer off loan 7/1985. Sold to: Percival. Oxford 7/1985.
ACA 297A	Sold to: G Ripley (dealer) Carlton, for scrap 2/1988.
HSF 555N	Returned to: E J Roberts. Meinciau, off loan 1/1987.
RLJ 89X	Returned to: DSB (dealer) Long Whatton, Leics. 12/1985. To: Globe. Barnsley 4/1986.

VNY 468G	Sold to: Davies Bros, (Pencader) Ltd, (185) with the business 6/1988. Ran on Eynon's licence until 31/7/1988. Transferred to Davies Bros licence disc; 1/8/1988. Withdrawn 11/1988. Used for spares by 1/1989, remains cut up for scrap at Trimsaran depot, 11/1990.
RVB 995E	Sold to: G Ripley (dealer) Carlton for scrap 3/1987.
JRB 188N	Sold to: Davies Bros, (Pencader) Ltd, (177) with the business 6/1988. Ran on Eynon's licence until sold 7/1988 to Stuart Johnson (dealer) Harthill, S-Yorks in part exchange for OUT 11W.
YUR 995K	Returned to E J Roberts, Meinciau, off loan 1/1987.
OKU 690R	Returned to: J Sykes (dealer) Carlton after re-certification 12/1985. Sold to: Wacton Trading (dealer) Bromyard, Herefordshire 10/1986.
ACY 119A	Sold to: G Ripley (dealer) Carlton for scrap 2/1988.
BWG 838L	Returned to: J Sykes (dealer) Carlton after re-certification 1/1986. Sold to: W Irvine. Law, South Lanarkshire, 7/1986.
TVA 481M	Returned to: J Sykes (dealer) Carlton after re-certification 2/1986.
FUS 169L	Returned to: 'D' Coaches. Morriston, Swansea, 10/1985 ex loan. In exchange, 'D' Coaches had borrowed BUF 528C for driver training purposes.
LVO 93E	Sold to: G Ripley (dealer) Carlton for scrap 3/1987.
78 HBC	Sold to: J Sykes (dealer) Carlton 4/1986. Sold to unknown film studio for a film set, where it was set on fire and burned out.
MSJ 379P	Sold to: G Ripley (dealer) Carlton for scrap 2/1988.
NCK 637	Licence changed to: E J Roberts, Meinciau, Carms, (The vehicle's owner) 10/1986.
GBX 57N	Sold to: Davies Bros, (Pencader) Ltd, (194) with the business 6/1988. Ran on Eynon's licence until 31/7/88. Transferred to Davies Bros licence disc; 1/8/88. Used as non PSV from 5/1989.
UCK 500	Sold to: Davies Bros, (Pencader) Ltd, (187) with the business 6/1988. Ran on Eynon's licence until 31/7/88. Transferred to Davies Bros licence disc; 1/8/88. Re-registered BDE67B, 4/1989.
PUF 173H	Sold to: Davies Bros, (Pencader) Ltd, (181) with the business 6/1988. Ran on Eynon's licence until 31/7/88. Transferred to Davies Bros licence disc; 1/8/88. Withdrawn 2/1990.
PUF 174H	Sold to: Davies Bros, (Pencader) Ltd, (182) with the business 6/1988. Ran on Eynon's licence until 31/7/88 when it was withdrawn and used for spares. Remains cut up 15/3/1990.
FWO 153L	Sold to: Davies Bros, (Pencader) Ltd, (179) with the business 6/1988. Ran on Eynon's licence until 31/7/88. Transferred to Davies Bros licence disc; 1/8/88. Withdrawn 3/1991.
PUF 163H	Sold to: Davies Bros, (Pencader) Ltd, (180) with the business 6/1988. Ran on Eynon's licence until 31/7/88. Transferred to Davies Bros licence disc; 1/8/88. Withdrawn 9/1988.
GAX 355L	Sold to: Davies Bros, (Pencader) Ltd, (176) with the business 6/1988. Ran on Eynon's licence until 31/7/88. Transferred to Davies Bros licence disc; 1/8/88. Fitted with bus seats (DP53F) 2/1992. Withdrawn 3/1995.
SGF 483L	Sold to: Davies Bros, (Pencader) Ltd, (178) with the business 6/1988. Ran on Eynon's licence until sold 7/1988 to Wacton Trading (dealer) Bromyard, Hereford. To: Sargent. Kington, Hereford, 7/1988.
OVK144M	Sold to: Davies Bros, (Pencader) Ltd, (188) with the business 6/1988. Ran on Eynon's licence until 31/7/88. Transferred to Davies Bros licence disc; 1/8/88. Withdrawn 4/1991. Sold to: Woolley. Llanedwen (Anglesey) 4/1991.
VLK 662S	Sold to: Davies Bros, (Pencader) Ltd, (193) with the business 6/1988. Ran on Eynon's licence until sold 7/1988 to Glyn Hicks a non PSV operator at Llanelli, Carms.
HCS 793N	Sold to: Davies Bros, (Pencader) Ltd, (183) with the business 6/1988. Ran on Eynon's licence until 31/7/88. Transferred to Davies Bros licence disc; 1/8/88. Withdrawn 12/1997 & sold.
SCS 328M	Sold to: Davies Bros, (Pencader) Ltd, (184) with the business 6/1988. Ran on Eynon's licence until 31/7/88. Transferred to Davies Bros licence disc; 1/8/88. Written off after accident at Cwmffrwd, Carmarthen on 7/12/1989.
SCS 327M	Not operated. Returned to G Ripley (dealer) Carlton, less engine & gearbox 6/1988.
NMJ 289V	Sold to: Davies Bros, (Pencader) Ltd, (174) with the business 6/1988. Ran on Eynon's licence until 31/7/88. Transferred to Davies Bros licence disc; 1/8/88. Withdrawn 1/1995 after a rear end collision and used for spares.

VEHICLE PHOTOGRAPH INDEX

Above: Eynon's ex WD Scammell Explorer 6 x 6 recovery vehicle, which operated for the company from 1974 to 1979 before passing to competitors Gwyn Williams & Sons Ltd, of Lower Tumble. It was fitted with a 'very thirsty' Meadows 10.3 litre **petrol** engine.

Above: The front line coaches in 1974 consisted of nine vehicles, five of which are captured here on the garage forecourt in June 1974. Left to right they are XTH 944M, OBX 1J, VTH 5L, PBX 700J and VTH 655L.

23313 A.E.C. RF Bus EYNONS OF TRIMSARAN ☐

Operating from Trimsaran in and around the Carmarthen area in South Wales this red and white fleet was well respected and known locally as 'The Hero'. Ex-London RF 512 registered MXX 489 is working on service around the Transaran Colliery. Limited production run of 1400 pieces.

Above: In April 2002, the die-cast model makers'Exclusive First Editions' brought out this limited edition 1/76th scale model of Eynon's AEC Regal IV (RF type), which is reproduced here from the EFE catalouge.

Above: This is my 'code 3' model of Eynon's former London Transport RT 190, HLW 177. It was converted from a 1/50th scale die-cast model manufactured by 'Solido' in 1980 to promote 'Coca-Cola'.

FAMILY TREE

Davies Bros (Pencader) Ltd. 6/1988

↑

Samuel Eynon & Sons
Bryn Villa Garage
Trimsaran.

↑

R. C. Lloyd	J. Hughes	J. Davies	E. Morris	O. Rowlands	Western Welsh O C	T.B. Gravell
Star Hotel	Mile End		Glasfryn	Brynamlwg		Pinged Hill
Trimsaran	Trimsaran	Carway	Llansaint	Carway	Pontyberem	Kidwelly
1923	1935	7/1936	1946	7/1964	1/1971	4/1976

Above: This neat little Plaxton bodied Commer Avenger 1 coach, registered **FBX 489** in September 1949 was regularly hired by Eynon's to help out at busy times. Fitted with a 6 cylinder, 4.75 litre side-valve petrol engine and constant mesh gearbox, this 32 seater was owned by Oliver Rowlands of Carway near Trimsaran, and was last hired by Eynon's from July to September 1964, when Eynon's took over Rowlands' operator licence. It returned to Rowlands in September and was laid up at his garage until sold to Thomas Jones, Perris Garage near Llanrhystyd, Cardiganshire five years later in September 1969. It was sold with T Jones' business in September 1975 to J A Evans, Tregaron and withdrawn in November 1976 with no further trace. It would have been nice to have seen this rare vehicle preserved.